Pickett, Plunkett and Puckett.

My 50 Years in Advertising

Larry Postaer

PORTLAND • OREGON
INKWATERPRESS.COM

Cover design by William Biderbost
Cover and interior layout by Masha Shubin
Cover photo by Steve Bao
Advertisement: "Words of Postaerity.", © WSJ, 1994. Used with permission.

www.inkwaterpress.com

Paperback
ISBN-13 978-1-59299-585-1 | ISBN-10 1-59299-585-3

Kindle
ISBN-13 978-1-59299-586-8 | ISBN-10 1-59299-586-1

LCCN: 2011926255

Publisher: Inkwater Press

Printed in the U.S.A.
All paper is acid free and meets all ANSI standards for archival quality paper.

5 7 9 10 8 6 4

Contents

Preamble

I made a mistake by hooking my wife on *Mad Men*, the Emmy-winning melodrama that takes place in the early sixties, precisely the period my career began. And though it was more than a decade later when we married, I thought she might be interested in seeing what advertising was like for me back then.

I had watched the first few episodes on my own and seen no reason to exclude her. But maybe the writers and producers were beginning to feel their oats, maybe the cable network had told them to raise the ratings temperature, whatever the reason, the fictional ad agency my wife is watching with me for the first time is turning into an erogenous zone. The sincere skinny ties are flying off along with the button-down shirts and trousers. Seemingly every actress on the show has become fair prey. And I'm squirming.

Finally my wife turns to me. "I knew about the smoking and the drinking," she said gesturing at the screen, "but I didn't know about..."

I raised my hand as if taking an oath and stopped her mid-sentence. "That's New York, dear. Chicago was a different story."

Introduction

My sons call me the Cal Ripken of advertising.

You may remember Ripken. In the mid-nineties, he dominated the sports pages by tying and then surpassing the great Lou Gehrig's once unreachable record of endurance by more than 500 games. All told he started at short or third 2,632 games in a row over seventeen seasons. No ball player will ever come close to those numbers again. But Iron Man that he was, I've got Cal beat. I just clocked my fiftieth consecutive year ducking high hard ones on the creative side of the advertising business. And loving, mostly, every oddball minute of it.

How do you find steady work for so long in a world as mercurial as advertising? Luck, for sure. And timing. And grabbing the brass ring. And all those other self-effacing clichés. But somehow my career path, with no Dutch uncle or calibrated inner compass to guide me, inexorably—and gratefully—headed north.

Professionally, such as it was, I began writing newspaper inserts for a department store in Chicago earning a whopping $65 a week. I soon moved on to a job as a copywriter for the Sears catalog. Believe it or not, there were eighty of us banging away on manual typewriters producing that monster tome. My moment of glory? The plum assignment to write the back cover announcement of an amazing product—the first ever Silvertone *Color* Television!

Two years at Sears and dozens of applications later I got my wish—a copywriting job with a small Chicago advertising agency one block removed from the Magnificent Mile. I figured I'd stay a while, build up a sample portfolio, then head for greener pastures. But the owners of the agency made leaving difficult. They promoted me, at the ripe old age of twenty-five, to the lofty title of creative director. Suddenly it was my show. And while the agency grew exponentially, fourteen years from the day I started, I gave in to the Siren lure of the big leagues. Unsolicited, a blue chip Chicago ad agency recruited me for a position as V.P. and group creative director, a major leap of faith for them—and for me. There were four times more writers and art directors under my wing than I had at the height of my last agency. It took me months to memorize all their names. Our group's client list included some of America's biggest brands, the likes of McDonald's, Anheuser-Busch, State Farm, Campbell, Wrigley, Dial, even Hamburger Helper up at General Mills. Early on the pressure was so intense I had to find myself a new and more effective underarm deodorant.

Five years into that challenging job, the agency offered me a transfer to their Los Angeles office. The lead client there was a small but promising car company called Honda. I mulled over the transfer for about fifteen warming seconds. Eventually, due to automotive client conflicts created when our parent company became part of the biggest merger in advertising history, my business-side partner Gerry Rubin and I had the chance to buy out the L.A. office while retaining the Honda account they were forced to jettison. We took that chance. Which takes us to the present twenty-four years later as I share the stodgy title of Co-Chairman of RPA (Rubin Postaer & Associates), one of the largest independent ad agencies in the country.

Retail. Mail order. Small agency. Large agency. Own agency. You can't write a script like that. Certainly not without the creativity of talented people, many still close friends, whose ideas made me look good along the path. Or the flashes of management style and wisdom I gleaned from my various bosses, individuals all and to all I owe everything.

And then there were the clients without whom there is no script. They paid the bills. They pronounced life or death sentences over the storyboards I held before them like Crusader shields. On a good day a client reaches into his or her own quiver of creativity and wisdom. By and large, they're an interesting group of achievers. Not to beat the baseball thing into the ground, but I may be the only creative director in the world who had as clients at one moment in time owners of three National League teams: Ray Kroc (Padres); August Busch III (Cardinals); and Bill Wrigley (Cubbies). They and others I've dealt with are stars in their own business galaxy. A very bright friend who became president of a large company with veto power over advertising told me he always felt the agency he had inherited treated him as though he was stupid and incompetent. I never viewed clients that way. It was our job to know their business almost as well as they did. It was also our job to instill in their advertising a freshness often derived from popular culture which most clients understood wasn't one of their strong suits.

Of course not all clients have good days every day. A wise boss tried to console me once on a long drive back from a brutal McDonald's meeting. "We get paid for the pain," he said. Perhaps. But a bad client day can make one forget Cal Ripken's record of longevity with thoughts instead of opening a hot dog stand.

For a creative director, losing a sale is not just a case of personal defeat. There also loomed what awaited back at the office when the team of childlike optimists who had conceived the black bag full of now-battered goods I schlepped would descend upon me asking the most vexing question in all of advertising: "How'd it go?" The subsequent look on their faces said it all. In their eyes I, too, had joined the ranks of incompetency.

Clients control the happy/sad switch. Sometimes they're not even conscious of their power. Twice I've been in a costly new business pitch—the crucible of all things gut-wrenching about advertising—and watched as the head guy fell dead asleep in the midst of the meeting. One was a major clothing manufacturer just off a plane from the Far East who gently put his jet-lagged head down on his arms at the table and began snoring. The other, the elderly founder of a well-known golf equipment company, just slid down in his chair and dozed off. In neither case, I hastily add, was I presenting at the moment their unconsciousness commenced. But in neither case did we win the account either.

Once I was asked to give an overview of past advertising to the newly appointed marketing director of STP, my small agency's biggest account at the time. New marketing directors tend to be the bane of our business. Like new guys on the country club greens committee, the first thing they want to do is change the configuration of all the traps. I had rehearsed for days. And had almost nine years of very successful work (STP is the Racer's Edge) to show off, for me a tight two-hour presentation. With not so much as a handshake, he removed his Breitling, set it on his desk, said he was swamped and told me to confine my comments to twenty minutes. We were fired three weeks later.

Another time, at a breakfast meeting, I watched as our research director ran through slides showing irrefutable evidence that the TV campaign we were running for the Chicagoland Oldsmobile Dealers Association (The Gallant Men of Olds) had achieved an astounding 90% unaided recall among viewers when, from the back of the darkened room, one of the dealers present, an opinionated and negative sort who we later learned had a brother-in-law in the agency business, began throwing chocolate doughnuts at the screen. A month later the account went "into review," a polite euphemism for You're Toast.

Lest anyone reading this now thinks I've been, for the last five decades, a masochist just grinding it out for the paycheck, let me say unequivocally that the highlights—winning a pitch, selling a breakthrough campaign, hiring a kid who becomes a superstar, collecting creative awards so ubiquitous in our business, even convincing a dour client that a clever pun is permissible—have far outweighed and outlasted the ephemeral rejections.

Besides, I had my survival tactic.

To wrest some solace from the sleepers, the clock-watchers, the pastry-pitchers et al., I'd chalk it up to experience and say to myself, "That's one for the book." I never kept a list or a diary though I wish I had. But after all these years in advertising, fortunately I still retain my faculties. And most of the memories—the bad and the good—remain for posterity.

And for The Book.

Pickett, Plunkett and Puckett.

A Lot to Learn

There are breech babies. There are premature babies. And there was me, a bargain baby, brought into this world by a Dr. Rubenstein at twenty-five percent off his asking price. I only learned this ten years ago when my mother passed away. My oldest son Steffan was helping my father move into a smaller unit at his retirement home and happened to come upon an old carton full of papers. One was the rough draft of a note my mother would send to the doctor. She was searching for a respectful tone. Words were scratched out replaced with better-chosen ones, all in her perfect secretary's penmanship, far more legible, I'd guess, than the good doctor's.

> *Dear Doctor,*
>
> *Enclosed please find check in the amount of $75 fully aware that your services are worth much more. However, because of unforeseen financial reverses this is the most I was able to scrape together. I hope you accept this as payment in full.*
>
> *Sincerely,*
> *Mary Postaer*

Mom had written her drafted plea on the backside of a phone bill for $21.50, their most recent and a huge amount in October of 1938 (my dad must've forgotten himself calling out-of-towners to broadcast my arrival). Stapled to the bill were Rubenstein's $100 invoice and the stub from Mom's $75 cashier's check. Clearly she presumed her copy would do the trick. I trust we were not sued for the balance. Those three fragments of the past are now displayed together in a frame. It's sitting on my desk as I write, a reminder of whence I came and how fortunate I've been.

Not that growing up in the heart of the South Side of Chicago foretold a dead end destiny. During the last presidential election, I discovered my old address is just blocks away from Michelle Obama's childhood home. She seems to have done okay.

Still, back then, my world was light years from the glitter of Michigan Avenue though I did get an occasional glimpse of it. My dad drove a bus, a big double-decker job, and his route, a half-block from our apartment, was South Park Boulevard all the way north where it ended in The Loop. Sometimes I'd wait for him to pull up at 72nd and climb aboard for a free ride downtown sitting in the "captain's chair," the high single seat over the right wheel well.

But that's as close as I got. Where we lived there were no mentoring neighbors with connections, no aspirational role models unless you count Ralph Capone, Al's younger brother, whom I'd see now and then getting a shave at the neighborhood barber shop. Most certainly, the concept of anyone having a career in advertising was literally unheard of.

My hard-working parents still talked about the Depression like it was yesterday. It almost was. Money was not spent on things like subscriptions for magazines so there were none in our apartment. Other than the product mentions integrated into Jack Benny and Fred Allen's radio programs, or the faded poster for Neolite heels hanging in the window of my grandpa's shoe repair shop down the block, or the cheesy Charles Atlas testimonials in comic books, my exposure to advertising—which today, for me, has reached the point of glut—was almost nil.

I say almost because there was one form of advertising that did attract not only my attention but my best friend Rippy Hudson's as well. Word would get out that White Castle was running their semi-annual coupon ad in the *Tribune*, the one entitling the bearer to six of their little square oniony burgers for a quarter, a colossal value since regularly they cost twelve cents each. We would find a couple of unopened *Tribs* lying around on porch steps, filch the coupons and race off on our bikes to feast at the Castle two miles away.

And I did know something about brand awareness. That bike I rode was a ninth birthday gift from my parents. I had nagged for weeks, peppering them with the Schwinn and Monarch names, both brands famous for their snazzy models I would have killed for. When the birthday arrived, my dad hollered up from the backyard of our building. He had a surprise for me. I raced down the stairs and there it was next to him—a shiny new stripped-down J.C. Higgins from Sears. Crestfallen as I was, I hugged him in thanks and took off down the alley to spare him my tears.

Ironically, when I went to work for Sears, I helped preside over the demise of J.C. Higgins. Sears had finally gotten the message and the temerity to broom that lackluster brand. They signed up Ted Williams, an all-star replacement, to shill for a number of their sporting goods lines. Because more than once I had mentioned my disappointing bicycle story to the head buyer of sporting goods, he saw to it that I was given the copywriting assignment for a catalog page that would launch the Ted Williams brand—an offer for a baseball glove, a medallion and ball autographed via facsimile by the Splendid Splinter himself—for just $9.95. I threw my heart into the copy. Sears sold a million of them. A year later that heartfelt page, displayed in my sample portfolio, was instrumental in helping me land my first agency job.

In the summers of our grade school years, Rippy and I, the original latchkey kids, kept busy. We played softball—the ball itself a taped-over sixteen incher the size of a cantaloupe otherwise known as a Windy City clincher—at the intersection of 72nd and Vernon, our bases the sewer covers at the four corners. When batting, you had to pull it dead left down Vernon or flare it right down 72nd.

Hitting it to straightaway center was a no-no. The windows of a six-flat stood in the flight path.

On weekends, when traffic picked up on our makeshift ballfield, we'd scoot our Radio Flyers over to the High-Low supermarket to hustle deliveries. Rippy's mom worked there as a cashier so the manager was okay about us hanging around outside. "Carry your bags, lady?" (Women didn't drive much back then.) At a dime per shopping bag we had all the business we could handle following shoppers home, their grocery bags snug in our wagons. Two bags, twenty cents though they'd always round it up to a quarter, sometimes more. On a good Saturday we could rack up three or four dollars. Not too shabby for ten-year-olds.

Of course, we spent it as fast as we made it on the usual kid stuff—comic books, candy, flat squares of bubble gum backed by trading cards. (I still have, locked away somewhere, a complete set of National Football League cards from 1948, the first year they commercialized professional football, at the time a second tier attraction comprised of just eight teams.)

There were a few more worthy uses for the money. Once I found my way to a bookstore on 79th, the southern extreme of the neighborhood, and plunked down $2.95 for a hardcover copy of *Black Beauty* by Anna Sewell. I didn't realize the book was first published in the late 1800's but that didn't matter. To me, it was brand new. And worth every penny. It had a textured grasscloth cover in black. The title and such were embossed in what I thought was solid gold. It felt good. It looked good. My very own book. When I showed it to my mother that night she seemed surprised and proud of me. My father, beyond the sports pages never a reader, thought I should be saving my money, for *what* exactly he didn't explain. That same week Rippy spent some of his money, too, investing five dollars for a BB-gun. (Last I heard he'd retired after an adulthood of barbering and was still an avid hunter).

Two years later, in 1950, the All-Star baseball game would be played at Comiskey Park, home of the White Sox. Rippy and I knew that place inside out; we had snuck in there a dozen times by sliding down the ice chute leading to the vendor supply area below the stands. Occasionally, we'd get caught, which meant the security guy, on the spot, would hand out our sentence: Take these push brooms and start sweepin' 'til the first pitch. For a big deal like the All-Star game we knew the ice chute was not an option. Instead we played it straight. Baseball announced a lottery for less desirable outfield seats. We sent in our money, three dollars each, and prayed. Amazingly, two tickets arrived in the mail, third row, right field foul line.

Day of the game, we got off the El at 35th Street and headed for Comiskey. A block from the park, a large, rather ominous man approached us.

"You kids got tickets to the game?" he asked.

"Yeah," we answered in unison, our right hands clutching the tickets in our pant pockets. "Right field, three rows up," I boasted.

"I'll give you fifty bucks a piece for 'em," he said flashing a hundred dollar bill. Neither of us had ever seen one before.

We looked at each other and thought about what awaited beyond the turnstile—Joe DiMaggio, Stan Musial, Ted Williams, Jackie Robinson, even Gus Zernial, the White Sox' version of Ozark Ike—then blurted out again as one "No sir, we're goin' to the game."

We never regretted that decision. Ralph Kiner tied it for the Nationals in the ninth with a homer; Red Schoendienst won it for them in the fourteenth with another. To this day, by all accounts, it was the greatest All-Star game ever. And to top it off, during batting practice one of the lesser-knowns, Cincinnati outfielder Johnny Wyrostek, tossed a ball up to each of us.

Books. And baseball. You can see where this is heading. The kid wants to be a sportswriter one day. And you'd be right. I'd seen my words and byline in our grade school's mimeographed monthly newspaper. A poem about Rapunzel. A short essay on the meaning of Thanksgiving. And I liked seeing them. The desire to express myself, however, did lead to several issues, one that actually brought my mother to tears.

In seventh grade, the school brought in a new gym teacher, a big jerk with an unmerited name: Mr. Charms. Until he showed up, gym class consisted of softball, touch football or indoor basketball, depending on the season. Mr. Charms must've studied Soviet methodology. His idea of gym was exercise. A non-stop fifty minutes of it. And yelling a lot. Finally, fed up, I wrote a petition seeking his dismissal, a version of the Declaration of Independence, and slipped it under the door of Stella Johnson, our principal, who already had it out for me. (Years earlier she taught high school algebra. Unfortunately for me, one of her pupils was my father, a student-athlete who, by his own admission, preferred football scrimmage to subtracting fractions.) I had autographed my petition with a flourish *à la* John Hancock, then coaxed a number of classmates to sign below it. Stella kept Charms. But she sent me home on a two-day suspension.

The next year, 1951, I had a run-in with Mr. Barch, owner of the local school store. I was there minding my own business when a friend came in to buy a set of tempera paints for art class. Barch overheard me when I told the kid the same paints were a lot cheaper at Woolworth's. It seemed like overreaction, but he came around the counter, grabbed me by the collar, shoved me out the door and told me to never set foot in his store again. This really upset me—his was the only school store in the neighborhood. I went home that afternoon, got hold of a big piece of cardboard and wrote on it in bold black crayon. I don't remember my exact words but they somehow impugned Mr. Barch's pricing policy. I then tacked it onto a yardstick and hid it under my bed. The next day, during lunch hour, I picketed back and forth in front of his store brandishing my inflammatory sign.

At that point, Barch brought humorless Miss Johnson into the fray. This time, no leniency. She expelled me for a week. My mother, bless her heart, called Mr. Barch seeking mercy on my behalf. It was then I saw her cry for the first and only time. She hung up in tears, turned to me and said, "He called you a Communist!" My recently deceased grandfather born in Russia might've cheered from on high. Perhaps Senator McCarthy added my name to his infamous list. Me? I had no idea what Mr. Barch was talking about.

⁂

Things began looking up in our household. My dad and his brother Harry partnered to buy a small grocery store in a black neighborhood not far from Comiskey Park. All through high school, I helped out there on Saturdays and the busy pre-holidays. Long before the term "ethnic marketing" was invented, I was somewhat of an expert on the subject. One of my tasks was spritzing water every hour or so on the loose greens displayed in the vegetable bins—leafy pyramids of collard, mustard, turnip and spinach—low-cost and down-home nutrition for our customers back then; featured today on the menus of America's trendiest restaurants.

I enjoyed working alongside Uncle Harry. He was my boyhood idol, the first person in the family to go to college and, more impressive for me, he went on a full football scholarship to DePaul, a local Catholic university. Like the University of Chicago, back then they had a team. Though his playing days were over before I was born, as a kid I spent hours poring through his yearbooks and press clippings, reading of his exploits as a star quarterback and punter. Given our singular and ambiguous last name (contrived for my grandfather by some official on Ellis Island), DePaul never knew Harry was Jewish. I learned that startling fact years later from my father. According to him, had anyone at DePaul known, there's no way his kid brother would've gotten the free ride. Such were the times. Uncle Harry not only threw a "Hail Mary" now and then, he also had to memorize the prayer itself so he could lead the team's recital of it before every game.

With better times my family moved to slightly greener pastures thirty blocks south on 102nd Street. No longer renters, my dad and Uncle Harry chipped in on a fairly new three-flat with a pale yellow brick façade; we took the third floor, Harry and Aunt Jean the first, the second they rented out. We could now have a dog, a Collie mix. My little sister Judy named him Lucky. And he was. He ate nothing but meat, the fresh scraps my dad brought home every night from his butcher counter. Even for 1953, the price of the property ($30,000) was a bargain mainly because it sat just a hundred yards away from the raised and very active Illinois Central tracks. The high school I had just transferred to played their football games at Gately Stadium, which was conveniently located, as it turned out for me, on the other side of the tracks.

As a junior, they let me sign up for journalism class, short for working on the school newspaper. I didn't know a soul at the new school so I tried to make my presence felt by grabbing an assignment for a monthly column. I called it "Larry's Ledger," an opinionated potpourri on topics like dirty washrooms and crummy cafeteria cuisine. From the lack of feedback I received, nobody except the angry lady who ran the lunchroom actually read it.

Writing in obscurity ended in senior year when I got what I really wanted: the Sports Editor's job. Fenger High School may have been academically challenged but it was a football juggernaut. That year, 1954, the Titans went 11 and 0, slaughtering all comers, then moved on to the City Championship game—the top public school (us) versus the top Catholic school (Mt. Carmel)—held at Soldier Field before 70,000 fans. We won 44–zip. Even more exciting was the contact I made with a young sportswriter working the prep beat, Jerry Holtzman of the *Chicago Sun-Times*. I "spotted" for him up in the press box during the big game. We hit it off. Naively, I asked if he could help me get a job as a copyboy for the summer after graduation. A few weeks later he called with the bad news: two kinds of kids get those jobs at the paper, he reported: bosses' nephews and big advertisers' nieces. This was not what someone with absolutely no clout wanted to hear.

As a sidebar, forty years later, I stroll into a SoHo art gallery killing time before a meeting. The artist, William Mann, a heavy-set bearded guy wearing a work apron, was busy installing his small found-object sculptures along the back wall. We struck up a conversation. Chicago. Advertising. Sports. What have you. He mentioned his brother, Jerome Holtzman, had just retired as Sports Editor of the *Sun-Times* after a long career. I told him about "Jerry's" fateful phone call back in 1954 and how I often wondered if my life would've been different had he gotten me that job. The artist patted my shoulder and said I had done the right thing going into advertising. His brother, he went on, "never made a dime" working for that paper. Right then and there I bought the sculpture he was just about to hang, one that had as its centerpiece the porcelain and curly electric element out of a discarded Sears hotplate. It is displayed on a shelf in my office at home. My wife hates it. But, for me, it has multiple meaning.

So how *did* I sidestep the sportswriter muse and go "into advertising"?

For one thing, as that glorious championship football season unfolded, a dark side emerged. On Monday mornings after the latest Saturday slaughter across the I.C. tracks, I'd take the bus to school, the story of the game, hot off my typewriter, stuffed in a folder ready to turn in for that week's edition.

I was proud of my prose; it was alliterative—and objective; as good as they were (even Holtzman said later they could have beaten half the college teams in the country; had Dick Butkus, who lived in my new neighborhood, chosen Fenger instead of a nearby vocational high school, I think they could've given Notre Dame a game), not every one of their plays was perfection. The Monday after the third win, a self-appointed editor, the Titans' monster right tackle, accosted me on the bus. "Lemme see whatcha wrote dis time," he demanded. Obviously he didn't like something in my account the week before. The lummox grabbed my story, scanning it for his name no doubt, then took menacing exception to an observation I had made about sloppy interior line play. That was followed the next week by a corridor run-in, this time with the B.M.O.C., a blond Adonis and bruising fullback, very unhappy with my pithy, albeit, factual snipes about his missed blocks. Scariest though was a confrontation with Coach Palmer, Fenger's version of Bear Bryant, revered and feared by everyone in the school. Unfortunately, he was also my gym teacher who, with a grunt, had the power to drop me down for twenty-five more push-ups or a few extra laps around the practice field.

"Why you knocking my boys all the time?" He was in my face. I could smell the Listerine on his breath.

"I know they're great, Coach. But it's my job to point out a few..."

He cut me off, his face turning red. "That's *my* job!" he roared. "Lay off of 'em."

Did all that piling on intimidate me? Sure. I began to watch my words, couching comments in rah-rah rhetoric, confining my criticisms to fan behavior. Hey, they were running the table, right? And were a lot bigger than me. But I was no longer a journalist. I was a fawning hack churning out glowing praise bound for their scrapbooks and college scholarship applications. And I didn't like myself for caving.

That same fall, a friend, Lyn Cini, who was a half-year ahead of me and one of the sharpest guys I'd met in school, talked me into checking out a program he was involved in called Junior Achievement. It sounded wimpy, or whatever the word for nerdy was back then, but I took him up on it. If nothing else, one night a week, it would keep me off the streets.

You may know J.A.'s premise: kids meet on a weekday evening at a Center (ours was located in a drafty one-time factory building within the historical Pullman Car Works complex on 111th Street); major area corporations provide volunteer executive counselors;

small companies are formed; "stock" is issued and sold to family and friends; a product is chosen and manufactured, usually simple handicraft items like potholders or trivets; and finally the company members go out and sell the product more often than not to the same people who bought the stock. Look, Ma, I'm a Capitalist!

Everything about it appealed to me including the chance to chat with the counselors, guys who showed up from their day jobs actually wearing suits and ties. One of them, a marketing manager at International Harvester, saw something in me, I guess, and suggested I give thought to an advertising career. He regaled me with stories about collaborating with his ad agency—the field trips, focus groups, creative presentations, casting sessions and photo shoots—and managed to make something as unglamorous as advertising to farmers sound exciting. Since I'd been floating along in a vacuum, it didn't take much of a nudge to alter my course. The more he told me about the business, the more I knew he was right. I began taking out library books: *How to Write Advertising that Sells*, Clyde Bedell's ponderous volume; and *Obvious Adams*, a highly motivating story by Robert Updegraff, as thin as Bedell's was thick. I leafed through copies of *Saturday Evening Post* and *Life* and *Collier's* and saw ad after copycat ad that even I knew were uninspired, many mere rote renditions of a product's TV commercial. I can do this stuff, I said to myself; maybe I can do them even better.

That winter my friend Lyn had moved on to DePaul as a business major. We'd often reconnoiter at a pool hall late at night. Between shots, we started talking up advertising, innocently musing about the future and how, maybe one day, he and I could start an advertising agency, something we knew next to nothing about. We had a simplistic plan: he'd run the business part; I'd write the ads.

That never happened. Lyn, ever the achiever, junior or otherwise, went into the Army after college to fulfill his ROTC obligation, met and married an Army nurse and kept re-upping. He wisely spent the Vietnam years writing white papers on logistics back in D.C., rose to the rank of full colonel (he had one ass to kiss to make General, he said, but couldn't bring himself to do it) and ended his career as Commandant of Arlington National Cemetery. Any similarities between that solemn role and running an ad agency are purely cynical.

Lyn had been our Center's representative at the downtown council of Junior Achievement. When he left, the Center's manager asked me to take Lyn's place on the council. As on any board, there were perks: a scholarship to the Dale Carnegie course, held downtown one night a week, where I learned how to win friends and influence people, an invaluable skill later in life; a spring-break convention trip to exotic Oxford, Ohio; and opportunities to rub elbows with important Chicago business leaders.

I'll never forget one of those occasions. It was the end-of-year Junior Achievement gala, several thousand strong, held at the International Amphitheatre. Oddly, both national presidential conventions were held at that place two years earlier in 1952. Illinois' own Adlai Stevenson and Dwight Eisenhower, a General if there ever was one, got the nod of their respective parties.

As one of the ten council representatives, I was seated on the dais. They had arranged it so a major figure in the Chicago business community would sit between each of us at the long table behind the rostrum. Eddie Fisher sang the National Anthem. (For those too young to remember, Fisher was a crooner known for his rendition of "Oh My Papa," which my grandmother loved. He married several hotties during his life. Elizabeth Taylor for one. And Debbie Reynolds for another. Debbie later married Harry Karl, who owned a chain of shoe stores out west. To complete the circle, Karl's Shoes wound up as a client at my first agency). Hizzoner Mayor Daley gave the greeting and Cardinal Stritch, the invocation. It was, without question, the biggest deal in my young life.

I wasn't sandwiched between executives; I had been placed at the far right end of the table. And the executive to my left was busy chatting with a fellow council member seated to his left, an attractive young lady who, unfortunately, I only vaguely knew. Despite

Dale Carnegie, I'm sitting there tongue-tied over my breast of chicken with no idea how to insert myself into their conversation.

Finally, he felt obliged to turn my way. A short jowly serious-looking man in his sixties, he wore a classy gray suit and vest with a gold chain draped across it. Edward G. Robinson came to mind. As we all did, he had a nametag pinned to his left lapel; he could easily read mine, I couldn't read his.

"So what do you plan to do when you get out of high school... Larry?" he asked rather perfunctorily.

"I'm thinking about journalism school, sir"

"Oh? What facet of journalism?"

"Advertising," I answered without hesitation.

"Hmmm. Why advertising?" His interest had piqued some. That should've been a clue.

"Well, I heard they work the least and make the most." I don't know why I said that but that's what I said. "And what do you do, Mister..." I leaned forward to read his nametag, "...Burnett?"

He cocked his head and winced as though I had just stabbed him in the eye with my salad fork. "I own the world's sixth largest advertising agency, young man. And you have a lot to learn."

Indeed.

Pier Pressure

Upon graduating high school my grade point average, like whale poo, nestled in the bottom quintile of my class. And for financial reasons I needed to live at home the first two years of college. Between the grades and the money, my choices were limited. The best available was the University of Illinois at Chicago, which in those days was a two-year program housed at Navy Pier.

Today, the Pier is one of the jewels of Chicago's famed lakefront. It's a festive place, braided with lights, an amusement park and convention facility adorned near its entrance by an enormous and radiant Ferris wheel and, at the far end, by a bulbous and ornate ballroom.

Then, it was a military remnant, a former loading dock and narrow warehouse converted into the world's skinniest school, which plunged out for a mile into Lake Michigan off a forlorn downtown street rutted by rusty rail tracks. Some disgruntled students called the non-campus "Grand Avenue with a hard-on."

But, and it was a big but in my case, they were mandated, at an improbably low tuition, to take on all comers possessing a pulse and an Illinois high school diploma. The word slacker wasn't in vogue yet, but however you'd characterize them, as each semester began the Pier had more than its share (in studious ways, myself included). The start of each semester you were given a random locker assignment somewhere down the mile-long corridor bisecting the classrooms and labs to either side. The locker might be located, as my first one was, two city blocks from your nearest class. You couldn't complain about it but you could wait it out. On Day One, students swarmed the place, pushed there in large part, I suppose, by prodding Old World parents. Invariably, a month into the semester the student body dramatically dropped; you could poach empty lockers close to all your classes because so many of the enrollees so soon had seen the scholastic future and for one reason or another knew they were not in it.

A case in point: Geology 101. As a liberal arts major, I had to choose a math or science course. No decision. Higher mathematics was definitely not part of my genetic make-up. Yes, like my father, I could add a column of figures scribbled down the side of a grocery bag as fast as an adding machine, but the complexities of anything more abstract put the left side of my brain on overload. Back in high school, my advanced algebra teacher, Mr. Hollister, who reminded me of Ebenezer Scrooge with a hearing aid, took me aside after grading final exams. He said I had earned an F in the course but that he really wasn't looking forward to seeing me again in summer school. He pulled a quarter out of his pocket and told me to call it, heads or tails. The coin in mid-air, I hollered "tails" with no idea where this was going. "Heads it is," he said, "you pass with a D." I shook his hand and left the classroom as bewildered by what just transpired as I had been all semester long blinking at algebraic hieroglyphs.

That first day in geology class I learned right away that here they took their subject matter far more seriously. The professor, a young bearded man sporting a corduroy jacket and a German-tinged accent, greeted us. "Good morning. I'm Dr. Danzer." Then he cut to the chase. He held up a rock the size of a grapefruit. "I found this chunk of quartzite on a fieldtrip to Montana. Carbon-fourteen dating has determined that it is approximately ten million years old. If any of you, due to religious beliefs, cannot accept that fact, please identify yourselves." Wow, what's this all about?

I heard movement behind me and turned to see three buddies, still loyally wearing their letter sweaters from a parochial high school in Little Italy, look at each other then rise from their chairs in slow motion as if they were about to be crucified.

"Very well," the prof said resignedly, unwilling to deal with their dogma. "You'll need to talk to your advisor about finding an alternative course. If you remain here you will fail." Just like that. The three nodded righteously, gathered their stuff and left.

Personally, I found geology fascinating. It brought to life the memories I had of the one time I'd seen mountains—on the only family vacation we ever took, a car trip to Yellowstone when I was eight. Beyond expository writing and poetry and such it was one of the few courses at the Pier that piqued my interest. To this day, I always try for a window seat on flights so I can gaze down on those stately formations millions and millions of years old.

For extra credit in Geology 102, a classmate—John Hennessey—and I decided to take our own fieldtrip over the Easter break to the Smoky Mountains. "Deliverance" hadn't been written yet, much less filmed, or some of the locals we bumped into down there might've given us pause. We pacified one half-drunk geezer by buying a jug (actually a repurposed bleach bottle) of moonshine he was aggressively pushing. He took the two bucks and disappeared into the dogwoods. As for his distillate, the bleach would've been a tastier chaser.

We had John's beat-up Plymouth and one old sleeping bag. The car was his so I volunteered to sleep under the stars. When I awoke Easter morning—Oh Jesus!—I could feel something moving near my bare left leg. I whispered loudly for John to get out of the car and begged him to slowly slide down the left side zipper. Out slithered a four-foot long diamondback, toasty warm and not looking for trouble. It was my first and last camping trip.

Thanks to geology, I avoided college math but could not dodge a foreign language, another subject area I dreaded. Again, back in high school, as a freshman and sophomore, Spanish meant *muerte*—death—for me. Fortunately, we had an extremely eccentric teacher, Miss Perette, an obsessive collector of *National Geographic* magazines going back to its inception in 1888 though, poor thing, she did lack an issue here and there that would tidy up her treasure trove. Every semester she passed out an updated list of missing issues. She never put it in writing but we all understood the deal—for every copy on her wanted list you could deliver she'd raise your grade one notch. No, I'm not kidding. In fairness to her, she did draw the line at A's; those you had to earn legitimately.

I've given my good fortune the nod already. This was one of those times. A couple in our old apartment building on 72nd Street had moved out, skipping on their rent. The janitor told me the people had left a lot of junk in their basement locker and, before he threw it out, I could rummage through it to see if there was anything I wanted. Knowing Stash, I was sure he'd already grabbed anything good. But lo and behold, I discover two very heavy boxes in there filled with—guess what? I came back down with my Spanish teacher's wish list and methodically went through the musty contents. Bingo, six of them, mostly from the '20's. As long as Miss Perette kept her job through my four semesters of obligatory Spanish, I had a C-average covered. *Gracias a Dios*, she did.

(I did absorb some of Miss Perette's obsession. Gratefully being on *National Geographic*'s "comp list" for years, I've never thrown away a copy. There's a five-shelf bookcase in my house bracing under the weight of at least 350 of those yellow wonders. It would dismay Miss Perette, as it did me, to learn you can buy today a boxed set of DVDs, a few inches wide, that contains every issue of that magazine ever published from Amazon for $49.95.)

Now that I conquered Spanish, it's off to college to take on French. On several levels I have no problem with foreign languages. I like their movies; subtitles work fine for me. My wife of more than thirty-five years was born in Shanghai and can speak on the phone to her family and friends in any of four Chinese dialects. No problem. It goes in one of my ears and out the other.

My problem was *studying* a foreign language. It took too much time. Despite Stella Johnson writing in red all over my grade school report cards, "Larry does not apply himself," I am applying myself—to jobs that will let me save enough money to go away my junior year to college, to the advertising department at the University of Missouri School of Journalism if they'll take me and yes, it's not up there tuition- or room and board–wise with an Ivy League school, but it's money I don't have and nobody else is offering and it's not going to happen unless I keep applying my ass off.

My two years at the Pier I worked three jobs. Helping out at the grocery store on Saturdays was one. I learned the Dewey Decimal System which I'm sure today is as dead as Dewey and worked Monday and Wednesday afternoons shoving books back onto shelves at the Pier's library. Best of all, from a "marketing standpoint," on Tuesday and Thursday evenings and all day Sunday not to mention full time at the Christmas break and summers, I sold small appliances and stereos at a place called Polk Brothers. (Thanks again to my friend Lyn who worked there first and got me the job interview with Maury Polk, the most lovable tyrant of all time.) In sheer size, Polk Bros. was a precursor to Best Buy and Good Guys but in spirit it operated more like Crazy Al's in New York.

All the name brands were there at a discount. For instance, tiny—and tinny sounding—Motorola and Zenith *transistor* radios, the latest rage. As a demo, you'd bounce one on the counter, catch the rebound and turn it on. It worked! Try that with your old vacuum tube portable. Selling them was a cinch; the real trick was how big the discount. The more of a price break you gave a customer, like maybe your mother, the more Maury's salemen's commission scale slid. You can imagine the conflict, the soul-searching, the ethical crisis this system created. And, in the midst of negotiations, if you screwed up your calculations and quoted the customer an obscenely low price, then tried to backtrack (or "Indian give" as they used to say in the old neighborhood) and the customer said "I heard'ja da first time," you'd excuse yourself and go see Maury in the backroom. He'd march back out with you, okay your errant quote, then fire you on the spot. You'd walk away head down and dejected. Without fail, the customer would tell Maury, "Hey, I don't wantcha firin' the kid on account of me. What's your real best price?" When the satisfied customer left with his transistor radio or Westinghouse floor fan or Grundig hifi, you'd come back out to the floor and start selling again. Maury would say, "Next time, kid, learn how to count." I knew how to count. The problem was percentages.

So I'm taking college French. No amount of *National Geo* back issues can save me. And I'm sinking fast. To get into Mizzou I need a C average. At best, I'm borderline. Then Bob Quinlan, a high school classmate who, like me, had been trying to stay afloat at the Pier, threw me a life buoy, actually two if you include the time, a week earlier, when he talked me into taking a walk with him over to the Naval Armory on the lakeshore a couple of blocks from school. Like so many students, Bob had had it with higher education. He wanted to join the Navy, a four-year hitch, and thought I might be interested in what they had to say. (He had caught me on a particularly bad day). Long and short, Bob signed up. I was actually mulling it over when one of the enlistment officers asked me to step outside for a cigarette. Maybe he didn't like the cut of my jib or had filled his quota for the day with Quinlan, but he told me I ought to count to ten and give school more time. You can always enlist later, he said. I don't recall his name but I owe him.

On his way out to sea, Bob mentioned that his girlfriend, still in high school, had met a fellow student newly arrived from France. Would I like to meet her? Maybe she could help you with your French. Perhaps you've noticed I've made no reference to girlfriends. Girls were okay. But like the act of cracking textbooks,

I had no time for them. Not to mention the fact that old Stella Johnson, despite her withering personal attacks, had double-promoted me twice in grade school (perhaps to accelerate my departure). Always a year younger than anyone in my high school class, I was insecure and awkward, bereft of even a driver's license. A month from seventeen when I started at Navy Pier, here I am a geographically disadvantaged townie in a school full of townies. There were no fraternities or sororities. There was no social life. There was only that long dank overcrowded corridor and icy Lake Michigan beyond and the coldest walk this side of International Falls from the school to the I.C. station a mile away. All just as well since girls weren't in my game plan. That is until Quinlan introduced me to Marie-Christine Françoise Montet.

Her mother had worked on an American Air Force base near Bordeaux so Christine's English was very good. She patiently held my hand through the two *tres difficile* years of French. Thanks to her* I eked out an overall average slightly north of middlin', sent the transcript and some samples of my writing to Mizzou and was accepted for that fall. Now all I had to do is figure out where Columbia, Missouri, was and how to get there.

* *Did I mention Christine looked like Brigitte Bardot? You can picture the rest. Four years later, though still way too young for either of us, we married, had two sons just fifteen months apart, struggled financially and emotionally, and sadly divorced.*

Coming of Age

Growing up, I was always surrounded by grandparents. No one ever heard of "assisted living for the elderly," certainly not in our family. All during the war years and into the early fifties it was my father's father, Grandpa Sam, who lived with us. He kept to himself most of the time. When he wasn't fixing shoes at his shop on 71st Street, he was next door at Joslyn's Saloon playing pinochle with his cronies, all neighborhood Irishmen. That open-minded kinship notwithstanding, he had a far less tolerant side he reserved for the family.

Once, I brought from school a Christmas wreath I'd made out of red and green paper and innocently hung it on the front door of the apartment. When he came home, no doubt with a little schnapps under his belt, he spied the wreath, speared it with his cane and chastised my poor mother for letting me put the thing up. One time, in an expansive mood, he tried to teach me how to trim out a new sole with his sharp scythe-like knife. I still have the scar on my left index finger to prove I wasn't cut out for his line of work. For him to walk the block back and forth to his store or Joslyn's was an arduous task requiring the aid of that cane and a cumbersome leg brace he sometimes asked me to help him lace up. He blamed smoking for his bum knee. Years earlier, when 71st was a streetcar line, he was crossing in the rain, he said, head down so his hat brim would keep his Lucky lit and never saw the streetcar coming.

A difficult and irascible man 'til the day he died, the family found what I thought was a counterintuitive way to lay him to rest. They buried him next to his wife who, in 1926, had deserted him and his three sons, a premeditated act. One day, when she knew none of them would be home, she hired a truck to move her and her youngest, her only daughter, and a lot of their furniture to the far Northwest Side. Why she left was never discussed. I do know my dad and his brothers deeply resented what had happened and refused to ever again see their mother or sister. I, on the other hand, was coerced into accompanying Grandpa, taking two streetcars and a bus each way, to visit my absentee grandmother and aunt once a month on Sunday. They'd serve us tea and a snack; he gave his estranged wife money when he thought I wasn't looking. None of it made any sense. All I knew was that after being separated for twenty-five years, they were now reunited forever.

I learned another deep, dark family secret when, soon after we moved to 102nd Street, it was my mother's turn as a caring child. Both her parents joined our household. I remember helping my dad and Uncle Harry carry her father up to the third floor, his wheelchair our gurney. He was in bad shape, both legs amputated some years earlier, hardening of the arteries the cause, they said (I have to believe there's a less barbaric treatment today). Understandably, he was even a bigger grouch than Grandpa Sam. In his shoes, or lack thereof, I would have been one, too.

On the other hand his forbearing wife, my grandmother, was as kind as she was strong, as close as I've ever known to an Eleanor Roosevelt; she even resembled Eleanor though her Old Country accent gave her away—patrician, she wasn't. Despite his disposition, Grandma was a saint (though that description she would not have appreciated) the way she treated her invalid husband, truly miraculous considering their history together. And apart.

As the story goes, in 1918 when my mother was five and her three brothers a bit older, they all lived behind a curtain at the rear of a notions shop Grandma ran on storied Maxwell Street.

Grandpa, who was a cigar roller by day, went out one night, he said, to buy a newspaper. And then disappeared. Unannounced, unrepentant and empty-handed, he showed up five years later. Supposedly, he had spent his hiatus in South Africa searching for diamonds. The crazy part is Grandma took him back.

Given my admitted language deficiencies, I didn't understand much of what she said to him in Yiddish but I had the impression that, now and then, when his demands grew irrational, her saintliness lapsed and she would emphatically remind him of his long and unexcused absence.

We played musical bedrooms when they moved in. My sister took over my small room at the back of the apartment, my grandparents took Judy's room and I switched to a foldaway cot in the dining room a bit removed from everybody else. I gladly agreed to that; my late-night comings and goings would less likely disturb anyone's sleep and my parents would less likely know of my late-night comings and goings. A win-win. Perhaps I had inherited some of Grandpa's errant ways.

He died in the spring of my sophomore year at the Pier. The burden of caring for him lifted, my grandmother gained new life and energy. In fact, she had just returned from her first airplane trip, all the way to California, where she'd spent the entire summer with her oldest son.

I had said the good-byes to my friends and Christine. All that remained was the packing and a run to Polk Bros. to shake a few hands, especially Maury's, remind him he'd see me again for the holiday season and pick up my last paycheck, which would be sizable since August was a scorcher and those expensive Mobil-Aire fans had flown off my sales book and out of the store.

The next morning, I saw Grandma for the first time since she went out West. I hugged her hello. She gave me a glowing description of life in Los Angeles. Then she noticed the half-filled suitcase sitting on my cot.

"Ver you goink, honey?" she asked as she instinctively started folding the shirts I'd tossed in with my underwear and socks.

"I'm going away to college, Grandma. To Missouri."

"Missouri? Vats der?"

What could I tell her? I barely knew myself.

⁂

I left at dawn on the last Saturday of August. The J-School had written that there would be people waiting into the evening to help get new students settled in. As a going-away present, Uncle Harry had given me—the second college student in family history—his '51 Dodge Coronet, a stick-shift six in decent shape. It took nine lonely hours to escape the pull of the South Side, make my way down Route 66 to St. Louis, then across U.S. 40 to reach that foreign place in the middle of Missouri. (I missed Eisenhower's grandiose Interstate Highway system by a couple of years. Today the same trip on I-55 and I-70 is much quicker.)

Over the next two years, I would make that drive in the Dodge eight or nine times, the last few on five cylinders and a can of motor oil every hundred miles. I'm not sure exactly where Bobby Troup got his kicks on Route 66. The section I took had to be the most desolate and boring stretch of road in America—save for the dead of winter when the snow turned to ice and the road definitely held your attention.

It's customary today to "visit" multiple campuses, parents in tow. In my case, that would have been an impossible luxury. Besides, once again, my options for an education, especially now zeroing in on advertising, were limited. Finicky and pricey Northwestern was out of the question. A hundred miles off to my left as I drove toward St Louis, even the University of Illinois at Champaign required a lofty 3.5 average. So Missouri it was. And though I couldn't answer Grandma's question, I was eager to find out what *was* there. Would the professors be disciples of Clyde Bedell, preaching over-starched theories about copywriting? Or would creative freedom reign? I knew the Ozarks were down there somewhere. Would the school be full of hillbillies? What would living in a dormitory be like and who was my mystery roommate? I'd read there were two other schools in town, Christian and Stephens, both women's colleges. Those odds held promise. And rounding out my priorities I wondered what the drinking age was.

And so it went until I arrived at the outskirts of Columbia in mid-afternoon. Driving into town, it hit me how clean and leafy overhead the streets were and how light the traffic and low the buildings were on Broadway, the main drag. With the help of a passer-by I found my destination on the northeast edge of the campus: the world's oldest School of Journalism housed, appropriately, in a dignified reddish-brown brick building trimmed in weathered stone, fairly lengthy but just two stories high. (I soon learned there was a third level below grade bursting with activity where the *Columbia Missourian*, a city daily and cornerstone of the J-School's learn-by-doing philosophy, was published.) A graceful archway cut through the ground floor and framed a large bright green commons beyond, the "Quad," surrounded on all sides by similar structures and other schools of the University. Casting long shadows at the far end of the quadrangle stood the six Ionic limestone columns I'd seen reproduced in the left hand corner of all their correspondence. What remained after a fire in 1892 that destroyed the University's main edifice—a fire reportedly started by an electric light bulb, the first ever installed west of the Mississippi—was now their logo.

The counselor was busy with somebody else so I went down the hall to check out the Advertising Department, my new home away from home. Creative samples from the previous year were still on display, tacked up on bulletin boards along the corridor. I knew there were no art students in J-School so it didn't surprise me that the ads and outdoor layouts weren't all that slick. But the writing was concise, some of it pretty clever. Seeing now what had preceded me, I thought I would be able to hold my own. I inhaled deeply, the old sigh of relief, and smelled the printer's ink wafting up from the floor below. For the first time, I knew for certain coming here was the right decision.

The friendly counselor gave me some paperwork in preparation for Monday's orientation, then pointed me in the direction of my dorm. A grad student advisor there told me my assigned room was on the second floor and gave me a key and the name of my roommate: Virgil Page. In my entire eighteen years, I had never met a Virgil. This should be interesting.

I went back to the car, grabbed my Smith-Corona portable and the suitcase and found the room up the stairs. I unlocked the door wondering if ol' Virgil had showed up yet. There he was, sound asleep in his skivvies on top of one of the unmade mattresses, crew cut and all.

He woke with the noise and lifted up, braced by his sinewy arms.

"Larry, right?"

"Yep, and you're Virgil." I went over and shook his hand.

He was squinting at me in a disapproving way. "That how they dress where ya come from?" He had what I quickly learned was a Missouri twang, an accent prevalent among those born a bit south of Columbia, below the arbitrary Mason-Dixon line.

"I guess. Chicago if you want to know. Is there some uniform here or something?"

"Nah, but those trow gotta go."

I figured he was referring to my gray Dickie work pants. They were cheap, no ironing necessary and that's what I wore, though, looking down, I had to admit they were saggy from the drive. I don't remember what kind of shoes I had on but he didn't think much of them either.

Assuring me there was hope he said next week he'd show me ("Show Me" state, right?) what to get at a store everybody went to.

"You gotta gun?" he asked out of nowhere.

"They legal here?"

He laughed. "G'wan unpack. Come all this way, you're prob'ly hungry. We'll go to the cafeteria, ain't great but we're payin' for it anyhow. Then we'll run over to Sears and getcha a twenty-two."

"Someone starting a war, Virgil?"

A good audience, he laughed again. "T'morrow mornin', we're goin' huntin'. It's Sunday, you got nothin' better to do anyway. Me, you and my friend Duane, we got a date with some big old 'coons."

It *had* been a long day. I wasn't sure I heard right.

He got up, threw a towel over his bony shoulders and picked a Dopp kit off his pile of stuff on the floor. I assumed the showers were somewhere down the hall.

"Be rabbit out there, too," he said all knowing.

Out of the Woods

Thanks to Virgil and Duane, I killed what could have been a very lonesome first Missouri Sunday. We drove about ten miles south of town in Virgil's swoopy and souped-up '49 Mercury to a wooded area on a farm owned by "Dewey's" uncle. Dewey was tall and lean, like Virgil a junior ag major, son of a farmer, and a devout independent who loved the noncommittal life in the dorms. He was the true hunter of the two, Daniel Boone incarnate. Despite my murderous Chicago mystique, he sensed I didn't know squat about shooting. And he was right. So he set an old Coke can on a stump about thirty feet away, came back and told me to take a few practice shots. I bolted a bullet into my brand new Remington single shot .22 (the rifle and fifty rounds of ammo had set me back twelve bucks at Sears) and brought it to the ready. Both stood back and watched. It felt like an initiation. I steadied myself, took aim and fired. First shot the can went flying. They yipped it up. "Dang, Larry, you'll do fine," Virgil hollered.

And I did. With Dewey Boone cautioning me about stepping on twigs and pointing out squirrel nests up in the hawthorns, I managed to bring one down. They bagged three more between them. We never did encounter any raccoons, thank God. These were fox squirrels, reddish and bigger than their gray Chicago cousins that, as a kid, I'd left food out for in the winter.

I knew this was my successful trial by fire but it felt wanton and pointless, that is until Virgil pulled his Merc behind a rib shack outside of town. They reached into the car trunk, each grabbing two of the squirrels by their tails. "C'mon, Larry," Dewey said, "let's get us some supper." Damn, not only did we have to shoot 'em, now we had to eat 'em! They saw the look on my face and started laughing. It was all just part of the rites. The black owner of the shack came out to greet us. He knew them. "Gotchu four, huh boys? Leave 'em 'side the door and come on in." It was barter, Missouri style. Four fresh-killed squirrels equaled three delicious pulled pork (at least that's what the menu board called it) sandwiches and all the trimmings. The Falstaffs were on me.

Sitting there chewing the fat, as it were, I learned they both were going steady with nursing students (they called them their "night nurses") who were driving in together from Kansas City as we spoke. It was a relief to hear that their spare time was thus spoken for; they were unassuming guys and I was grateful for the macho experience they so brotherly shared but starting tomorrow I was heading out of the woods in a different direction.

And Virgil would never have to fret again over his roommate's Dickies. The tromp through the burr-laden tangle of underbrush had taken its toll. My pant legs were shredded beyond redemption.

It took root in a farm field in the middle of Missouri when Martin Van Buren was President, the first public school of higher education west of the Mississippi.

Chalk up 170 years and a bit of history accumulates. To wit:

The first teacher in their School of Art was George Caleb Bingham, famed realist who focused on everyday life in the Old West. Had Dewey been around in 1851 he could well have posed for Bingham's "Daniel Boone Escorting Settlers Through the Cumberland Gap." Stark and front lit, it's as if Boone is leading his followers out of the darkness into the promising light and damned if he doesn't look just like Dewey.

Missouri's football coach from the mid '30's until just before I arrived in '56 was Don Faurot. He conceived the split-T formation, its many permutations still called today at all levels of the game. He also had this chauvinistic albeit crazy idea that if you played football for Missouri you ought to be *from* Missouri, one reason his teams remained in the doldrums for decades. Another reason, though perhaps not his doing alone, is that it wasn't until Dan Devine replaced him as coach that the first African-Americans received football scholarships: Mel West and Norris Stevenson, both running backs, both Missouri natives. Norris lived down the hall from me in the dorm. West went on to play pro ball with the old New York Titans for a couple of seasons.

And, of course, there was the School of Journalism, in 1909 a revolutionary concept. Given the recent plight of newspapers, their steep decline in influence and revenue, the idea of building a curriculum around a functioning city daily today would be an anachronism. Though when I arrived in 1957 it was anything but. Student reporters raced in with their notepads and began pounding out stories. Others manned the city desk, editing the rough copy, passing it up to the supervising professor, and getting it back for headline writing based on the allotted space a given story would command. Then down to the pressroom where, from a bank of clacking, mesmerizing Rube Goldberg–like contraptions called linotype machines fed by molten lead, the story, no matter how insignificant, was set (in a way, immortalized) into hefty column-wide chunks of Times Roman type in reverse, ready for all the other arcane steps required before the presses rolled. Even for me, the avowed ad man, my junior year there—when it was compulsory that every J-School student work on "the paper"—was pretty heady stuff.

We had our "beats" regularly rotated to broaden our experience—the local hospitals checking for births and/or deaths (serving a small town, it was axiomatic that everyone was entitled to have his or her name in the paper at least twice in a lifetime); the police blotter from which no one wanted to see their name repeated in the paper; the fire department; local high schools for sports results and academic honors; one of the three schools of higher education; Little League officials; the Boone County permit department where development deals unfolded; the City Hall where the best chance for a byline might occur; even churches to get news of upcoming weddings and confirmations.

It was Journalism 101 and we were not expected to come back from any of those beats empty-handed. For one thing, our grade depended on our perseverance. For another, we were up against a competitor, the *Columbia Tribune*, which had a full-time professional staff covering the same territory. A year later when we, the ad majors—no longer involved with news gathering—were out there competing with them for newspaper ad dollars I learned the hard way just how formidable an opponent the pros at the *Trib* were.

Meanwhile Missouri offered other courses I found stimulating and yes, gratefully, up my alley.

There was Ad Principles where, whether I remembered every principle or not, I aced the ad writing assignments and was engrossed by the various guest speakers, mostly alums employed at big-time ad agencies, people like Wally Armbruster, the hot-shot creative director on Budweiser at D'Arcy MacManus in St. Louis and Morris Jacobs, who only "attended" J-School long enough to start his own agency, Bozell-Jacobs, famous for Mutual of Omaha's "Wild Kingdom" TV show starring the scintillating Marlin Perkins.

And Typography. On the go-in I had no idea it existed as a course—required by both news and ad majors—worth three credit hours at that. And I loved it. In grade school, I was the one always asked to draw the posters. I had that overlapping balloony lettering down to a science. Perhaps the midnight artists defacing our byways and freight cars stole it from me. It blared forth on the picket sign that got me in trouble. It was on the posters I created when I ran for grade school mayor:

Brains, brawn, curly black hair (I was twelve)
That's our candidate
Larry Postaer

A toothy kid named Bucky Hill beat me by a whisker but my posters kept me in the hunt.

The typography lab at J-School fascinated me. The myriad of fonts and their mysterious names: Bodoni, Baskerville, Caslon, et al. How could someone have sat down hundreds of years ago and created from scratch a work of art as demanding and intricate as a type face where each letter works in harmony with all the others and words and sentences form to make a statement that still speaks eloquently today? We mastered the California Job Case, so logical in its perplexity. You see them today hanging on walls, their well-crafted wooden compartments, like an elaborate Mondrian, the perfect frame for collections of knick-knacks. Then, a single case held type of a certain font and size: lower case, upper case, numerals, punctuation marks, ligatures; each in its designated cubby hole; the more prevalent a given letter (i.e., e, a, i, s, t) the larger its compartment. We had to learn it blindfolded. The *Missourian* employed the larger point sizes of this antiquated handset type for news and advertising headlines that the infinitely faster linotype machine could not produce.

History and Principles of American Journalism, a required course, sounded dry as dust. But taught by Professor William H. Taft, a lively and erudite lecturer right out of central casting, it grabbed me the way no other history course had. I still refer to our textbook written by a former dean of the School of Journalism, Frank Luther Mott. From Ben Franklin's wisdom, to the newspaper wars of Pulitzer and Hearst, to the sardonic drawings by Bill Mauldin, U.S. history sprang to life for me from a far more relevant and personal perspective. To this day, whenever *Jeopardy* puts up a category remotely related, I kill.

It wasn't all J-School. Across the quad I took Shakespeare, taught by a wonderful elder named Hardin Craig. He actually wrote the book, all five pounds and forty dollars of it, filled with the Bard's plays and sonnets and Dr. Craig's pithy annotations that he theatrically and lovingly embellished in his lectures. I was lucky to get in. His was arguably the most popular class north of Ag School.

And Modern Poetry taught by a garrulous guy who claimed to be a New York drinking buddy of Dylan Thomas, the semi-sober Welshman who wrote the lyrical "Poem in October"—*High tide and the heron dived* et cetera. It's the one lengthy poem I still have committed to memory.

Things were going well. For the first time since grammar school, my grades were not an issue. The money I had made at Polk Bros., including a two-week return stint that Christmas, was holding up well. Back then, Missouri was truly a bargain. Board was nominal, tuition next to nothing, about eighty dollars a semester (it actually *was* nothing if you were a Missouri native!). I met new friends, fellow ad majors, several close to this day. One, Ed Cristal—who still has his own retail agency in St. Louis, another Cal Ripken—asked if I wanted to move out of the dorm and share an apartment with a friend of his who was coming down that second semester to attend Business School.

Other than an occasional Sunday hunt, I barely saw Virgil, certainly never saw him lying around our dorm room studying, and moving out would not be traumatic. I do have one lasting memory of him. It was a pair of his blue jeans that miraculously stood—upright and unsupported—against a corner of the dorm room near the window. Virgil, like his namesake, ever the farmer's son and poet, called them his "humpin' pants." Stiff as they were, he managed somehow to climb into them before heading out on his early evening rendezvous with the night nurse (curfew for women was

10:30 weekdays). These were pre-Pill times; why he called his jeans what he did and how they sat up like a *papier maché* sculpture, I'll leave to the imagination.

So sight unseen I have a new roommate arriving in a week. I found an inexpensive apartment, actually one end of an unfinished basement in an old Victorian close by J-School. It had two primitive beds, a night-stand between them, one moth-eaten couch stained from God knows what, a pipe rack for hanging clothes and a ratty curtain separating it from the furnace, hot water heater and the lunatic landlady's laundry appliances. Since he'd left the site selection to me, I felt obliged to spend several nights trying to scrub the place clean. His mother had driven him from St. Louis. I encountered the two of them for the first time. One look around and his mother, who was Old World, lit into me. "How could I let her son live in dis kind of dump?" It was downhill from there.

Almost immediately we began arguing over privacy. There was none. On nights when we both needed the other guy to get lost for a couple of hours, tempers flared. Even if you won the toss and had the place to yourself, the landlady, who must've had our side of the basement wired, would spoil the moment by clomping down the stairs screaming about rules and regulations.

Once, in an ill-conceived attempt to overcome the privacy issue, we tried double dating—to a drive-in movie—with two young ladies from nearby Stephens College. Before picking them up, I drove to a liquor store. Parking was bad so I pulled into the alley, a no parking zone, and told him to move the car if the cops showed up. When I came out with the Ancient Age in a paper bag purchased *sans* identification, a police car, lights flashing, now sat facing my Dodge. I threw the bag into the back seat and approached one of the officers. "What's in that bag?" he asked. "Mix," I responded. He wasn't buying it and went on to explain that unless I opened the car door and showed him the bag, they would make us follow them to the station until they could get a warrant which would kill the entire evening (Stephens girls had an even earlier curfew). I retrieved the bag and handed it over. "Mix?" he asked rhetorically when he pulled out the bourbon. Half-heartedly, I replied, "Well, you gotta mix it with something."

After taking me into the store and eliciting from the sad sack clerk that I had not been asked for proof of age (I was 19 at the time), they double-crossed us. We still had to follow them to the station and fill out a bunch of paperwork, which killed the evening anyhow. The aftermath turned into a brouhaha: the Dean getting on me over my reluctance to cooperate as a witness; the uncomfortable hearing where I saw several J-School reporters doing their job taking copious notes; in the end, the poor liquor store was shut down for the ensuing Homecoming weekend, a costly punishment I felt horrible about. And, of course, there was our snoopy landlady who heard my name in a radio report of the crime and threatened to evict us if she got wind of any more trouble.

As for my roommate and why he had not moved the car when the police arrived; he had forgot to tell me he didn't know how to drive a stick shift. From Day One our relationship had never been good. Now it completely unraveled. We went the last two months of the semester without uttering a word to each other.

On the other hand, I did hear from Virgil. Indirectly. He had given my name to a friend of his, the rush chairman of the Kappa Alpha fraternity. Missouri was the K.A.'s northernmost outpost. Throughout every home football game, their pledges were made to stand at the top of the stadium incessantly waving a gigantic Confederate flag. The frat sponsored a cotillion each year in consort with one of the halls at Stephens College and, before the ball, drove down Broadway in a procession of open convertibles, the brothers all dressed like Rhett Butler, their dates, natch, *à la* Scarlett O'Hara.

So I get a phone call from Virgil's buddy. Evidently their house did not have representation from within the prestigious halls of the School of Journalism. No surprise there. He'd heard I was a good guy and though he knew I only had one year left he said they would be willing to waive all the "hazin' bullshit" and, after a face to face, just might have me come move in there for my senior year.

I interrupted his sales pitch. "Did Virgil mention I was Jewish?" It dawned on me that, as little time as I spent with Virgil, the subject had never come up. What's more, I doubted he had even the slightest familiarity with the subject. In his eyes, I was just this dumb-dressin' okay J-School guy from big bad Chicago.

"Well, say Larry, it's been real good talkin' to ya."

Click.

Senior Moments

It happened that my senior year coincided with the fiftieth anniversary of the School of Journalism, a very big deal. The Postal Service got into the act, issuing a four-cent stamp commemorating the occasion. Coming from them, it was unusually stark and simple, a black and white design depicting a quill pen above a printing press. I still have the first day cover from September 22, 1958, postmarked Columbia, Missouri.

First Day Cover honoring Mizzou's Freedom of Information Center, 1958

Throughout the year we were treated to prominent speakers, the likes of Eleanor Roosevelt (she really did look like Grandma). As part of the festivities they held something called the World Press Congress attended by journalists from, well, around the world. Tip-off for the Congress took place in the basketball field house, the keynote speaker former President and Missouri's favorite son, Harry S. Truman. Somehow I was chosen to be part of the small cadre who would escort Truman to the stage. I actually held one of his bony elbows as he climbed the steps to the rostrum.

Given what I now know of the Japanese—after extensive and often intensive client meetings over the years—what happened next that morning in Truman's presence was stunningly uncharacteristic. After his introduction and the warm standing ovation, just as he began to speak, on cue, the Japanese delegation of seven, seated to one side close by the stage, rose as one to the deliberate sound of scraping chair legs, then single-filed it down the aisle and noisily headed for the exit. The audience's reaction was awkward silence and ol' Harry continued his speech on the Freedom of the Press—the theme of the Congress and the postage stamp—perhaps unaware of the affront. But fourteen years after his fateful decision, the pervasive radiation from Hiroshima wafted over the hall.

⁂

Back in the advertising department of J-School, I had signed up for Magazine Design, another course taught by my Typography professor, Dr. Paul Fisher, a true New England iconoclast. I thrived in that course. And several fortunate opportunities came my way because of it. For one, Dr. Fisher and I got to know each other well.

We shared similar opinions on a number of issues including the dire situation that had cropped up south of us in Little Rock: we both opposed Governor Faubus's stand against desegregation and applauded Eisenhower's forceful counter-moves. I mentioned my shock at seeing, other than the two football players, no black students in J-School, or for that matter, anywhere on the campus. I told him I had always attended integrated schools in Chicago; Jesse Owens' daughter graduated from grammar school with me (her daughter was one of the last torch bearers inside the Coliseum at the '84 Olympics in Los Angeles). Fisher, visibly chagrined, offered no defense other than to quietly say there was a historically black college fifty miles from Columbia and that "Traditions die hard down here." He asked me to take on the job as his paid assistant in Typography (fifty dollars a month as I recall) to work with the latest batch of juniors bewildered by the California Job Case. And to proctor the pop quizzes and exams he contrived.

The latter role led to a moral dilemma, one I would be forced to face in many permutations and occasions down the road. Typography was a requirement; without a passing grade you could not graduate from the School of Journalism. It happened that two of my ad major classmates, a dating pair, had avoided the course until they had run out of time, the second semester of senior year. There they sat in the last row of the final, a mere eight days away from graduation, theirs and mine. I watched as they passed crib notes back and forth, blatantly cheating and assuming, I suppose, that I would empathetically look the other way.

An hour later I discussed the episode with Dr. Fisher. "What did I think?" he asked. I thought I should not even grade their exams. I thought they should have their ungraded tests returned topped by a sanitized one-word explanation: "Incomplete." Fisher agreed. The two never raised an objection with him nor, not surprisingly, ever spoke to me again. I heard they hung around that muggy Missouri summer retaking the course.

On a brighter side, at least initially, Fisher had been approached by several news majors who were about to launch a new campus humor magazine, a sequel to one called *Showme* that the university had banned two years previously on grounds of obscenity. The upstarts needed an art director and Fisher recommended me. With "Magazine Design" freshly under my belt, I felt up to the challenge.

Besides, this job had a sixty-dollar-a-month stipend attached to it. My savings from the past summer at Polk Bros. were running low and I still had a semester to go.

Giving birth to a magazine is painful. I had my ideas. The originators of *Harlequin*, their name not mine, had theirs. Using the rudimentary tools of the time, and getting by on an extremely limited budget, I designed the masthead, the index, the various page layouts, the monthly covers and made the thirty-mile run back and forth to Jefferson City several times a week holding the hand of a less-than-gifted printer.

Though the university had no direct editorial control (Freedom of the Press, remember?) they were subsidizing the venture so the very bright staff of five kept away from controversy, almost to a fault, in my closely held opinion. To them I was the Art Director, brought on to make them look good. I bit my tongue over the tepid material, did my job, and only once chipped in editorially with a poetic ditty called "An Ode to Ale" when I found myself at the last minute a half-column short of editorial material. But in the third and, as it turned out, final issue of the publication, the boys let go some and crossed

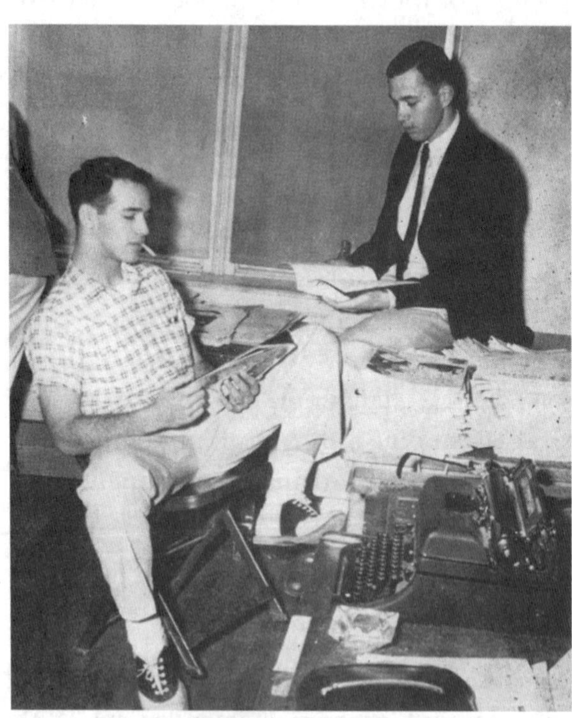

In the makeshift *Harlequin* office, saddle shoes and cigarette, 1959

an invisible line, the Mason-Dixon line, one the university-at-large still stumbled over.

The offending piece, which I really liked and positioned far forward in the magazine, was a simple allegory the editor himself wrote. The gist of it was that in a faraway land there lived two factions: the Igs and the Ogs. If an Og dared break with the pack by befriending an Ig he was chastised as an "Igger-lover" and beheaded.

That did it.

I had busted my butt getting the issue out in time to garner sales before the school year ended. And the issue did disappear off the newsstand racks—a handful actually purchased. The vast majority, however, were confiscated by campus security.

⁂

AT THE BEGINNING OF SENIOR year, I embarked on the most crucial subject of the two-year curriculum—Advertising Sales. We again had a "beat," though rather than chasing down stories at City Hall or where-have-you, we were given a short list of clients, mainly retailers, who advertised in the *Missourian*, some more heavily than others. The objective of the course was highly defined: "handle" your assigned accounts for the year; call on them regularly; bring them ideas in layout form for sales, seasonal events, Homecoming specials, ads *ad infinitum*; assuage any unhappiness over positioning in the paper; in short, become their friend. Your grade—worth four big credit hours each senior semester—was based on your ability to maintain, better yet, increase their advertising expenditures.

For me, Ad Sales was as close to the real world as any college course could possibly be. It also provided the *Missourian* with a non-commissioned (sub free) sales staff, a point the combative *Tribune* complained so long and loud about over the years that today the course does not exist. These days, the *Missourian*'s ad sales are handled by professionals. Too bad. In my case, the course was life altering.

On the surface, my assigned targets seemed innocuous: a lumberyard out by the highway, the Dairy Queen near campus and, the biggie, the grandest haberdashery in Boone County right on Broadway.

The cruel and, no doubt, inadvertent joke came via the names of my three clients. Mr. Pickett owned the lumberyard. Mr. Plunkett, the D.Q. And Mr. Puckett, the eponymous Puckett's Men's Store.

Pickett. Plunkett. Puckett.

Try keeping those three straight. Even I knew, thanks to Dale Carnegie's course, how hard it is to sell a man something if you can't get his cornpone name right. I remembered a technique Carnegie taught us: word association. It worked beautifully. Picket fence... lumber yard...Mr. Pickett. Plunk down a quarter for a cone...Dairy Queen...Mr. Plunkett. Puckett was a no-brainer; his name was emblazoned in gold on both sets of windows of his doublewide storefront.

Mr. Pickett took a liking to me. I guess he approved of the half-page seasonal sale newspaper ads I created for him—gratis—and asked if I'd take on a freelance assignment knocking out direct mail pieces for his new line of Lawn Boy power mowers on a predetermined fee basis. Of course I accepted though I never dared calculate how little shrewd Mr. Pickett was actually paying me per hour.

Mr. Plunkett's needs were the easiest for me. As a Dairy Queen franchisee, he was required to use the ad mats provided by the corporation. We just sat down with the binder full of reprints they'd sent him and picked out something to run whenever the temperature was cooperating.

And I hit it off with Mr. Puckett too. He doubled as the dollar-a-year mayor of Columbia, certainly good for his business. Physically, he reminded me of Dick Daley, still Chicago's mayor at the time, though he was nowhere near as ornery. Fortunately Columbia's mayor never put my name together with the heinous liquor store incident of the previous spring. He was one of the paper's most loyal and important advertisers; historically, he ran a full-page ad every Thursday about forty weeks a year.

We had our routine. We'd talk on Friday, he'd tick off some items and prices he wanted to feature and I'd come back Monday afternoon with a layout that I had pasted together from stock art provided by manufacturers like Hart Schaffner and Marx. I'd write some florid copy and my idea of a clever headline. And, hopefully, he'd buy off on all of it for Thursday's scheduled insertion. He rarely asked for changes.

One eventful Sunday morning I went into J-School planning to put the ad together for my Monday meeting with Puckett. And I see the banner headline spread across the front page of the Sunday *Missourian*—they'd hauled out the especially large hand-set type, carved from maple, normally reserved for the start and finish of wars—"PUCKETT'S ROBBED!" Below the big black type was a photo of Mr. Puckett's wall of emptied suit racks. After the store closed Saturday evening, some perps pulled a truck up to the loading dock, broke in, and left with every suit and sport coat in the place.

Jeez, he's gotta be pissed, I thought. No way I can bring him an ad tomorrow. I'll just let him simmer down 'til Friday. He'll miss one week. No big deal.

I made that decision unilaterally. I did not discuss it with my professor slash sales manager, Miss Bratek.

Tuesday morning, I stroll into the ad sales office only to be greeted by a rather stern-faced Bratek, who waves in my face that day's edition of the *Columbia Tribune*. She suggests I take a look at their back page. What I see is a blow to the groin, a chop to the Adam's apple, the worst thing that ever happened to me in advertising then, or since.

Obviously, the *Trib* had no problem calling on Mr. Puckett that Monday. Or selling him an excruciatingly clever ad. It was a reprint of the front page of *their* Sunday edition. The treatment of the robbery story was not quite as sensational as the *Missourian's*. Their format was conservative, a small-town version of the *N.Y. Times* while ours was more splashy, a precursor, in fact, to the not-yet-invented *USA Today*. Nonetheless, there it was, their four-column Page One account. The only addition my competitor made to the reprint was sheer genius. Below their photo of the empty suit racks they had routed out a burst, an oblong starry-shaped space, and inside it they had inserted this copy:

"People love our suits so much
they can't wait for the store to open."

Excuse No. 1. I had no clue Mr. Puckett's business insurance more than covered his losses. Not only that, in one swift act, the burglars had rid him of several racks of pawed-over inventory destined shortly for a clearance sale. Turned out, he had a boffo Saturday night and he wasn't even open!

Excuse No. 2. I was twenty years young.

There are no other excuses. One-upped, scooped, splattered across the ad sales office, the nail standing tall unmercifully hammered into the ground by both Miss Bratek and my classmates. It was the low point of my career, a career that had yet to begin. Even Mayor Puckett felt sorry for me.

There have been no known relapses. Or scoops. I was never again caught napping or slacking off. Nor did I ever again miss an opportunity to create an ad that fed off the momentum of current events.

It was a hard lesson learned.

⁂

Now that Opportunity's knock was permanently implanted in my head, I began to debate whether or not I should hang around for graduation. Leaving before the pomp might give me a leg up in Chicago; I could start pounding the pavement before other job seekers from graduating classes around the country hit town. Besides, the trip down to Columbia would be near impossible for my parents now that their grocery store was a true mom-and-pop operation. In the end, I didn't attend the graduation or beat anyone back to Chicago.

Instead, I came down with a withering case of mononucleosis (regrettably, the "kissing disease" label did not apply). Between the course load, the magazine fiasco, my several side jobs and Messrs. Pickett, Plunkett and Puckett, I was purely and simply fried.

Ed Cristal and I now shared a nicely finished basement apartment in a brand new house owned by a Stephens College professor and his young family. Eddie was as sorry as I was over the roommate disaster. And despite our conflicting personalities—he the social director of the advertising class; me more the grump—we got along great. He was the one who saw me struggling and insisted I go to the University Clinic. The people there knew the symptoms well. After drawing blood, they immediately sequestered me for a week. Eddie packed up my stuff. My dad flew down solo on Ozark Airlines to drive me and my old Dodge back home.

My father coming to my rescue was like something out of Philip Roth. Worrying about me driving the car; volunteering to be my chauffeur; finding someone to help Mom in the store; booking a flight—all that paternal hassle was just not in his wheelhouse. He worked hard. I knew it and never intruded on him with my problems. We functioned, father and son, at a respectful remove. Other than the roof over my head when I came back to Chicago on breaks, I never asked for his help with expenses nor did he ever offer. Perhaps if I'd played football instead of writing about it... who knows? But there we were alone in the car despite the clinic's objections (I told them I had technically graduated three days earlier and was no longer their issue). Now, still fighting a fever as J-School slipped away in a sea of green treetops, I would spend half the ride stretched out, dozing on the back seat; the other half, up front, talking with my father about the chances ahead: for me finding a job and facing the draft; and for the '59 White Sox finally with a chance to win a pennant.

Good-bye Columbia.

The Retail Reality

With a steady infusion of Grandma's chicken soup, I willed myself well the second day back from Missouri. Now, though, there would be no summer backpacking across the Pyrenees or trekking to Machu Picchu. Nor would I take Maury Polk up on his open invitation to come back and sell appliances. With a folder full of J-School samples and degree in hand, it was time to establish my advertising career. I knew I was the only grad in my class who had set sights on Chicago. No competition there. So, full of myself, and boasting my résumé from Missouri, I was certain I'd land an agency job by week's end.

It's an old and cyclical story which I would soon learn: times were tough in the summer of 1959.

My first stop was the Chicago office of D'Arcy-MacManus. Aware of their connection to J-School, I didn't call or write. I just showed up at their fancy high-rise offices. (The Leo Burnett agency was located in the same Prudential building but I didn't think Mr. Burnett was ready for me yet). I told the D'Arcy receptionist, a gorgeous blonde with remarkably rigid posture, that I had just graduated from J-School expecting that fact alone would get me past her desk. It did not. I dropped Wally Armbruster's name. It cut no ice. "I think he's in our St. Louis office," she said dismissively as though St. Louis were St. Lucia (this was my first encounter with the so-called *interdependence* of advertising agency networks. There wasn't any then. There isn't any now).

She did bother to ask whether I was an art director or copywriter. I said I was both. She said it didn't work that way; you had to be one or the other; but either way they hadn't hired anyone in months. Out of sympathy, she accepted one of my naive résumés.

I have another stop nearby in mind but it was approaching lunch hour and I needed to think this through. Wimpy's was two blocks west on Randolph Street. I went in there for a burger and some soul searching.

Copywriter? Art director? At Missouri, I *had* been both. While I certainly wasn't Picasso I knew layout design and typography well enough to cobble together a passel of passable newspaper ads and three issues of a magazine. Then again, writing had always been my salvation. I'd survived a myriad of tests on the strength of my mini essays. And had found writing the headlines and copy in class and for Pickett and Puckett to be challenging and enjoyable. So until such time as somebody makes me The Creative Director and I can play both sides of the street, I need to forget the one-man-band approach and make book on copywriting. P.S. Wimpy's was as good as ever.

I wasn't panicking—yet. Hell, the lady at D'Arcy, beautiful or not, was just a receptionist. Still, she seemed to know more about the agency business than I did. All I knew was I had more clout at my next stop. Morris Jacobs had mentioned my name to his son, who ran the Chicago office of Bozell-Jacobs and now I am in Don Jacobs' office, greeted like a long-lost friend and we're talking about his father and how I *volunteered* to pick him up in my beater Dodge at the Columbia airport on his frequent visits. He was as down-to-earth as his dad and seemed comfortable in his unassuming second-floor office on State Street, a few doors from Fritzel's, back then, Chicago's version of the 21 Club or Brown Derby; his gritty view, the Lake Street el tracks just to the south.

He took his time looking through my samples, commenting favorably here and there. He thought I had talent. I thought I was in! He set the work down, removed his reading glasses and began to recite the facts of life: This was a terrible time to be looking for an agency job. The economy stunk. Everyone's cutting back—including him. Better to take what you can get, any kind of writing job would be better than nothing.

Then he mentioned he knew of an opening, at least it was open that morning, at Goldblatt Bros. Department Store a few blocks down State. Was I interested? No, I thought, been there and done retail newspaper ads. But I remembered that Doyle Dane Bernbach in New York, a new shop gaining fame by the day as the Second Coming of advertising, had earned its spurs on some highly creative Ohrbach's department store advertising. In Ad Prin, we had studied the breakthrough campaign. I knew enough about Goldblatt's—my entire family shopped there—to know it was no Ohrbach's. But Jacobs' assessment of the job market had deflated me. And his reassuring comment that "there were no small copywriting jobs, just small copywriters" made sense. (I've used that line on young writers dozens of times since.) I asked if he would call his contact over there at...that department store...on my behalf.

Marge Strauss, the Goldblatt's copy chief, did not make me cool my heels. She saw me straight away. As I soon learned, everything around there happened fast. Miss Strauss, call me Marge, she said, had a bouffant of bright red hair that belied her age and the nervous moves of a hamster. She whipped through my samples and declared them "pretty good for small town stuff." I'm sure Jacobs' blessing hadn't hurt. Just like that, elapsed time maybe ten minutes, she offered me the job. I wasn't thrilled. Either she was desperate for help or I was better than "pretty good." I wasn't proud. I felt like the guy who was dragged to the prom by the homeliest girl in the school. And I wasn't suddenly rich either: my salary would be $65 less taxes paid every Friday in cash (obviously, they had plenty lying around the store). Despite the misgivings, I accepted.

And would start the following Monday, perfect timing, she said, because she held a staff meeting first thing every Monday, a chance for me to meet my fellow workers. And, oh, she almost forgot, there was no overtime pay but, on the other hand, with my employee I.D. card, anyone in my immediate family could buy anything in the store at a ten percent discount.

As I rode down the elevator from the eighth floor, I wondered how my classmates were faring out there in the real world and who, beside my mother now ten percent better off, would be impressed by my new job.

THE STAFF MEETING WAS, IN actuality, a highly democratized bitch session. No one minced words in deference to me, the new guy. Boiling over the weekend, the staff couldn't wait to vent. Oscar, the overweight production manager and old-timer of the crowd, complained about deadline indifference. A groan rose in unison. A layout lady, bird-like and dressed almost as well as Marge, repeated, she said, "for the umpteenth time," that none of the art supplies she ordered ever showed up. She was seconded by her immediate boss, the head art director, a gnarly sloppily dressed guy with a thick Northwest Side accent. (George Botich became a good friend. I stayed with him and his dirty socks for a month once between apartments. An accomplished artist, but ever the retailer, he lives in France to this day painting vivid scenes of Parisian storefronts.) A svelte black lady copywriter with the air of someone who had worked at higher altitudes (J. Walter Thompson, she bragged to me later) loudly reminded Marge about her promise to puh-leeze! get a cleaning crew to visit our floor. Two middle-aged writers, a thin man with a thin mustache and a somewhat voluptuous woman, giggled the meeting away passing (love?) notes back and forth like fourth-graders. Marge, the peacekeeper, agreed with everyone; from the expression on everyone's face it seemed she always agreed with everyone. For some reason, I felt I'd found refuge in a white-collar penal colony.

Puckett's did serve me well there. Rather than the kindly mayor handing out assignments, here I had various and harried buyers hovering over my cubicle, each demanding their job come first.

The guy in the cubicle next to mine, Jack Badofsky, was a godsend. Just out of the Army, he was a few years older and far more facile a writer than me. He had a temper he tempered with caustic one-liners. In a war of words, no buyer could intimidate him. He worked there because he had never finished college and figured no agency would hire him. If someone with his skill as a wordsmith—certainly none of my classmates came close—worked at a place like Goldblatt's, then maybe it wasn't so bad after all.

Being the new guys, Jack and I worked on the dregs—those annoying newspaper inserts that fell out of the fat Sunday editions, those colorful blasts Goldblatt's relied on to goose business on slower Mondays and Tuesdays. Since there was an incessant barrage of them and so little time to write them and even less time for anyone like Marge to oversee what we wrote, we'd sneak in as many puns and word plays as we could get away with. We'd yell them out for approbation—our latest and greatest—across the short wall separating our cubicles, two little brats playing "keep-away" from Marge. It made the day pass quickly and besides, we both knew most of our prose ended up lining the bottom of kitty litter boxes all over Chicago soaking up the pee.

Marge's boss, Max Applebaum, the Advertising Director, was forever hounding her for new promotional themes, really new excuses for presenting a value proposition to the public. We never saw Max but it seemed odd that the two rank beginners in the department were being asked to influence the chain's entire marketing effort. Were the other writers burnt out? Storewide Clearance Sale. Labor Day Liquidators. Budget Busters. 63rd Street Store Parking Lot Fire Sale. August Sizzlers. You name it. We soon wrung the English language dry. Whether Max, in his wisdom, chose one of ours, or recycled a previous winner (retailers are superstitious that way), Botich would waste his God-given artistic talents tying into the latest theme, framing the front page of the inserts with his hand-drawn designs, flashes of flying type and brilliant borders. And that "look" would be picked up throughout the eight-store chain for displays and window dressing.

Speaking of August Sizzlers, heading into that month, Chicago was on fire again, running a hundred-degree temperature day after day. No overtime, I knew about. But Marge had not mentioned the part about no air conditioning. Or windows that opened. Of course, the retail floors, all the way down to the bargain basement, were air conditioned. Otherwise, financial suicide. But for us laboring in the advertising vineyard on the eighth floor closest to the searing sun, we sweated it out. I began dressing for work like a beach bum. Shorts and sandals notwithstanding, I developed severe jock itch. I visited the first floor drug section to buy ointment at ten percent off.

The heat—and the filthy floors—finally got to C.C., the anal black copywriter with the big league credentials. She had been working on an assignment, a page ad for garden supplies, so her office, larger than our junior cubicles, was crammed with the products to be featured. When last seen, before security took her away, she was careening down the halls of the sweltering department, an open ten-pound bag of Goldblatt's grass seed under one arm, tossing handfuls of it in the face of everyone she passed and all the while screaming "If they're not gonna clean this goddamn dump, I'm growin' grass up here!"

To cool off, several times a day, Badofsky and I embarked on research trips to the retail floors. We rode the escalator down through the reviving air, a leisurely way to take in the scenery, such as it was. One morning there were promotional stanchions we hadn't seen before on every landing announcing the (temporary) back-to-school College Shoppe on the third floor. To lend some panache, they had wisely pasted an eleven by fourteen headshot of one of the new—and, sadly, no doubt temp—co-ed salesgirl cuties on each sign. (Goldblatt's was hardly a sorority girls' haven.) We hopped off the escalator on three. As we neared the empty little Shoppe tucked in a corner of Women's Wear, two of the cover girls approached, eager for customers. In the flesh, one was decidedly better looking than the other, or her own picture, but the way we were aligned she would be walking right into Jack. A delicate elbow to his ribcage and I had moved him off stride. We struck up a conversation, told them we wrote for the company newsletter and needed to know all about them for the next issue. Sensational Joyce Johnson, in from small Central Michigan College and staying with her aunt in a close-by suburb, would be mine for the rest of the summer. Graciously, Jack admired my athletic move; he didn't know I had it in me. Not to mention he had a girlfriend.

Meanwhile, back up in the torrid penal colony, another lady copywriter, the one passing notes in my first staff meeting, totally lost it. Apparently, a proofreader missed a typo in one of her headlines. The word brassiere was innocently misspelled. Her line, that ran in all the city dailies, read "Too bad the world can't see you in our scintillating brasserie." First of all, why was she so upset? Nine-tenths of Chicago had no idea what a brasserie was. And why go stab Oscar's big fat arm with that sharpened pencil just because he was an easy target? Oscar wasn't the proofreader; Oscar never read anything. And now Marge was minus two lady copywriters in one week.

I felt this might be an opportune time to ask her for a raise. I didn't like the idea of hitting her when she was down. On the other hand, in my tan little pay envelope every Friday nestled, to the nickel, $53.65. At Polk Bros. there were *days* I earned three times that much! I kept Jack out of this. I didn't know or want to know how much he was making. If I *was* successful, I'd tell him about it.

As I stated my case, Marge squirmed and made all kinds of faces. In the end she obfuscated. Only Max can give raises, she said. I've never even seen the man, I responded. He's at the other end of the building, past the buyers, in the corner office. Go ask his secretary, Edna, if you can talk to him. He won't bite, she assured me.

No surprise, Edna reminded me of a lady prison guard. I asked to see Max. She told me to go wait for him in his office, definitely a surprise. I opened the fancy oak door and, surprise number two, I was hit with a blast of thick cool conditioned air. There were other closed-door offices along Max's wall. I assumed head buyers occupied them hoarding their own secret stash of frosty air. Max's office was all-around cold: his thermostat read sixty-eight; his décor said austere. Impeccably maintained, though (either Edna did the dirty work or a cleaning crew actually set foot on certain parts of the eighth floor). He had back problems. There was some sort of contraption off to the side that I think could turn Max upside down.

Oh, that's Max, I said to myself when he entered a few minutes later. I'd seen him a few times down on one. He looked so out of place there I'd assumed he was one of the Brothers Goldblatt. He was short, with a vainglorious comb-over haircut and a handsome seersucker suit I'm sure he didn't buy with his discount card.

We shook hands. He told me to call him Max (he and Marge must've gone to the same finishing school).

"Nice office, Max. Air conditioned and ever..." I was saying before he jumped in.

"That's the trouble with you young guys. Work here a couple months..." He acted like he knew me. No doubt Marge gave him a heads-up with a quick call. "...and first thing you want is the corner office. I know the big picture. I earned this office! Copywriters... you're a copy guy, arntcha?" I nodded. "Okay, I'll tell you about copywriters. All year, they've been up and down the elevator shaft, from all the big shot agencies, lookin' for a fuckin' job. Tell you what, kid. Copywriters are a dime a dozen." He lowered his voice. "Now what do you want?"

"I think we're worth at least two for a quarter, Max."

He looked relieved. I'm sure he knew I knew they were short two writers and instead of asking a specific and exorbitant price, I gave him a wisecrack.

"Okay, kid," he said with the hint of a smile and looking me straight in the eye. "Five bucks a week. Now get back to work."

For another month I did as Max suggested. Then, choosing the lesser of two evils, I joined the Army.

Catching Ditties

Fall of 1959. The Korean War was history. And Vietnam was nothing more than one-third of the answer to the trivia question: What three countries were formed by the partition of French Indochina? Exigencies or not, Congress and the Army hung on tenaciously to the dreaded draft, the Cold War now the culprit, a hammer (and sickle) over the head of every able-bodied non-student childless man in the prime of his American way of life. Unless you had maimed yourself, the draft intruded on your short-term plans like a bayonet to the backside and was, potentially, no further away than tomorrow's mail.

There were options. You could become a professional student. You could rush to the altar and quickly make babies. You could have an occupation, say rocket scientist, that the Draft Board deemed worthy of permanent deferment. You could pretend and/or pray the Army forgot about you and your two-year active duty obligation. You could run off to Canada though an option that final didn't really catch on 'til the bullets started flying in Vietnam. You could enlist (as my friend Quinlan did) in one of the other branches—Navy, Air Force, Marines, Coast Guard—all sporting jazzier uniforms but all demanding four full-time years out of your life. Or you could join a National Guard or Reserve unit, signing up for six months of active duty followed back home by five-and-a-half years of weekly training meetings and annual vacation-erasing summer camps.

I chose the latter of the latter, the Army Reserves.

Besides the shorter active duty, the Reserves offered another big advantage. When drafted, your M.O.S. (military occupational specialty) was left to the fates and some tobacco-chewing sergeant pushing a pencil. You...rifleman. You...cook. You...tank mechanic. With the Reserves, you had a chance to name your own poison. If you did your homework, you might find a unit that specialized in something fairly interesting and remotely related to your civilian occupation.

I remembered John Marquardt, a career salesman back at Polk Bros., who told me once how much he liked his reserve unit. Now that Max Applebaum helped me decide to bite the bullet, I gave John a call for details. He was still selling hard. His unit had an intriguing name—The Army Security Agency (ASA). And a convenient Chicago meeting place near lots of my haunts. He couldn't reveal exactly what they did, just something about "communications." Hey, that's up my alley, right? Like every other unit located in the Midwest, there would be eight weeks of basic training at Fort Leonard Wood down the road from my *alma mater*. But after basic, he assured me, it got better. The last four months of active I'd be sent to Fort Devens, thirty miles northeast of Boston, near all those famous girls' colleges. And if I timed it right—like soon!—I'd catch weekend skiing in nearby Vermont (for this elite unit, he boasted, there was never any weekend duty like peeling potatoes).

In his estimation, the ASA was as good as the Army gets. But because of that, he said, it was tough getting in. On the plus side, John told me he was tight with the commanding officer, Col. Coleman (he had recently prevailed on Maury Polk to give the good colonel the "clergyman's price" on a washer and dryer) and would put in a good word for me.

Add John Marquardt to my list of saviors.

Col. Coleman had suggested we meet during lunch hour at his family's fur salon (yes, a furrier) on North Michigan Avenue, a ten-minute walk from the Goldblatt sweatshop to another world entirely. A true citizen-soldier, trim and fit and suited in gray flannel, Coleman ushered me by the spare display of opulence, the tumbling folds of fur unmarred by tacky price tags, then past the imposing bank-like vault door where I imagined the killer stuff was, then into his office, which was enclosed in shoulder-high glass.

Either due to the confidential nature of his military affiliation or the natural sound-muffling effect of sable and mink, it felt as if our entire conversation was conducted in a stage whisper. He took notes while casually asking questions about my education, marital status and so on. Things only turned weighty over one issue: Did I have relatives living anywhere overseas? None to my knowledge, Colonel, I responded without hesitation though, in truth, I had no idea if any of my grandparents still had family over there who somehow survived the pogroms and the Nazis. Hopefully, I was right, he said matter-of-factly. Otherwise I would not be given the ASA's mandatory cryptologic clearance. He threw the strange term out like common currency while I—ignorant of its meaning but impressed by the sound of it—am thinking Holy Cryptologic Clearance! Wait 'til I lay that on my buddy Badofsky. Or Max, on my way down his elevator for the last time.

⁂

More good fortune. It turned out Coleman was about to send four new inductees down to basic training but had just been forced to delay one of them because of a wrist injury. If I got my act together in a week, the Colonel said, I could join the other three on the train ride to Ft. Leonard Wood. Before swearing me in though, he once more cautioned me about the foreign relative question. They (whoever "they" were) would be conducting a thorough background check while I went through basic training. If something cropped up, he warned, I'd be out of the ASA and into a conventional infantry unit—he snapped his fingers—just like that.

My traveling companions were college chums from Notre Dame who'd learned about the ASA from one of their cousins. All south suburbanites, they struck me right away as good guys, smart and just as leery as I was about the basic training part of the deal beginning with the haircut we all knew was coming. By the time we got down there—about ninety miles due south of Columbia—we had become the four amigos and, as we learned shortly and to our surprise, the only guys in our entire two hundred–man company, a mix of draftees and reservists, who would go on to Ft. Devens, Massachusetts.

We were assigned to the same barracks, one of four in our company. By day, we commiserated on smoke breaks over the Army's incredibly numb nuts teaching methods aimed at an eighth grade intellect: the grainy films on the perils of venereal disease and the importance of hygiene that most guys slept through; our den mother, Sergeant Gibson, and his high-decibel and repetitive lessons in bed making, shirt tucking, brass burnishing, boot shining, close shaving ("Next time stand closer to the razor, Soldier!), rifle cleaning, about-facing, field stripping, floor mopping, saluting, sir-ing—and keeping a straight face through all of it. At night, when the rest of the barracks had dozed off, we'd sit around a butt can discussing sex and religion.

We four amigos, slightly older and more informed it seemed than most there, had our "nevers" down pat. Never volunteer. Never be caught sleeping in Sunday mornings when almost everybody went to church; heathens would be gathered up for some kind of make-work detail. And never complain in the mess hall about the food. It was amazing how many of our fellow trainees, mostly blue collar or farm kids, knew nothing about the "nevers." A ranch hand from Enid, Oklahoma, who slept in the bunk above mine, feeling ravenous after our morning run, made an innocent comment to a server as we passed through the breakfast line. "How come all's we ever gets just *two* eggs?" He was immediately yanked, told to sit down and wait until the mess sergeant himself brought over a big cookie sheet covered with what looked like at least two dozen fried eggs sunny side up and then glared down at my bunkmate until he ate every last one of them.

I didn't overtly curry favor with Sgt. Gibson but I did like him. Despite his short stature, he didn't have the Napoleonic thing—in fact, considering his tough guy role, he was pretty good-natured—though when he marched along with us counting off cadence he had to strain and stretch those stubby legs to keep up with us. And much to the envy of my three Fighting Irish friends, I became one of his favorites. For one thing, he was a huge fan of the Missouri Tigers and was genuinely impressed that I actually graduated from that school. For another, my shooting prowess back with Virgil and Duane was not a fluke. While it had a lot more kick than my .22, I was deadly with my Army-issue M-1, consistently scoring highest in our company. (Not too shabby for someone who had worn glasses since he was eight; but terrible if they find some great-uncle of mine in Siberia and start thinking rifleman for me.)

Sarge even sent me to a battalion shoot-off where I missed second place by a millimeter. As a reward, he authorized me several times to go to the PX, off limits to trainees, so I could watch the Dodgers beat my beloved White Sox in the World Series. And he did something unthinkable for me, a lowly trainee. He knew Homecoming at Missouri was around the corner and, without my prompting whatsoever, he cut me a weekend pass so I could go up to Columbia on a Greyhound for the football game (and a much needed reunion with a Stephens College friend. She commented favorably on my newly acquired military physique).

Sarge was so taken by my soldiering he decided to send me, along with a few others, to a try-out for the Regimental Drill Team. He seemed to think there was a correlation between shooting a rifle and knowing your left foot from your right. In my case, there was none. I tried to dissuade him. I even suggested one of the amigos, Dick Bringaze, who was far more coordinated than me. He wouldn't hear of it. So off we marched to the trials where his handpicked warrior performed precisely—as Sgt. Gibson's red-faced head drooped in dismay—precisely like a Keystone Kop. Of the sixty odd candidates out on the parade grounds, I was the first sent packing by the officiating drill sergeant.

There was a snafu in the transportation arrangements to Chicago for the four of us now finished with basic training and ready for our Christmas furlough. We had to kill an extra night at Ft. Leonard Wood. Sgt. Gibson seemed to be staying put, his small private room at the far end of the wide-open barracks apparently his holiday home as well. To cheer him up we invited him out for some beers. He gladly accepted but he didn't need cheering. He was just one of those people, career Army to the core, a combat veteran of Korea with the stories to prove it and not a tinge of bitterness over the civilian success of others. He knew nothing about the Army Security Agency but wished all four of us the best.

Thinking about it today, if it were mandatory for every young man in America to go through *just* the eight weeks of basic training with a Sgt. Gibson calling the cadence, this country would be in a much better place.

⁂

Thirty miles from Boston Bay
Lies the home of A-S-A.
We came here to cloak and dagger
But all we do is drink and stagger.
Sound off...one two
Sound off...three four

EVEN A FOOT OF NEW snow did little to brighten the ominous feel of Ft. Devens as our bus pulled up to the main guard gate. The place was sealed off like a concentration camp by a double row of cyclone fencing spaced a few yards apart, each at least twelve feet high and topped by nasty whorls of razor wire presumably electrified.

Framing the low-slung military buildings ahead were two immense four-legged steel towers Eiffel might've designed on a slow day. Like twenty-story Christmas trees both were decorated with all manner of antennae and electronic gewgaws. In the strict sense of the word, we soon learned, these were not *communication* towers. They weren't used for transmitting. They were only used for receiving or, more to the point, intercepting. Given the state of the art at the time, they were sophisticated ears piercing the sky seeking out encrypted military messages meant for others and sent via good old-fashioned Morse code.

Dit dit dit. Dah dah dah.

There were forty of us from hither and yon on the bus. We'd followed orders and met at Logan International. We all shared a maturing buzz cut and a certain eagerness about this cryptologic mumbo jumbo. But not one of us had the faintest idea we would be spending the next four months of our lives learning to discern arbitrary combinations of Dits (dots) and Dahs (dashes) coming in on a headset at a rapid rate and then to transcribe them in real time on a typewriter into familiar letters and numerals ready for deciphering. Nor did we know this arcane feat of hand and ear coordination, in typical military lingo, would have a belittling sobriquet: catching ditties.

THERE MUST'VE BEEN AN AGREEMENT between adversarial nations—a Geneva Convention for communication spies—that all code would be sent in five-letter groupings: i.e., HRU2Q JL7EP XSW21. Unlike *Wheel of Fortune* where you can get a sense for the mystery sentence by the length and order of the blank words, coded letter groups give nothing away that easily.

But I'm getting ahead of the program. We would only receive a glimmer of code deciphering in our four months at Devens. That aspect of the "cloak and dagger" would happen back in Chicago at our weekly meetings.

Here, and every weekday morning for the next three months or so, we are seated in rows, each of us in front of a low console and a pair of revolving knobs. We have spent our first week in an all-day class memorizing the dots and dashes of Samuel Morse's ingenious code. Now we can hear the instructor, a studious looking Specialist 4, through our headsets.

First he tells us to listen to pre-recorded code being sent at twenty-five five-letter groups per minute. There must be a technical glitch. All we hear is crackling static.

He has anticipated our reaction. "No, gentlemen, that is not static. That's 125 individual characters of Morse code sent in sixty seconds. Believe it or not, in three months, give or take a week, all of you will comfortably catch ditties sent at that customary speed. But we're gonna walk before we run."

That's where the knobs came in. On the left a volume control. On the right, a speed control that allowed you to listen to as slow as one letter group per minute all the way up to that daunting twenty-five. The sooner you could master the latter, the sooner you'd have a lot more leisure time.

I should mention that the ASA intended that our afternoons be spent boning up on our typing skills. After all, you couldn't intercept and transcribe 125 characters a minute if you couldn't accurately type that fast. In typewriter talk, that's 25 mistake-free words per minute. The curriculum must've worked for them in the past. As students increased their ability to catch ditties in the morning, they would be increasing their ability to type them out in the afternoon. One problem with our over-achieving group: when the typing instructor gave us a test the first day, to his shock, all forty of us easily exceeded the passing requirement.

Around this time we learned we were something of a grand experiment for the Agency, the first class they'd ever taken on composed entirely of college graduates.

The truth was they had no Plan B for our afternoons. The instructor told us to just keep typing. None of us wanted to cause trouble. On the other hand, we thought the Agency ought to put our skills to better use. We complained to the instructor, who talked to a lieutenant, who talked to a captain and so on, we supposed, because a week later a major was waiting for us as we walked into typing class.

He complimented our typing skills and told us that, after taking it all the way "to the top," it had been decided we would be given a new challenge—we would now spend our afternoons learning Speedwriting (U cn gt a gd jb 4 mo pa, etc.). None of us knew what those afternoons of secretarial school had to do with the security of our nation, but it was better than something else they might've cooked up like calisthenics or shoveling snow and honestly, it is one aptitude I learned in the service, and then only by happenstance, that I actually put to good use in my future lifetime of terminal meetings.

Back in the code room it was amazing how the gibberish coming through my earphones began to separate and speak to me. Being able to set your own pace, moving the knob to an ever quicker click, made a game of it and led to friendly competition with my three amigos. In a month we were all nailing around fifteen letter groups per minute and, according to our instructor, were well ahead of the curve.

Every class I ever attended had a curve raiser and we had ours—a New Yorker who'd done his basic at Ft. Dix. Like the rest of us, he had never given Morse code a thought. But, incredibly, in one week he had taken the speed knob to the limit and was now coasting along in his own brilliant daydreams. That is, until the day two spit-shined M.P.'s entered the code room and whispered something to the instructor; then one called out the genius's name. He left with them and never returned. The instructor told us nothing. When we got back to the barracks, our classmate's footlocker was cleaned out. We figured he'd been secreted away to the C.I.A.

A week later, Dick and I are heading to the PX after dinner when an empty troop carrier pulls up in the slush. Who else was at the wheel of the clunky vehicle but the genius. He said they'd uncovered a long lost aunt living in Moscow and, worse yet, she was a party member.

We shared Ft. Devens with the Second Infantry Brigade, primarily made up of tough regulars from Spanish Harlem, their mission seemingly to protect us wimps in the ASA. Just as Col. Coleman had forewarned me, the infantry was now the fate of the unveiled genius. He was hoping, he said forlornly as he ground the truck into gear, he could get through the next three months without any of his new barracks mates discovering he had graduated *magna cum laude* from Harvard.

Back then the Army Security Agency was housed in Army facilities but was actually under the wing of the National Security Agency. Therefore we were treated with kid gloves by the regular Army personnel at Ft. Devens. No K.P., no marching, no weekend duty whatsoever. Only once in the four months there were we required to pull guard duty, albeit a bitter cold walk with an unloaded rifle in the middle of the night through the well-trampled snow back and forth between the two towers theoretically protecting them from a sneak attack.

My pal Bringaze, an accomplished skier, encouraged me to join him hitchhiking up to Vermont and Mt. Snow a couple of times. We had no equipment and very little money but the military rates for a weekend ski pass and rental gear were maybe ten dollars and we found a Spartan boardinghouse up there for three dollars a night. I went up the lift the first time *sans* experience or lessons other than, down at the base, Bringaze showing me how to slow down by forming a V with the skis. My premier run was catastrophic. I was in free fall; it was called *schussbooming* and it was *verboten*, two facts I only learned later. Then, to prevent a body-to-body collision with an older chap gracefully traversing the slope, I slid into him like he was home plate. One of his ski poles snapped in half. He was furious, but thanks to my slide, unhurt. I somehow got myself up and out of there. When I finally reached bottom, I joined a beginners' group lesson for the rest of the day.

There were plenty of snow bunnies at Mt. Snow though no stories to tell. Most were unpatriotic, instinctively put off by the Army issue dress green wool pants we had tucked into our ski boots as though we possessed serious ski garb.

I made several trips to Manhattan taking advantage of military room rates and the USO's largesse, once being handed a ticket to the revival of *Death of a Salesman*, and on another weekend, receiving a front row seat at Carnegie Hall directly beneath the great Leonard Bernstein's shower of perspiration. A third trip there, I had arranged an evening with a J-School classmate who, I heard through a letter from my friend Eddie, had swung a copywriting job at a big-time Madison Avenue ad agency. I must admit I had admired her from afar all through school though regarding me, at least, she always seemed aloof. But when I called her from Devens she sounded genuinely excited to get together. Naturally, I harbored certain pent-up fantasies on the bus ride into Manhattan that were dashed when she opened the door of her apartment and introduced me to her roommate, an attractive girl she called her "partner," a term new to me then. The three of us had a nice chatty dinner at their favorite place in Little Italy. They paid.

The daffodils were poking through the last vestiges of snow surrounding the officers' quarters as our four months at Ft. Devens were drawing to a close. Now, at last, came the chance to put our spy skills to the test. Instead of the make-believe static we'd been listening to for months, our headphones were, for the first time, hooked up to the probing ears of the towers. But we didn't zero in on encrypted five-letter groups sent by an enemy power. The Morse code we heard and transcribed was merely unguarded chit-chat concerning the Stanley Cup playoffs originating from several remote outposts of the Royal Canadian Mounties.

Cataloging Events

When you're in the army and you're half the writer you think you are and you're writing letters back home, you fall in love with your words. Which I did. So thanks to those increasingly torrid letters I'm in love with my French tutor Christine. In love, in Chicago and out of a job.

Perusing the newspaper, I saw a want ad from Spiegel's for a catalog copywriter. Remembering there was no such thing as a small copywriting job, I made the call and got the interview. They tested me in a windowless room. Word association. Psychological multiple choice questions. Typing skills (which I destroyed). A simple copywriting exercise—write a paragraph selling a clock radio. Overall, driving home, I was convinced there was no way in hell this second-tier mail-order house would not hire me.

Three days later I called for the verdict. A woman in the personnel department, choosing her words carefully, told me Sorry, but I had not met their requirements. There had to be a mix-up. I drove back to Speigel's, barged into the personnel office and demanded to know why I had failed their test. They asked me to leave. They threatened to call security. I stood firm until someone qualified would talk to me. Finally, I was ushered into the corner office. The head guy, mousey and nervous and shuffling through my paperwork, gave me the circumspect news: I was over-qualified for the job and "would not be happy working here." I wondered how happy he was.

With Christine's rekindled love and encouragement, I pressed on, this time walking in unannounced to the antiquated West Side headquarters of Sears, Roebuck and Company. For some odd reason, I was greeted like a long lost relative. They looked at my schoolwork and Goldblatt's stuff, asked me to go into their testing facility, gave me a sheet of bullet points describing the virtues of a Kenmore wringer-less washer and told me to write a headline and paragraph selling this modern convenience. Bingo. A day later the job was mine: $425 a month, the "most they had ever paid a starting catalog writer," that's how scintillating my copy apparently struck them.

My first day on the job, they told me I would be assigned to Department 611, Sporting Goods. Terrific. But first, there was one more test to take. When it was set before me, I shuddered. It was the identical psychological test Spiegel's had foisted on me. The woman asserted that I was hired and that this test would just go into the file for future reference. Taking it, I tried to anticipate the responses they wanted to see. Did I want to write the play, act in the play or sell tickets to the play? Of course, sell the damn tickets.

I was escorted through the massive old brick complex to the Merchandising Building, where all the many buying departments were housed, then up to the Sporting Goods group on the fifth floor. Unlike Goldblatts's, where all the copywriters were gathered in the advertising department, at Sears, copywriters were housed within their assigned merchandise group, meaning the real clients in this case, the all-powerful sporting goods buyers, were eyeballs away.

Like Goldblatt's I was given a desk in a cubicle, next to the other writer, an odd and much older duck named Carl Olafsson. All catalog business was conducted through pneumatic tubes hissing over our heads. By gravitational magic, a foot-long metal missile would drop into a receptacle next to my typewriter. Opening it I'd find a layout for a page in the catalog. On the layout there were rectangles outlined in red pencil. These were the copy blocks. My job was to look over the reference materials from the buyers along with similar efforts from past catalogs, then meticulously type the descriptive copy within the designated rectangles ending, of course, with the catalog number, shipping weight and price. And, I was warned, not one elite character over the border. It mattered more that the copy fit inside the red lines than if it was in any way inspired.

Just as I had been challenged by Jack Badofsky at Goldblatt's, Olafsson showed me the light here. He had worked at highly regarded ad agencies in Minneapolis, he said, without explaining why he had landed at Sears. But he took this job seriously, never influenced by the prevailing acceptance of mediocrity. Polyester shirts were the latest rage. Carl took them seriously too. The more we worked together, the yellower his white shirt became. An avowed bachelor, he told me he washed the same shirt every night in his bathroom sink, hung it to dry, then wore it to work the next day. Wash and wear, a modern miracle. He also revealed his real ambition: to save his money and open a laundromat back home. Like a parking meter attendant, he couldn't wait to empty the coin boxes full of quarters every night, quarters Uncle Sam would have a difficult time keeping track of, he said with a wink.

But he could write. Down the pneumatic chute dropped a two-page fishing lure spread. There were at least forty lures for Carl to wax poetic about, forty copy rectangles to fill. Almost all the lures were old reliables but not once did Carl refer to previous catalogs for pick up copy, a tactic, I learned, that was not only permissible but expected particularly if, in the buyer's opinion, previous copy had done the job. Carl attacked each lure—colorful bead eyes, shiny spinners and spoons and swivels all camouflaging multiple hooks—like it was a work of art. Never could the notion of "no small copywriting job" have been more exemplified than by the fresh take Carl spun for that spread. The fishing equipment buyer who always had plenty to say was rendered speechless. I never checked but my guess is that, until the day thirty-three years later when they buried the Sears catalog, Carl's copy for those irresistible and deadly lures was still intact and, no doubt, still titillating gullible anglers across America.

Once I felt secure at Sears, I left my parents' place to share a furnished apartment Near North with two guys, one a fellow Sears writer, named John Clark, the other John's old high school chum from back in Michigan, Kyle Richards, who was a hotel management trainee working at Chicago's biggest, the Conrad Hilton. Christine lived with her mother just a block away. In short order, mindlessly brief in retrospect, we decided to get married. No one tried to tell us we were too young.

Finding someone to officiate, short of just going to City Hall, was not easy given the Catholic/Jewish dichotomy. Finally, her mother came up with an acquaintance, a municipal judge who happened to be Jewish but was born in France. Judge Braude had no prejudices concerning us. And offered the library of his very elegant apartment on Lake Shore Drive as the venue. He suggested August 4th, the next Thursday evening, an odd day and time for a wedding, but my parents, her mother, and two friends who would serve as witnesses were all on board. Christine's mother was leaving for an extended trip back to France so we could use her apartment while we looked for our own. And as a wedding gift, my roommate Kyle said he could, especially on a Thursday night, get for us *gratis* the honeymoon suite at the Hilton. Cool.

My ASA meetings fell on Thursday evenings. I stopped by Col. Coleman's fur salon to blithely request an absence from the next meeting, my wedding night. Who are you marrying? he asked. This French girl, I told him. She immigrated here with her mother four years ago. Does she still have family over there? Her mother's divorced. But her father, is he still there? Yes, I said, suddenly realizing France and Russia were one and the same in the eyes of the ASA. I'm happy for you, but you're going to have to find a new unit. You can't stay with us and you can't go to summer camp (two weeks away). And you need to find one quickly. The way things are with the Russkies, the balloon could be going up anytime now. Find a new home or you'll end up in the infantry. We shook hands and I left thinking I'd get onto the quest for another behind-the-lines unit once I'd settled in as a married man. But, honestly, I hadn't taken his sense of urgency all that seriously and didn't until precisely one year later when his last words to me would prove frighteningly prophetic.

On my three-month anniversary at Sears, the personnel department asked that I stop by to review the results of the test I had taken back on my first day. I remembered they said it had no bearing on the job, but still, I was now a married man with rent to pay. The assistant personnel director took me through a series of small charts. In permanent black ink were the so-called "Sears' norms" for various responses to the psychological and personality questions. Their evaluations of my answers were superimposed in red pencil over their norms. It didn't take a psychiatrist to note that never the twain did meet. The interviewer sensed my anxiety looking at the divergent black and red lines but, in a comforting tone, assured me those differences would change as I grew with Sears and that when they tested me again in five years I'd be pleased to see how much more closely my lines on the charts would align with their idea of the ideal. It was at that moment I knew I would never become a lifer at Sears.

⁂

INSPIRED PARTLY BY JFK'S "ASK not" speech, partly by my days spent filling little red rectangles with less stirring words, I decided to make a run at Edward R. Murrow's United States Information Agency (USIA).

Half the battle was passing a language proficiency test. I signed up for a refresher course, French 104, at DePaul's downtown night school. Again, with Christine's help, I actually aced it and then went on to get a passing grade in a government-administered written test conducted in the Federal Building.

Next came the orals described in the materials as a free-form examination of my political and historical knowledge and personality traits. I didn't know quite how to prepare for this test other than riffing through my college World History textbook. The book happened to end on the then-recent partition of French Indochina. I bet they ask me that one, I predicted to Christine.

Now I'm in an empty courtroom again in the Federal Building. Across from me are two stern-faced men in their forties both wearing somber suits that might've been ordered from the last Fall/Winter catalog. Other than introducing themselves, they did not reveal their governmental affiliation. My guess was State Department or F.B.I.

They took turns firing at me. Describe five of the ten Bill of Rights. Name the last five presidents and their political parties. Who's third in line for the presidency? What three countries were formed from French Indochina. Laos, Cambodia and Vietnam, I fired back punctuated by a self-congratulatory grin.

Why you laughing? one asked. I knew that question was coming, I replied. Big mistake. Instead of favorably commenting on my intuitive skills, without so much as a smile, the other man said, "Very well, then, name the seven countries of Central America." I blew it on Belize.

And so it went. I thought I was doing okay. Then their questions became less scripted. They asked about the ASA. I said I couldn't discuss that. The right answer. Was your wife aware your first duty station would not be someplace cushy like France? How would you two feel about a place like Upper Volta? I didn't admit it, but they had me there since I never heard of the place. Did we know there was no air conditioning and that the average temperature was ninety-seven degrees? Harking to my Goldblatt's inferno, I said we'd get used to it. Then one of them jumped in saying "You know countries like that are run by niggers. Could you handle that?" I mentioned my experiences in the family grocery store and that that wouldn't be a problem. Wrong, wrong. What I should have done (and did, in fact, feel at the moment) was take exception to officials of the U.S. Government using the "n" word. I fell into their trap and knew it leaving the courtroom. It was confirmed when the letter arrived. I would not be considered a candidate for the USIA. But thank you for your interest. *Merde.*

MEANWHILE, CARL HAD MOVED ON to start counting those quarters. I'm now the senior Sporting Goods writer. J.C. Higgins was going the way of all flesh, the great Ted Williams was hanging around our offices and I was making my mark, steadily receiving small raises. I even learned to ignore the constant hissing of the tubes overhead. I discovered later, at my first ad agency job, how literally out-of-touch those tubes were. The creative department of an ad agency operates like Noah's Ark, the people work in pairs—a writer and an art director. Everybody has a partner, a collaborator, someone to concept and commiserate with.

But at Sears, writers were on their own. Yes, there were layout people at the other end of the pneumatic tube but we didn't know who they were or even where they were located. They got their marching orders directly from the department's merchandise manager. He designated what percentage of a catalog page would be given to a specific item, e.g., a newly designed tent might get fifty percent of a page, four sleeping bags might share the remaining half. If I questioned a layout that had dropped onto my desk, like wondering where the space for a headline was, my only recourse was to scribble out a constructive, pleasantly worded comment, put it back in the cylinder and send it off to who knew where. Sometimes the mystery layout person would actually make an adjustment based on my comment and shoot it back to me.

The front cover of the big Fall/Winter and Spring/Summer catalogs always featured a gorgeous model attired in something unexpected from Sears, an item chosen to make some sort of inflated fashion statement for the company. Invariably, the item was well over the head and taste level of the average Sears customer. My wife had that figured out. She saw a suede outfit on a cover and knew there soon would be hers and thousands more on sale in the Sears employees' store at a huge discount.

It was the back covers of those catalogs that were coveted by every buyer in every merchandise department, not to mention the lucky copywriter who'd end up with the assignment and a chance to shine. In my two-and-a-half years there, I managed to snag two back covers. One, the Spring/Summer tome of 1961, introduced Ted Williams and his special glove, ball and medallion, all for $9.95. It didn't take much to be a star writer there. My copy describing the offer began with the words: "Sniff the new leather smell." No big deal. Every kid did that with every glove they ever owned. But somehow, and embarrassingly for me, it was the talk of the Sears complex, this slight nod to emotionalism, particularly in the employee lunchroom where the eighty writers working on catalogs congregated every noon hour. How did I slip that one by the powers-that-be? Huh?

There was nowhere else to go for lunch. Years later, Sears was headquartered downtown in a Skidmore Owings and Merrill 108-story edifice. But our complex, similar in appearance to the old Pullman Works where Junior Achievement met, was built in the 1880's. Homan and Arthington was a grand Westside area back then; now, in 1961, it was hemmed in by the worst slums in Chicago. Like hunkering down in the trenches, we swapped stories at lunch, all us erudite and misplaced writers, just waiting for the chance to escape. I met several friends at those lunch tables, one in particular, Marv Stern, who eventually engineered my exit from Sears and has remained a close friend and golf buddy to this day.

One steamy August day that year, I was leaving work. I passed the sign in the lobby announcing the closing price of Sears stock, important to every employee since, well before the rules changed, every dime of our profit sharing was invested in it. There were legions of anecdotes about Sears elevator operators who had retired from the firm with a million dollars' worth. (My father constantly reminded me of that every time I mentioned my determination to leave Sears for an agency job.) I'm now in front of the building heading for the parking lot. Like a scene out of an old movie, a young black kid was hawking the afternoon edition of the *Tribune*: "They buildin' a wall in Berlin. Prez-dent callin' up duh Reserves!" It wasn't my habit, but that day I plunked down the dime for the paper. Walking to my car, I'm reading the list of reserve units on Page One. There it was, alphabetically leading the list, the Army Security Agency. Holy shit!

Back at the apartment, a yellow telegram was sticking out of our mailbox. The all-cap words were loud and clear enough: REPORT TO O'HARE AT 0530 AUGUST 20 TO RETURN TO FT. DEVENS. STOP. *Don't they know? I lost my cryptologic clearance!*

The next morning, I made a beeline for the fur salon, telegram in hand. Coleman asked if I had joined a new unit yet. I said I was close. He told me if I followed orders and went back to Devens, as he was about to do, the mistake would be discovered immediately and I would be placed in the infamous Second Infantry Brigade. Colonel, can you help me out of this? I don't know why but he said he would. Now get yourself into a unit, he urged, because, like I told you before, the balloon is up.

Sunday, August 20th, our phone rang at 6:45 a.m. I could hear airport sounds in the background. It was a very short call, five words worth, from Bringaze, one of my three amigos. "You son of a bitch." That's all he said. I didn't know if it was uttered out of jealousy or contempt. I do know those guys spent the next year at Ft. Devens doing absolutely nothing. It was all a political ploy. And that ultimately, out of frustration, the wives of thousands of recalled Reservists, including those of two of my three amigos, marched on Washington to protest the wasteful interruption in their husbands' lives.

⁂

THAT OCTOBER I WAS SENT on my first ever business field trip, to Washington, Missouri, where Sears tents and sleeping bags were manufactured. I would be driving my own VW Beetle down there. No one minded when I asked if I could bring my wife along for the ride. We, especially my wife, weaseled out of a perfectly reasonable offer to spend a night experiencing life in their newest, most luxurious tent. With some lame excuse about her sore throat, we opted for a nearby motel. I'm reasonably certain our first son, Steffan, was conceived in that precursor to Motel 6.

Soon after my return, I was promoted from Sporting Goods to the Radio/TV Department. I had been very comfortable where I was but someone had bothered to check my résumé and saw I had sold radios and such at Polk Bros. It was then I had the chance to write my second back cover, this time for the Fall/Winter book and a product first for Sears: *color* television, a tiny 12-inch screen enclosed in a fake oak cabinet the size of a small refrigerator.

⁂

CHRISTINE WORKED FOR A COMPANY called Auto Europe. She arranged the sale of high-end cars to people traveling abroad. They'd avoid the cost of a rental car, drive the new one for a month or so, then Christine would have it shipped back to the States as a used car at a substantial savings in duty and taxes.

We had been saving, too, for a trip back to meet her family in France. And Sears was kind enough to give me a two-month sabbatical. My wedding witness and good friend from Polk Bros. days, Hal Slan, made us a tremendous offer: buy him a Sunbeam Alpine over there, drive it all we wanted (the more miles the lower the duty) and ship it back when we were leaving.

So we tooled around France in a bright red sports car, a point of interest for every kid in every village we passed through. In Biarritz, a seaside resort town south of Bordeaux, we stayed with her father, René, a ringer for Cary Grant, and his new young red-haired Italian wife. We went on to her mother's family in a tiny village near St. Emilion, Christine's birthplace. Her uncle was just installing a copper water pipe leading to the kitchen sink, their first taste of indoor plumbing.

I went fishing one long night with *Tonton* Joseph and several of his old *Resistance* buddies. We smoked foul-smelling Gauloises and I listened as best I could as they talked about the *Boche* like it all happened yesterday. At dawn, in came the net they had stretched across the Dordogne. It was laden with squirming lampreys hissing in unison far louder than the pneumatic tubes at Sears. Joyously, the men in their *bleus* tossed the eels into an old wine barrel at the front of the skiff. They would sell the writhing delicacies to a seafood wholesaler in Bordeaux for a nice evening's profit.

We left her family behind and traveled on to the proverbial South of France racking up kilometers for Hal. One evening at our small hotel in St. Paul de Vence, Christine was washing out some of our underwear in the tiny sink when she turned toward me with an admission—that she never said anything at the time, but was glad I flunked the USIA exam; that she and her mother had lived before in a France without laundromats; and that she didn't want to deal with that again in some Godforsaken third world country. I flashed on Carl Olafsson and his quarter-gobbling machines up in Minnesota. Smart as he was, I wondered if he had given any thought to international expansion.

I had been very cautious driving that Sunbeam through the narrow roads over there. For one thing, Christine was quite pregnant. And, of course, it was somebody else's car. Without a scratch, we delivered it to the ship in Le Havre, then took trains to

Luxembourg where our bargain-basement Icelandic flight departed for Chicago. Weeks later, with word the car had arrived, I drove Hal down to the dock at the southern tip of Lake Michigan. Despite the voyage, the car, upon inspection, remained in pristine shape. Hal and I handled the paperwork transfer, I thanked him for his generosity and we went our separate ways. No more than an hour later, Hal's mother called. On his way home, a short drive north, a full-size American car going south flipped over a center divider and landed flush on the little Sunbeam. Hal spent two months in a hospital and is lucky to be alive; the car was totaled. We had put 3,300 miles on it in France. Hal said he hadn't even got it into fourth gear when he was pancaked.

I WAS GREETED BACK AT Sears with open arms and a stack of layouts filled with those demanding red rectangles. After Europe, my first time there, everything at Homan and Arthington felt ponderously anticlimactic. In earnest, I began sending letters and résumés to every ad agency I could think of. Then, as if I had willed it, Marv Stern mentioned that his older brother Jerry, who ran a small agency downtown, was looking for a copywriter. I wondered why Marv wouldn't take the job himself. He said he didn't want to work for his brother and, besides, Sears had just offered him a promotion to assistant merchandise manager in the high-volume Hardware Department. Personally, I couldn't imagine a life parceling out catalog space for nuts and bolts but Marv, never really bitten by the writer's muse, saw opportunity there. (And right he was. He retired from Sears decades later as President of Hard Goods—that's hardware, sporting goods, appliances, et al.—with over 100,000 people under his wing.)

Stern Walters & Simmons was indeed a small firm, just twenty-five people. They were located on the third floor of a four-story building a block east of Michigan Avenue.

It happened that one of SWS's largest accounts at the time was Grundig-Majestic, a German maker of high-end radios and phonographs known mainly for their glossy Euro-style cabinetry. Back at Polk Bros. I'd actually sold a number of their largest consoles at a considerable commission. Jerry and his two partners, Lee Walters and Marty Simmons, all three account men, grilled me for a hour. I think what won them over was my Polk Bros. experience and that back cover catalog copy for the color TV, two things they could merchandise to their Grundig client.

I asked when I would meet my immediate boss, the creative director. The partners said they didn't have one of those at the moment—the last creative director had just been "let go"—but were in final negotiations with a new guy currently in New York. They were certain I would like him and vice versa. I knew exactly nothing about the agency business. Still it seemed odd they weren't giving the new creative director the opportunity to approve me. Apparently they had work piling up and weren't concerned with nuisances like protocol.

And so I was hired for $2,000 more than I was then making at Sears, $8,500 per annum, starting two weeks hence if not sooner.

Back down in the small elevator lobby, curiously perusing the building directory, I noticed the impressive name of the occupant of the fourth floor. My first agency writing job and there I am, just one level below Mortimer Adler and his Great Books of the Western World.

Flying Solo

Stern Walters & Simmons, like every place I'd worked to date, had its cast of characters starting at the top with Jerry Stern, the charismatic president, who in many ways reminded me of a fleshy Frank Sinatra.

He had a tough veneer, an oldest brother command of a meeting, a confrontational demeanor even his two partners, equal shareholders, treated with diffidence.

He pushed back on the tides of change. He dressed old school and expected every man in the agency to show up in a jacket and tie. He faced a long commute yet was always the first to arrive. He'd walk the halls in the morning, growing angrier with every empty office he passed. During my divorced years, I had an apartment literally across the street from the office. It infuriated him that I strolled in late almost always. When he'd confront me about it, I'd piss him off more by saying if he had as good a time as I did the previous night, he'd be late too.

He was a throwback, the War vet who smoked three packs of Luckies a day. If he stopped by my office and grabbed one of mine (Kool Filters at the time), he'd unconsciously snap off the filter as if it was an unmanly intrusion. I tried one his way once; it grabbed at my throat like ground-up razor blades. He did his share of drinking too, though never before 5:00. Precisely then however, he would call out to his secretary, "Helaine, my nana please," and she, well-versed in the routine, sashayed in with a bottle of Johnny Walker, a cut-glass bowl of ice and seltzer bottle, fully charged, on a silver tray. My guess is Ol' Blue Eyes greeted that hour the same way.

On the subject of women in advertising, he only grudgingly acquiesced. When it came my time to do the hiring in the creative department, one of my first recruits was a young copywriter from Boston's Italian North End. She was feisty and highly liberated—a state of mind Stern could not fathom—and, of course, she refused the need for a bra. This became obvious when the office heating system was slow to kick on. Seeing her on one such nippy morning, he roared into my office demanding I tell her to start wearing something under her sweater. I told him her perkiness was good for morale and suggested that if it bothered him that much he ought to tell her himself. He left shaking his head in frustration.

For some reason, I did have a knack for getting under his skin. And getting away with it. Perhaps because his youngest brother was my friend. Or that he was just giving the next generation a little rope. Or maybe that he saw something of himself in my disregard for authority.

To wit, the agency Christmas party held in a private room of an Italian restaurant on Rush Street just three months after I joined the firm and barely knew more than half the staff. For me, there were several "firsts" that night. My first agency Christmas party. And my first and second and third martini straight up and straight to the brain. At which point, a well-endowed woman, ten years my senior, in a pronounced German accent, asked me to dance. We stumbled around the tiny dance floor to something by Tony Bennett, she more inebriated than me. "Who are you, dah-link?" she asked slobbering in my ear. And being told her name and department—Magda Gruennegger, in media, dah-link—I asked if her surname meant anything in German. "Great knockers," she said laughing and pressing ever closer to prove her points. Just then I felt a tap on the shoulder. Someone cutting in, thank God. It was the boss, Jerry Stern. He stood to my side and said that I was married and that I had had too much to drink and that I ought to take a taxi home. *Now*. I disentangled myself from Magda, turned to him and brazenly asked, "Why? Am I stepping on your toes?" I never knew if I was or wasn't. I do know that for as long as I worked for the man—fourteen years to the day—he never forgot that remark and every time we had a jurisdictional disagreement he would say, "Careful, you're stepping on my toes."

Under the crust he did have a softer side. A great storyteller, he was a master of dialects and could imitate the voice and mannerisms of every key person in the office, including Miss Gruennegger, not to mention our clients. He'd do it for laughs. Though he wasn't above a mocking barb if a client demolished a presentation. But he was man enough to turn the tables on himself especially after Helaine had delivered his "nana."

Holding court one night in his office, he got on the subject of the dumbest thing he ever did. After the War, he had landed a job as a copywriter in the promotion department of *Esquire* magazine, headquartered then in Chicago. He, too, shared cubicle space, his fellow writer a gawky pipe-smoker with secret and grandiose plans.

One day the guy came in with a bulky, scotch-taped dummy of a new magazine he'd been working on at home. He asked Jerry what he thought of it and whether he'd be interested in quitting *Esquire*, putting in some money and partnering with him to launch the thing. Jerry, a newlywed living paycheck to paycheck, took a look, and then a pass. Disappointed, Hugh Hefner left with his mock-up and found approbation elsewhere.

Stern was not the type to miss a second opportunity however. Buoyed by a few potential client connections he had made—one, the U.S. distributor for a line of German hifi's; another a no-nonsense entrepreneur named Jack Levant who marketed a skin lotion called Dermassage; the third, a small-time liquor wholesaler with a fancy British name, Park & Tilford—Stern left his dead-end job writing direct mail subscription offers for *Esquire* to start a one-man ad agency.

He struggled. The income from Grundig catalog sheets and small space ads for Dermassage and third-tier liquor brands did not amount to critical mass.

Networking with media salesmen in the Wrigley Bar, he was introduced to two other one-man agency guys: Marty Simmons, a squeaky-voiced tight-fisted ferret whose father-in-law owned TVTime Popcorn, an innovative (pre-microwave) snack food; and Lee Walters, handsome as a B-movie star, who handled advertising for Northern Electric, a maker of electric blankets, a big fad back then and run by a neighbor of his on the Northwest Side. The three joined forces in the fall of 1954. (The commemorative paperweight I came up with for the agency's 20th anniversary still functions on my desk; a 3x4 rectangle of hefty bronze, like a miniaturized magazine ad, with a bold raised headline: "Cast in bronze." Natch. The father-son foundry I prevailed on to make the keepsake almost went broke adhering to the production budget we were saddled with by Stern.)

The agency's first big break occurred when Colgate-Palmolive acquired Dermassage from Jack Levant. Along with the financial windfall, he was asked to move to New York to oversee the brand and a few other personal care products Colgate had waiting in the wings. Levant insisted he retain his small-time Chicago ad agency, an extremely loyal gesture. Colgate didn't need another ad agency, they already had a handful of giants, but swallowed Levant's deal point while disdainfully chirping from their Park Avenue perch: Who are those guys?

Now "those guys,"—Jerry, Lee and Marty—were thrust into the big leagues, easier said than done when the unwritten agency philosophy, and I mention this affectionately, was "Dress British, think Yiddish." Hiring credentialed media and research people, finding a respected creative director (oops, first try a bomb) and a legitimate art director or two, moving to larger quarters, all these wrenching investments took place just before I, the only copywriter, joined the firm.

Obviously, and oddly, copywriters per se had not been a priority at SWS—perhaps the Max Applebaum school of advertising? Account guys, including the three partners, "wrote" the copy, such as it was. And it was hackneyed, declarative, tell it like it is, devoid of anything resembling inspiration. Seemingly, their clients wouldn't know it if they saw it and certainly didn't demand it. I had the feeling when I settled in that I was the only person in the place who was aware of the cloudburst of creativity now raining on both coasts.

They gave me an office to share, windowless but my first ever with a door. The other occupant was a freelance artist, a munchkin of a man. He worked there rent free. In return, he reduced his fees to knock out illustrations for various collateral materials. To this day, he is the only man I've ever known who wore a toupee that somehow emitted dandruff. He was someone to talk to though so I tried to engage him on the subject of the coming creative revolution. He had no interest in that "adsy" stuff. His real passion was his large collection of daguerreotypes that he found prowling flea markets; his specialty was, you guessed it, circus midgets. In his downtime, he would sit there hunched over his child-sized drawing board doodling out dozens of Bruegelesque nudes. They were *engaged*, decidedly so, in a mass and ever expanding orgy. Lost in a world of his making, he giggled over every new and anatomically impossible position he conjured up for his little people.

A few months later than advertised, the Lone Ranger finally arrived to rescue me. And the partners were right. It was hard not to like the new creative director. Clark O'Shannahan was big in every New York way. A tall and portly red-faced Irishman, he had, for his sixty years, an enviable shock of white hair—though he did remind me of a financier who had missed his last two barber appointments. His hair flowed over the collars of all five of his pinstriped double-breasted black suits, one for every day of the week. I could tell the day by the color of the stripes and matching ties, from Monday's off white to Friday's deep purple. They were expensive suits, but they were frayed around the jacket and trouser cuffs; my guess was he'd been wearing them a long time.

And the man could entertain. He wove his ready yarns around his own loud laughter: his glory days on Madison Avenue vying with Ogilvy and J. Walter; his stormy marriages and three monthly alimony payments; his evening exploits on the tab at all the storied places. What he didn't talk about were the campaigns he conceived or the ads he wrote. Modesty didn't seem to be his mantra. Blarney was it then? I assumed the partners had seen his work. Then again, what did that prove? On the other hand, they hired me, didn't they? If blarney is what he's about, I hoped he'd use some of that charm pushing my stuff up the mountain here—and with the clients who would surely love this guy.

Sooner than anyone imagined, the Colgate business boiled up. They were keen on a new product for teen boys, a tube of clear gel that supposedly helped cure acne. Clearasil was out there but that product, a cosmetic really, was targeted to girls. Clark asked me, being closest in age to the market, to tackle Tackle (their name). In fact, Clark steered clear of the client almost as though a skeletal vestige of him remained in Colgate's closet.

Now came immersion in the maelstrom: the trips to New York traveling with Jerry and Marty, the interminable marketing and research meetings at 333 Park, the hand-wringing and nervous pacing that accompanies the birth of any packaged goods product, and sage Jack Levant shepherding us like his children through the maze. While visions of Volkswagen ads danced in my head, this product and this client weren't waltzing. Not yet anyway. And so we turned to Sunday comics as the place to reach kids with a series of problem-solution strips featuring cartoon portrayals of people like Yogi Berra advising his zit-blotched fifteen-year-old son Larry to tackle his skin problems. Awards? No. Sales? Boffo.

One fine St. Patrick's Day, Simmons and I were meeting with our Dermassage brand manager, George Rooney, a gangly and mostly gloomy Irish-American. He looked at his watch and said, "Hey, let's take a break. The parade will be passing downstairs any minute." The three of us squeezed into the throng along Park Avenue as the lead bagpipers approached. Rooney leaned down to warn us, "Watch your wallets, guys. Pickpockets work these crowds." Forgetting his thin-skinned sense of humor, I quipped up to him, "C'mon, George. They're all out there marching." He didn't laugh and then, back up in his office, he suddenly had all kinds of problems with the ads I'd been presenting.

⁂

WE WERE APPROACHED BY SUZUKI, an upstart motorcycle brand fairly new to the States. Would we do an on-package promotion with Tackle? They'd pony up fifty 50cc cycles as sweepstakes prizes. The contest worked well for Tackle. And just as significant for SWS was the relationship that developed with Suzuki and the invitation to come out to L.A. to talk to them about their business, which was currently at the San Francisco office of Dancer-Fitzgerald-Sample, a very good agency back then.

Stern and I and Bill Lowney, a terrific account guy Jerry had just hired, saw Suzuki as a huge opportunity, a chance to spread our wings to the West Coast in an exciting full-throttled product category, a chance, given the Colgate business, to truly become a "national" ad agency.

Meanwhile, Clark, the creative director, avoided all this "kid stuff," the acne cure and this motorcycle shot, opting instead to work on some of our softball accounts like the electric blankets and, not surprisingly, the liquor business. I knew he was stumbling back from longer and longer lunch hours, hiding the rest of the day behind closed doors. And telling me what a great job I was doing and then hitting me up for a spare ten or twenty which he diligently paid back on paydays.

The Suzuki meeting was two weeks away. They called it "exploratory," meaning just talk, but we thought since we're going all the way to California we ought to shoot craps and show up with some ideas in hand. Suzuki's competitor, entrenched then for several years with their "You meet the nicest people on a Honda" campaign, was formidable. We didn't need a meeting to tell us that. I knew nothing about motorcycles, if anything they frightened me, but I had the feeling that the mystique behind them had nothing to do with meeting nice people; that it was more about a man and his machine riding off into the sunset, hot throbbing cylinders under his crotch.

I was looking for a word that would encapsulate the mystique and that would work with Suzuki, a name unknown to most Americans. I walked into Lowney's office, he a decorated WWII fighter pilot, with something I'd scribbled on a notepad. "Fuck the nicest people. Get out there and Solo Suzuki." Lowney stood up and hugged me.

Jerry was on board. We pulled out all the stops. Jack Levant's son Howard was a prominent commercial photographer in Chicago. We put him to work on the magazine ads. I'd never written a jingle in my life but I wrote lyrics to "Comedy Tonight" from *A Funny Thing Happened on the Way to the Forum*. I knew that melody was all wrong for Suzuki's market but I didn't know how else to do it:

Solo Suzuki
Solo Suzuki
Spirit you'll feel it
When you wheel it around.

Someone from a radio station suggested I take my lyrics to Bernie Saber, then Chicago's pre-eminent jingle writer. Bernie was right out of Tin Pan Alley, his upright piano in a cramped office lined with framed copies of sheet music from his commercial hits like "You'll wonder where the yellow went when you brush your teeth with Pepsodent." Big time. Except Bernie looked like my Uncle Milton on my mother's side, bushy mustache, shiny pate and kept giving me the condescending "Kid" schtick. I told him I wrote the lyrics to that Broadway tune but I did not want anything remotely like that. We needed something stirring to get the Suzuki clients up off their asses. "No problem, Kid," he said and told me to meet him at Universal Studios in a week, the next Tuesday. He'd have a band, singers, the whole bit.

In the midst of all this, I get a call—the personnel director of Leo Burnett. Yes, I had written them impassioned letters when I was at Goldblatt's, and from Ft. Devens, and while at Sears, relating in several of the letters my encounter with Mr. Burnett umpteen years ago and my immature remark. Whatever it was that prompted them, from out of the blue they wanted to talk to me. Guilty as hell, I walked over there on a Friday lunch hour. Say what you will—Green Giant; Snap, Crackle, Pop; Marlboro Man et al.—Leo was Advertising in Chicago. The personnel guy, in his big corner office overlooking Grant Park and the lake, seemed to know more about me than I did. He asked what I made, then doubled it as though it was chump change. I was stunned and told him I would think about it. He said no one turned Leo Burnett down twice. I got his drift.

On the personal side, Christine was expecting our second child, snap crackle pop. And I was still helping out at my folks' store every Saturday to pick up an extra $20 cash. I'd grown to like the people at SWS and was feeling very confident about the Suzuki pitch. But simple math said $17,000 was two times $8,500.

Walking north across the Michigan Avenue bridge, past Col. Coleman's fur salon, on up three blocks to our new offices on Superior, I felt like Brutus, Benedict Arnold and the Rosenbergs all rolled into one. I went straight to Jerry's office. He immediately asked Helaine to get hold of Lee and Marty. The three of them then stared at me as if I was the Hope Diamond. "You can't quit," Jerry finally said, "we just fired Clark an hour ago. He came back from lunch drunk once too often. You're all we got."

Quitting Goldblatt's was close to euphoric. And Sears viewed the catalog copywriting job as a steppingstone to a career in merchandising; they were accustomed to avowed copywriters moving on. But right now I feel like a rat leaving the three forlorn partners on a sinking ship.

They offered to raise my salary to $15,000 (a substantial savings over Clark) and, if we landed Suzuki, they'd even match Burnett's number. Furthermore, they would promote me to Creative Director, an absolute stunner.

"I'm not ready for that job, guys," I protested. "I've got a lot to learn. At Burnett, I'll have mentors in the creative department."

Gerry parried. "You told me Missouri gave you 'on-the-job training.' Well, so will we. And I promise nobody's gonna cut your head off if you screw up."

I was twenty-five at the time. Accepting their offer would, most likely, make me the youngest, albeit lowest paid C.D. in America. I grabbed the ring. Adios, Leo Burnett.

Back in my office, an envelope rested on my Royal. In it was a short note from Clark. He said he told them I ought to get his job. And wished me all the best. Thirty dollars were tucked in there too, a ten and a twenty, his latest borrowings. To my knowledge no one in the agency ever heard from him again.

⁂

I HAD AN IDEA WHILE we were shooting Suzuki stills at Levant's studio. I'd met their top guy during the Tackle talks, an all-American motorcycle racing fanatic named Jack McCormack, along with several of his scarred-up associates. I had a line, totally inappropriate for advertising, which I thought might start our meeting off with a good he-man guffaw. "You get more nookie on a Suzuki." By no means a perfect rhyme. But these were motorcycle guys, not poets. Howard grabbed two gorgeous models who had sauntered in by chance, sent an assistant out to buy two of Rudi Gernreich's scandalous swim suits—topless save for the two thin strategically placed suspenders—and set to work shooting the girls in a sultry pose leaning against a white Suzuki cycle. We blew the shot up as big as we could get on an airplane and topped it with the "Nookie" headline.

On the Tuesday before our Friday Suzuki meeting in L.A., I went to the music session full of anticipation. Bernie was excited about what he had wrought. "You're gonna love this, Kid," he said heading out to the studio. He tapped the rostrum like Paul Whiteman. The twenty-piece orchestra and quartet of vocalists took up his beat. I couldn't believe it. They were playing and singing nothing more than "Comedy Tonight," note for note. He came back into the booth. "What do you think, Kid?" he asked. "I think you're a musician who doesn't listen good, Bernie," I answered and walked out feeling robbed.

In desperation, I called Chuck Blore, a brilliant commercial production guy in L.A. who'd made a presentation at our office a few weeks previously. I gave him the concept and asked the impossible. Could he come up with some kind of music track in the next forty-eight hours, something I could play at our meeting?

The firsts were piling up. My first trip to California, my first new business presentation, my first whiff of night-blooming jasmine as we climbed out of the rental at the meeting site, the Sportsmen's Lodge on Ventura Boulevard. As promised, there was Blore, in a blue jean ensemble, waiting for us in the lobby and looking like he just pulled an all-nighter. We went to the meeting room we'd booked for the next morning to hear what he'd thrown together.

As Blore threaded the Wollensak, Stern, Lowney and I prayed for salvation. Then out of those tinny speakers came the perfect anthem, as if the "Ghost Riders in the Sky" had hopped off their horses and onto two-wheelers:

He was soloing Suzuki
He was roarin' down the street
The whistling wind it combed his hair
The engine warmed his feet
A lively spirit moved him
To escape the old routine
He lived a love affair
Between a man and his machine
Solo Suzuki
He geared down at a traffic light
The mighty engine purred
He saw a girl in tight capri's
He knew that this was her
She climbed aboard and held him tight
They took off like a jet
That's soloing Suzuki and winding up duet.
Solo Suzuki

These days jingles are most definitely not in vogue. But that was then and Blore had nailed it; that, or he had signed on Johnny Cash at the eleventh hour. He even worked in the "duet" mention, something Stern, worried about the exclusionary implication of "Solo," insisted I shoehorn into the copy. Blore's tribal chant brought us to our feet. I went to sleep almost positive we would blow those guys away.

The next morning, waiting in the conference room, we heard them arrive, all seven Suzukis roaring into the Lodge's parking lot, revving for effect.

I had shrouded the mounted "Nookie" board with red velvet. It sat on an easel at the head of the table. The Suzuki guys marched in, lean and tan and Waspy as a Presbyterian church choir.

After the obligatory set-up by Jerry and Bill, I took center stage. Milking it for all it was worth, I told them we thought we had the perfect foil for Honda's campaign. "Screw the 'nicest people,'" I said flinging back the shroud, "You get more nookie on a Suzuki!"

No doubt, I overdid it. Maybe it was the two babes all but exposing themselves next to their cycle. But these guys were whooping and hollering like they'd just witnessed the Resurrection. I looked over to Jerry for help. He played the wizened ad man card, telling them that the "nookie" idea would work great as an ice-breaker at a dealer meeting, just as it had in this room; but, in fact, no respectable medium would or could accept it. And just wait 'til Larry takes you through our "real" campaign idea; guys, you ain't seen nothing yet.

Whew, I thought, Jerry's fatherly advice seemed to make sense to these young Turks. And I won't ever again risk the backfire misdirection can cause. (Except I made the same stupid mistake years later in a pitch for the brand-new Luxor Hotel in Las Vegas. I was trying to illustrate how predictable and similar all Vegas advertising was at the time, setting them up for our unexpected approach. We put together a video using snippets from all the competition's commercials—twelve babes diving into a dozen different swimming pools, six blackjack tables at six different casinos full of chip-laden winners laughing and scratching, champagne bottles popping one after another, etc.—all cut to Elvis's rendition of "Viva Las Vegas." Halfway through the video, watching the tapping of alligator shoes in the roomful of shiny suits, I knew I'd blown it. They did not see sameness. They saw their exciting lives flashing before them. They saw greatness. Which is not at all what they saw when I hauled out our simplistic, urbane and unanimously rejected campaign.)

The Suzuki Seven settled down. I took them through the thinking behind "Solo Suzuki" and read them the copy off the comped-up magazine ads I tacked on the wall. The finale was Blore's radio track cranked to full volume. I was new to this game but I could tell—they liked what they saw and heard. The head guy, Jack McCormack, asked the three of us to go down to the cocktail lounge while they "talked behind our backs."

By now it was late morning. Jerry, Bill and I are each on our second Bloody Mary when McCormack and his two senior guys come into the bar stone faced. And then they erupted. They loved everything. Will you open an office out here? Yes, Jerry said. And who wrote that copy? Most of it, me, I said. Well you sure as hell know motorcycles. We want you to stick around an extra day. We've got this really hot new bike, our fastest ever, the X-6 Hustler. We'll want to promote it big time so come down to our test track in Santa Ana tomorrow and give it a ride. And you know that "Nookie" poster, we all want it downsized for the back of our business cards. And maybe frame some 9 by 12's for all the guys' offices. Great, great and more great. With handshakes all around, they left, a cloud of blue fumes hovering over the parking lot.

It was my initiation in the new business barrel and, for the rest of my life, there never was another win more decisive or elating except…

"Guys, what about this test ride thing Jack wants me to do?"

"What about it?" Jerry said beckoning for a third celebratory round.

"What d'ya mean, 'what about it?' I've never been *on* a fucking motorcycle. I don't even know how you stop the damn things!"

Bill, the old pilot, chimed in. "You'll get the hang of it. Just like riding a bike."

I tossed all night. I would make a fool of myself not to mention a liar in the eyes of this enchanted new client. But once again, the fates intervened. The phone in the room rang around 8:00 a.m. I thought it was my wake-up call but instead it was McCormack and he had bad news. Christ, we're already losing the account! "What's up, Jack?" I asked, waiting for the sledgehammer. "There's a smog alert," he said, "and it's backed up here in Santa Ana. Opening your eyes, it hurts. I'm sorry but it's just not a safe day for riding. We'll do it next time you're out." Another first: a smog alert. For me, heaven sent.

We'd taken space east on Sunset in a quaint old building next door to a casting office for future soft porn starlets. And hired a guy to run the West Coast operation, Jerry Thompson, perhaps the only full-blooded Cherokee in advertising. McCormack had shipped three of their tamer 50cc models to Chicago to give our people a chance to "Solo Suzuki," his note said. I grabbed one and forced myself to learn how to ride the damned thing over a weekend in the empty parking lot across from our office. As it turned out, I never did get to Suzuki's test track, things were moving that fast. Two years into our relationship, Suzuki was going great guns. Their X-6 Hustler won race after race and they were chipping away at Honda's huge share of the market. After their biggest victory yet, I wrote a headline for a long copy "win ad":

"How a lonely Hustler won the heart of Daytona."

Totally unrelated to advertising, McCormack had fired, for whatever reason, one of the Suzuki Seven, a regional sales manager. It was a point of interest but of no consequence to us.

Until we were hit with the lawsuit.

When the guy left Suzuki, apparently he took along his framed copy of the "Nookie" poster as a souvenir. An enterprising sort, he started a company, the poster his only product. He reproduced thousands of them adding a little white space below the photo. He visited Suzuki dealers and sold them quantities of the flyers (as Stern had foreseen, dealers loved them). They would stamp their store info onto that little white space and hire neighborhood kids to slip the "Nookie" message under windshield wipers.

Suzuki management knew nothing about this rogue sales guy's activities. We knew nothing. But a Chicago lawyer, who had recently married one of the two models adorning the flyer he found one day under his Cadillac's wiper, he knew. And sued Suzuki and

SWS for defamation of character and unauthorized and unpaid-for use and depiction.

We were called on the carpet in Santa Ana when Mr. Suzuki, actually the son of the founder, came from Japan to discuss this face-losing litigation. I sat across from him and his bushy unibrow. He had one of the copies we were asked to frame in his hand; I could see our logo pasted on the back. I free-associated with Alec Guinness's interrogation in *The Bridge on the River Kwai*. Right before he landed in the hotbox. There was no small talk, no congratulations for putting them on the map of the United States. As relayed by his translator, he had just one question to ask of me: "Mr. Suzuki say, what mean nookie?"

I turned toward the two Jerry's, Stern, seated down the table and next to him, Thompson, my Tonto, for guidance. None was forthcoming. Every last person in the room except maybe Tanaka-san, the translator, knew we were innocent, which somehow made me feel more guilty. Aware the term emanated in the Far East after WWII, as in "Soldier, you want some nookie?" I found it hard to believe that Mr. Suzuki was so uninformed. In my mind he was really chastising his American employees at the table for involving *his* company in such tawdriness.

Directing my answer to the harried Mr. Tanaka, I said, "Tell Mr. Suzuki that young men in America..." I paused for the translation, "...they have many words to describe females." I bowed my head, nothing more than a nod, toward Mr. Suzuki. "And that 'nookie' is just one of them." Pause. "Tell him the sentence on the picture in his hand means you attract more girls when you ride a Suzuki. That's all." Stern chimed in saying the agency would take full responsibility for the Chicago-based lawsuit. (He already knew we could settle out of court for $10,000.)

With that, Suzuki stood up and said, in perfectly uninflected English, "Thank you very much." He then left the room tailed by Tanaka-san.

I don't remember which came first, the dismissal of McCormack and his remaining cadre of five—replaced by a whole new group sent over from Japan*—or our demise. The timing was close.

I do remember the memo to staff I wrote for Jerry's signature and its bittersweet heading: "So long, Suzuki."

* *Of course, the new team included a bean counter. One of his first actions was to demand we ship those three gift motorcycles, beat up as they were by then, back to Santa Ana. I thought that was rather niggardly of them. Jerry Thompson called them "Indian Givers."*

Goomba

I WAS GROWING COMFORTABLE IN MY CREATIVE DIRECTOR'S SKIN—IT just didn't stretch far enough. There were trips to New York for Colgate. And California during the Suzuki years. And, with the "buzz" the Chicago marketing community sensed we had going, along came a flock of new business leads. I needed help.

First, I reached out to my old Goldblatt's buddy, the wordsmith Jack Badofsky, at the time cranking out catalog sheets for a local paint manufacturer. He was amenable to a change but asked that I call his wife to convince her an ad agency equaled job security. Whatever I said pacified her, a fortuitous turning point for our creative department.

Then I placed a want ad in *Advertising Age*, the trade bible, seeking a few more young (and beginner salaried) souls. The ad had a brutally candid headline—"At 29 you're too old for this job"—with copy explaining that ours was a very young creative department and that, at 29, you'd be four years older than the creative director (despite being comfortable in my skin, I remained self-conscious about the age of it). The ad attracted some bona fide candidates. And a lot of unintended flak. Citing my teeny two-inch ad, *AdAge* wrote an editorial denouncing age discrimination. And our anonymous post office box was filled with letters from the unemployed, 30 and above, who thought we ought to be ashamed of ourselves. I hadn't suffered the "nookie" reprisal yet; this was my first lesson in the power of ill-chosen words.

We *were* saying something right however. Andy Granatelli noticed our new Suzuki ads in gearhead magazines and called one of the pubs to find out who the Suzuki agency was. (Those were the days when clients did their own homework. Today they invariably rely on outside consultants to assemble lists of compatible ad agencies for their perusal). After several get-acquainted meetings—today known as "chemistry checks"—with Andy and his team, he asked us to present campaign ideas for his nascent STP Oil Treatment, at the time a $5 million niche brand.

Granatelli was a character larger than life literally and figuratively. His girth was enormous; pear-shaped barely described it. He attributed his physique to a racing accident years earlier. What one had to do with the other he never said. Another time he told me there was nothing wrong with him; it was everyone else who was misshapen.

The man was an auto racing fanatic. Along with his brothers, Vince and Joe, they'd done it all in open-wheel racing, from inaugurating midget car races around the dirt running track at Soldier Field in the forties to hauling their own hand-built entries down to the Indy 500 in the fifties. In the early sixties, Studebaker-Packard, who owned the fledgling product, saw in Granatelli the perfect dynamo to run their STP Division. And, girth aside, run he did.

He had prevailed on his Indy 500 contacts, the team owners and drivers, to add his product to their crankcases and slap his dark red STP oval decal on the side of their racecars. Friendships notwithstanding, they had an incentive: a cash bonus from Andy if they finished in the top ten; the closer to the top, of course, the larger the bonus. The decals became a hot item at track souvenir stands and began to appear on race fans' rear windows. He was creating his own buzz though the average driver spotting one of those decals in traffic had no idea what STP stood for. Andy figured it was time to advertise.

Badofsky, a new art director I'd hired named Sol Levine, and I were working on it. Sol was a real find. Despite his artistic mien, he was amazingly collaborative and even-keeled. And considering Jack and I didn't know a carburetor from a percolator, it helped that Sol was mechanically minded. (Before "going green" existed, he was the first guy I ever heard of who rigged a stationary bicycle to a generator and a small television; to watch Captain Kangaroo, his kids had to keep pedaling off the potato chips.)

Plugging away at the office, I hit on an STP slogan I liked: "Pour it in and pour it on." Jack, the irrepressible punster, had one far more cerebral I liked even more: "The Racer's Edge." Having learned from the Suzuki pitch how much clients love the sound of their name set to music, we wrote lyrics for an anthem, okay a jingle, and handed them off to a youthful competitor of Bernie Saber:

From the Indy to LeMans
STP
Champions depend upon
STP
They pour it in and pour it on
STP
STP is the Racer's Edge!

We hammered out ballsy copy to sandwich between two choruses of the lyric and hired Don Gallagher, a Shakespearean-trained announcer gifted with stirring timbre, to growl out the promise of better engine performance. Meanwhile Sol crafted a stack of magazine ads and outdoor billboard concepts oozing with oomph.

Clearly, Andy Granatelli had no knowledge of the works of Somerset Maugham (or his sexual preferences). He bought into "The Racer's Edge" at face value—the ads, the outdoor, the music—he was excited about everything except Gallagher's voice, which he found offensively unfriendly. We had to come back with several other announcer auditions plugged into the jingle to prove our point. Accustomed as he was to having his way, Andy had to admit the other voices paled by comparison. Now it was left for Stern to work out the financial arrangements. For the creative department, it was off to the races.

Inspired in part by his new advertising slogan, Andy was determined to truly dominate the Indy 500. It wasn't enough to have his decal on nearly every one of the thirty-three cars on the starting grid; he wanted his own STP-sponsored team and car to win the race.

Ever the showman, Andy would not settle for just another vehicle. He cut a deal with Pratt & Whitney and unveiled at the 1967 Indy the world's first turbine-powered racecar, Parnelli Jones in the cockpit. It didn't look like the other cars. Or sound like them. It didn't roar, it whooshed around the oval. (Later that year Andy asked me to create his company Christmas card. Sol drew a sketch of him dressed as Santa behind the wheel of the turbine car. The greeting read "Best Whooshes for the Holidays.") It led most of the way and damn near won except for a two-dollar part that went south on the second to last lap. A.J. Foyt swept past to steal the checkered flag. But as though Andy wrote the script, his revolutionary car stole the show. And the headlines.

We were there with a camera crew prepared to quickly get on air with a "win" commercial. That didn't happen, not that year.

Account exec Mike Miller, Andy Granatelli and me on location at the Indy 500, 1969

But we had already filmed our first STP TV spot that we planned to run as a back-up to take advantage of the publicity we knew the car, win or lose, would garner.

The spot was simple: the Indy 500 track, dead empty save for a solitary figure, Granatelli in a custom-made trench coat reciting his lines as he ambled toward camera and the famous brickwork finish line. Andy had balked at putting on the trench coat. For one thing, it was hot the day we shot. For another, he said we were selling STP, not raincoats. I told him the director thought it made him look more heroic but I think he knew—deep in his gut—why we wanted him to wear it. I do know when we wrapped that day he left with the trench coat over his arm saying he'd paid for it anyhow. And from then on, every time we shot him, he showed up—unasked—wearing it.

⁂

Around the office his affectionate code name was Goomba but he wasn't all that Italian. Vodka was his drink. And he loved Mexican food. He did have one Godfatherly trait, a surreptitious streak, a keeper of secrets he'd occasionally divulge for all-knowing effect.

Once, he had me thread up and run a small 16-mm reel. In grainy black and white, for sure a home movie, there was Andy demonstrating how STP was slipperier than motor oil alone. He dipped the business end of a screwdriver into a can of motor oil, then held up the beveled edge between his thumb and index finger. He held on, no problem. Now, after dipping the oily tip into STP, he repeated the procedure. Oops. He couldn't hang on to the screwdriver; it dropped onto the table before him.

"This would make a great commercial, pal," he said. "Write some words and get a pro to reshoot it in color."

"Dunno, Andy. It's too pat. I mean, you're the judge and jury," I said as diplomatically as possible. "It needs a foil, y'know some big strong guy trying to do it. Maybe first you arm wrestle him, he wins, then you challenge him to the screwdriver test and he loses." I figured all this rigmarole would make his hokum slip away.

"That's good, pal. Would Rocky Marciano qualify?"

"Yea, he'd be perfect," I had to admit. "But he's got agents and all that bullsh..."

"No problem. He's comin' to the house for dinner tonight. He'll do it."

And a few days later, he did. Other than the fact it was difficult to tell who was who since Andy and Rocky looked like twin brothers (Andy was the one in the trench coat), and that Ralph, Rocky's five-by-five-foot black belt bodyguard kept looking at his watch and glaring at me because the shoot was cutting into their cocktail hour, it worked out better than I thought it would. Unfortunately, it was short-lived. Just a month after the spot began running, The Rock was killed in a small plane crash somewhere in Iowa.

Andy was inconsolable and, of course, we immediately pulled the commercial. Not to be undone however, after a respectful interlude, Andy comes up with another "big guy" crony, a Hawaiian named Jesse Takamiyama, the first American ever accepted as a full-fledged sumo wrestler in Japan. To make a bizarre scenario even more so, we shot the spot in Japanese (thanks in large part to a very patient lady translator who spoon-fed Andy his lines) with English subtitles.

Andy, a true believer, swore that STP helped engines start easier in the coldest of temperatures. Over the nine years the agency had the account—before Studebaker fired Andy for hogging the headlines and the company jet—we shot a number of cold weather commercials.

One in particular was all his idea. "There's a consumer product testing facility in Indianapolis with a huge freezer that can hold a car," Andy informed us. "We'll keep my Lincoln in there overnight at ten below, then in the morning I walk in there shivering and start 'er right up. And I'll get someone from USAC (United States Auto Club) to witness the whole deal and sanction the results. Just come up with the words for your guy Gallagher, pal."

So off once again to Indy we went to film Andy's demo precisely as he envisioned it—a convincing proof positive of STP's credibility. The man from USAC was there clipboard in hand; he'd already agreed to the hot camera lights inside the freezer for the brief finale. The camera rolled as we all watched Andy in trench coat and gloves come through steel freezer hatch, open car door, turn key in ignition and—and nothing.

We're all stunned and stuck in place. Except Granatelli. Moving rapidly given his bulk, he jumps out of the Lincoln, runs to the front and pops the hood. He peers inside and, car guy that he is, instantly identifies the problem. "Battery's dead," he shouts, "get another one." And as if by magic, one of his underlings races into the freezer with a nice warm brand-new Diehard. He exchanges it for the "dead" one while Andy and the USAC guy oversee the action, then closes the hood as Andy, vapor spewing from his ice-cold nose, jumps back into the driver's seat, hollers out, "Okay, now run the camera" and, presto, starts the engine just like it's the middle of May.

After we covered close up inserts of the freezer's temperature gauge and Andy's gloved hand turning the ignition key, it was a wrap. I took Andy aside to ask whether we were going to have problems with the USAC guy and his documentation of the "demonstration."

"Don't worry, pal. I'm flying from here to the race in Phoenix. He's my special guest on the plane. Besides, he knows even God couldn't start a frozen engine with a dead battery."

USAC WASN'T AS KIND TO Granatelli when it came to his turbine cars. After the near win in '67, fearing a field full of "whooshmobiles" and the derision of noise-loving racing fans, they decreased the allowable air intake dimensions to the point that a turbine-powered car could not be competitive. Andy gave it a go the next year with a rule-abiding version of his turbine but, as USAC hoped, came up way short.

In '69, Andy bent to USAC's rule. He bought Mario Andretti's racing team, lock, stock and four-barrel carburetors. And Mario returned the favor, winning the Indy 500 convincingly, a first for him and Andy.

Anticipating the victory, my guys and I and our film crew had moseyed down to the Winner's Circle already jammed with television and press people. Now Mario pulls in raising a victorious fist. He's handed the traditional container of milk and begins to swill it. I'm looking around for Granatelli. I can't believe he's missing this once-in-a-lifetime photo op.

I look back down pit row and rub my eyes. From their location at least a thousand feet away, Granatelli and Mario's pit crew are running hell bent for glory toward the Winner's Circle. An enterprising photographer grabbed a series of shots as they approached with Andy, incredibly, leading the pack. (We bought three of those photos—far, medium, close—and put an ad together headlined "Fastest quarter mile in Indy history.") For Andy, the sprint was worth the potential health hazards. He got there just in time to squeeze through the throng—no mean feat for him—and breathlessly whisper something into the ear hole of Andretti's helmet mere seconds before the track announcer asked the obligatory "How'd you do it, Mario?" Without hesitation, Andretti shared these immortal words with the 400,000 screaming fans and the world at large: "I couldn't've done it without STP on my side"—Andy obviously had remembered the double entendre lifted right out of one of our radio commercials. A news photo of a grateful Granatelli kissing Mario, still seated in the winning car emblazoned with oversized STP decals and surrounded by pit crew and press people, appeared everywhere at the time and remains today a classic Indianapolis 500 moment.

⁂

Andy's love for auto racing began and ended with open wheel cars on an oval track. European style road racing would never make it in the States, he told me, because they didn't go fast enough and fans only saw a small portion of the race no matter where they sat. About that, he's been right. And stock car racing, in his opinion, with its enclosed cars just didn't have the wind-in-your-face thrills real race fans wanted. Not exactly. NASCAR was beginning to make big waves, growing in popularity every year. Regardless of his personal prejudices, Andy couldn't fight the current—or Studebaker management's badgering—any longer. Typical of his *modus operandi*, he surprised the racing world, jumping in with both feet. He cut a major sponsorship deal with Richard Petty, the preeminent NASCAR driver of the time.

We were asked to create a design for the paint job on Petty's new STP Special. Sol came up with a red, white and blue beauty, really an STP can on wheels. And just as Andretti had done for Granatelli, Petty immediately went out in that car and won the biggest race in his sport, the Daytona 500, for an unprecedented fifth time. We ran a strong, simple ad to commemorate the victory: a dramatic overhead shot of the car and the massive STP logo adorning its hood headlined "King Richard, the Fifth."

Now it was time to do a commercial featuring the King. We decided on a re-enactment of a race, Petty weaving past a half-dozen cars to the checkered flag, the action narrated in his own Carolina twang. The film location was a place called Eastaboga, Alabama, at the Talladega Superspeedway, an unusually short track severely banked like a teacup. As always with STP, we were shooting on a limited production budget and, therefore, a skeleton film crew.

For driver's point-of-view footage, the crew had rigged an auxiliary camera to a roll bar support behind Petty's helmet. I don't recall if remote-controlled cameras had been invented yet; if they were we weren't budgeted for one. Somebody would have to sit on the floor in the back of his stripped down racecar and operate the camera. The problem was we were out of film crew; the few guys we brought down there already had their hands full. Uncharacteristically, I volunteered.

My task was simple. If I saw a filmic "money shot," say Petty passing down low or high up on the bank, I turn on the camera. To save film when nothing was happening, I turn off the camera. Easy. Except these simple tasks required the camera operator to keep his eyes open. That part I was having difficulties with.

Belying his fame, Petty was a polite and friendly guy, and knowing I was hanging on back there, just an old beat-up blanket between me and the steel floor and no restraining belt whatsoever, he wasn't going, as they say, "balls out," maybe 130 mph. I knew he was one of the world's great drivers; it was the six guys steering the other cars I wasn't so sure about.

To maintain human contact after one hairy inches-away inside pass, I hollered over the roar, "How fast we going, Richard?"

"Dunno," he hollered back, "ain't no speedometers in these thangs. But don't worry none. You die with me, you gonna die famous."

No argument there.

⁂

By late 1969, STP sales had grown twelve-fold. Studebaker decided to spin the division off through an Initial Public Offering. Andy urged a number of us at the agency to buy the stock. It was pegged to open around $18, he said, and should take off from there. I had absolutely no clout with a broker and was unable to buy any at the opening price. So I'm left at the gate as the "hot" stock—a brand I helped build—leapt to $28 that day.

A week later (the stock now in the high thirties) I'm still doing a burn when I bump into an ebullient Andy in the corridor of his headquarters. "Hey, pal, did'ja buy the stock like I told you?"

"You had to know somebody," I replied dejectedly.

"You do," he said. He pulled a folded sheet of parchment out of his inside jacket pocket and handed it to me—an STP stock certificate for 300 shares, worth that day close to $12,000. And there on the dotted line was my name.

"You owe me 5400 bucks," he said grinning ear to ear.

Andy Granatelli, my goomba.

Retail Reality Redux

One fine morning in New York, I'm walking down Madison Avenue with my boss, Jerry Stern, heading toward a meeting at Colgate to present a breakthrough magazine campaign for Dermassage nestled in the flat black valise I was toting and I'm looking up at all the tall buildings lining the famous street, their myriad of windows gleaming in the sun, and I'm thinking how the agency is suddenly growing like crazy and I'm still holed up in a drywalled tomb back in Chicago, my only view the dandruff-laden gnome sitting across from me drawing lewd little revelers, when I had a big idea.

"Know what'd be cool, Jer? A photographic poster shot from high up in one of these buildings looking down Madison. There'd be a faux frame around it, some kind of window frame. It'd be for people in the biz who don't have a window (like me, for instance). Run an ad for it in *AdAge*, nothing big, four, five column inches. I bet it would sell (yeah, to people like me)."

"Do it," Jerry said instantly though my self-serving inspiration for the poster seemed lost on him. "Get it produced and placed through the agency. We'll go halfsies with you. What do you want to call it?"

And so the Madison Avenue Window Poster was born.

I BOUGHT THE PERFECT STOCK photo from AP for $25. And prevailed on George, my old Goldblatt's artist buddy, to illustrate a simple wood frame, its venetian blinds pulled all the way up but slightly tilted to one side. Our production manager said the clergyman's price to print a thousand on heavy stock would be around twenty cents each. With mailing tube and postage, we're in business for a buck. Shades of my Junior Achievement days.

Now for the ad itself. Like naming your own baby, objectivity can be challenging. Every headline I came up with sounded like something out of the Sears catalog, flat footed and uninspired. I sucked in my pride and asked one of our new copywriters, Lane Larrison, tall as he was droll, to chip in some ideas. He hit a home run, a take-off on the famous carpet ad of the fifties: "A title on the door rates a Bigelow on the floor." Lane's version had more attitude:

No title at all?
Get a window
for your wall.

We priced the poster at $2.95, postage paid. And as a fillip, thinking there would be groups of disgruntled office mates who might bite at a quantity discount, the copy suggested one could build a corner office, six posters for $15.

To keep the agency's name out of it, purchasers were asked to mail requests to my apartment address and make checks payable to POSTER (close enough for my mailman to figure out and my bank to cash).

I hadn't accounted for the extent of pent-up claustrophobia out there. Or the size of my puny mailbox. Within days, and for months, it was stuffed to the gills with envelopes, many containing impassioned notes of gratitude, some near-Marxian diatribes.

Always on the prowl for new products, several mail order houses, precursors to The Sharper Image, requested prices for bulk quantities shipped flat directly from our ecstatic printer. No stuffing mailing tubes. No post office hassle. We gladly obliged. They saw potential beyond the lure of Madison Avenue and described the poster in their catalogs simply as a bustling view of Manhattan. And they reordered often.

Then one night I'm watching Johnny Carson. He had been venting show after show about NBC moving him out of his window office. Why the network would do that to their cash cow I have no idea. Why I didn't think to send him one of the posters is another good question. But somebody did. And to my astonishment, Carson pulls my poster out from under his desk, unfurls it and proceeds to do a four-minute bit about it and his grievance—an incalculable amount of free publicity.

The next morning, I raced into our media director's office. "Get hold of your NBC contacts. Tell them Johnny's poster is ours and to please forward any inquiries they get so we can follow up on them."

A week later she reported back to me: NBC had been deluged with requests, mailbags full of them in fact but, unfortunately, it was against their corporate policy to pass any of them on, even to us, a paying customer. I immediately switched viewing allegiance to CBS.

⁂

THERE WAS SOMETHING UNDERLYING THE success of that poster—a way, a tongue-in-cheek way, to improve one's status for mere pennies. It led me to think about other ideas that might supplement my funds to facilitate the alimony and child support I was, regrettably, now paying.

What about a possession absurdly out of reach, a seat on the stock exchange for instance? The real cost for one of those back then was a half-million dollars. But by silk-screening a photograph of the New York Stock Exchange's imposing facade onto a cheap vinyl stadium cushion we could run a small ad in the *Wall Street Journal* headlined:

Seat on the Stock Exchange, $5

Clever as I—and at least two underhanded mail order houses who knocked it off within weeks—thought it was, I overestimated Wall Street's sense of humor. In my wildest dreams, a firm like Merrill Lynch would order thousands to mail to customers at Christmas. That didn't happen. And orders from individuals barely covered the cost of advertising. (Imagine what a dud that gag gift would be these days!).

⁂

HAVING MY USUAL PRE-LIPITOR-DAYS LUNCH of two eggs and a hamburger patty at O'Connell's on Michigan Avenue accompanied by a recent hire, a clever young copywriter named Gary Klaff, we came up with another rags-to-riches idea that seemed to have broader appeal.

"What if a cologne smelled like money?"

"Does money smell good?"

"Always has to me."

"Yea, Cash Cologne."

"That's got cachet."

"Smell like a million bucks, yeah."

"From the root of all evil."

"Alright!"

And so our impromptu brainstorming session went. Now the serious part: making it—and for how much?

Somebody suggested we start with International Flavor and Fragrance. Clueless really, I drove out to their north suburban lab, a couple of new twenty-dollar bills in my pocket.

Like a pharmacy, I went right up to a counter manned by a professsorial chemist in a white coat. Behind him were thousands of identical vials arranged on shelves in some scientific semblance of order.

"Can you replicate this smell?" I asked handing him the twenties.

He squinted at the bills suspiciously.

Finally, it dawned on me. He thinks I'm a counterfeiter.

"For a cologne. We want to make a men's cologne that smells like money."

That resolved, he couldn't have been more helpful. He said he'd have a sample for me in a week and recommended a contract packager he'd worked with before who could incorporate his essence into a cologne, bottle it, label it, box it, no problem.

Klaff rode back with me to get a whiff of the formulation. Treating it like liquid gold, the chemist put an eye dropper into a beaker, squeezed out a few drops of his dark green liquid onto blotter paper, diluted it with a touch of alcohol and told us to rub it on our wrists. A sniff of it and then a sniff of the money and, yep, he nailed it. Unlike, say, Coco Chanel, we didn't consider whether it was a world-class fragrance, just whether it smelled like cold hard cash. Out of curiosity I asked how he did it, what stuff back there in those vials went into it? "Well, I shouldn't tell you," he stammered, "but it's the same ingredients, only slightly different proportions, we use to create new car smell." Hey, what guy doesn't like that?

We stopped off at the packager and selected a stock bottle and cap they had on hand. And got down to business on what it would cost to produce a trial run. Amazingly inexpensive, it turned out. We'd be able to sell a four-ounce bottle at wholesale for less than three dollars and still make a tidy profit. I envisioned the fortune old Coco must be making.

Back at the office, we asked another recent recruit, art director Bill Biderbost, to come up with a label. His masculine design had a look of substance, the typography and color damn near did counterfeit U.S. currency. He even worked in the "Smell like a million bucks" line along the bottom. His suggestion that each label have a different serial number—just like money—was a nice touch but the agency production guy said that trick would send printing costs soaring.

We needed real money to get started. Klaff and I asked an account guy at the agency, Mike Miller, who looked like a banker, to join us when we walked over to First National seeking a $5,000 loan. For a requisite company name, we had landed on BFD, Unltd.

Don't ask. Though the banker did, comparing our three last names with the company initials.

"What's BFD stand for?" he said. Klaff jumped in with youthful exuberance, "Big (PAUSE) Deal." The loan officer pursed his lips, thought about it for a moment, then smiled ever so slightly and authorized the cash for Cash.

In six weeks, we had a small run of the cologne, a mock-up of the twenty-four-bottle carton and a retail display card designed to rise above the back of the carton. On the card, Bill had drawn a *New Yorker*–style cartoon of a guy lying in bed, covers strewn about, a very satisfied grin on his face. Behind him, a bare lady's leg was seen exiting through an open bathroom door. (If this sounds vaguely familiar, it is—a visual version of the famous and woefully politically incorrect linen ad of the 1920's starring a satiated Native American and this risqué double entendre: "A buck well spent on a Springmaid sheet.") Our headline, of course, was different. In a big, bold typeface that smacked of money it read

Was it you or your Cash?

Mike and I made a call on the trade, my first and last. We're at Walgreen's headquarters in the office of their cosmetics and fragrance buyer, a rather chic middle-aged woman. She didn't like Cash Cologne, she loved it, so much so she insisted on exclusive sales rights for a year.

She promised the carton including the "clever" sign would be placed right next to the cash registers in 300 stores for starters; that meant an initial purchase order for 500 cartons (in round numbers, $35,000 to us). We could use her purchase order as collateral back at First National increasing the loan to cover our costs and then some. Wait 'til Klaff hears about this!

Oh, there was just one thing she had failed to mention: the display allowance. When it came to a new product, she said, it worked the same at every retailer. To cover, really to "rent," Walgreen's valuable display space, the manufacturer was required to immediately reimburse the retailer the full amount of the purchase order (the $35,000 we thought we just pocketed). This paper swap would only apply to the initial order, she explained. On ensuing orders—and she was sure there'd be many—we kept all the proceeds.

Feeling robbed, I said nothing. More the businessman, Mike played the partner gambit. The "exclusive" she asked for was a bit of a hiccup, he lied. We'd have to discuss a deal point so restrictive with the other investors and would get back to her shortly. She understood but just *knew* Cash Cologne and Walgreen's were made for each other. As we were packing up, she asked to keep one of those "cute" bottles.

"Talk about 'Catch 22,'" Mike said walking to the parking lot (the movie had just opened).

If I really believed Walgreen's would reorder and reorder, I was sure there was a way to raise the manufacturing cost of her order. But I knew in my heart—and my nose—the cologne was a gag gift, a one-shot with no shot as a perennial. We might've gone back to the poster model—just sell the bottles individually through small-space ads. But the post office had issues; they deemed Cash Cologne a flammable substance and would not mail them. So it was wholesale or no sale.

My days as a *parfumeur* were over before they began. Coco was safe.

Win Some, Lose Some

Though still a boomlet compared to Chicago's giant packaged goods agencies like Burnett, J. Walter, Foote Cone and Needham, we were making noise and growing fast. From where I sat, now in a corner window office in our new, larger quarters a half-block off Michigan and directly across Superior from Gino's East, the best pizza joint in the best pizza town in America, things were looking up.

Not so for Jerry. He harbored apprehensive demons born, I suppose, in the dreary Depression. To wit, the day he rushed into my office, bummed a cigarette, snapped off the filter, lit it, then stared out at my view—a thin slice of Michigan Avenue. He turned back to me and, out of the blue, said, "I wonder when the other shoe's gonna drop." He didn't wait for a response. I had none. He just left. Either he knew something I didn't know or the success he never expected had gone to his head in a bad way.

Over time, I learned to cope with his trepidations especially when the subject was adding people—and, for him, worrisome overhead. It wasn't a question of stepping on his toes, more a case of dodging that imaginary shoe. I hired promising kids right out of school. And convinced proven talent disenchanted elsewhere to hop onto our rising star at a salary I could assure Stern was worth the investment.

To complement our mainstay clients, we had attracted a number of smaller brand names—Le Creuset cookware, Dopp Kits and

Scholl's footwear—that gave my creative staff (and their relatives and friends) even more of a chance to see their work in national media.

Beyond the growing client list, there was one somewhat arcane benefit in the area of television production that I could dangle before candidates. Most of our large competitors clung to a system whereby agency producers held sway over the making of commercials, literally calling the shots. Burnett, in fact, had a staff of such people residing in Los Angeles and New York. An approved storyboard was sent out to them (via long distance pneumatic tube?) and they took it from there, often cavalierly. With no glamorous—or from management's perspective, expensive—trips to the coast to cover a shoot, the creatives who conceived the commercial were relegated to a secondary role, anxiously waiting back in Chicago for whatever it was The Producer made of their baby. Understandably, it was a sore point, one I was able to capitalize on.

The word was out: at SWS, if you sold a TV spot, you produced it. This wasn't something I dreamed up one night. Jerry and his partners had very limited experience with television commercials; the few local spots they had been involved with in the past, they produced themselves. It had never occurred to them to dole out good money to hire a TV producer. Today, some of my best friends are TV producers. But then, not even *knowing* one helped me attract a surprisingly strong staff.

Along came bigger client opportunities. For one, my favorite retailer—Sears. Initially, we were asked to help them introduce an upscale line of children's clothing carrying the powerful Winnie-the-Pooh name, a brand they had just licensed from Disney.

Klaff got out his guitar and put notes to a lyric we wrote, okay another jingle, that poured honey on the proposition:

If Winnie-the-Pooh were a kid at heart
Although he is a bear, that's true.
He'd go to Sears to dress the part.
It's Sears for Winnie-the-Pooh.

We shot the intro commercial at a posh playground in Beverly Hills, the kids swooping down a slide in their Sears finery, last one down an animated and endearing Pooh, all edited to the beat of the music. And followed that up with a series of stylish (for Sears) magazine ads based on the concept of "No-no's for Mommie from Winnie-the-Pooh" written by a young lady, actually a summer intern. Around elegant photographs of children (my sons, six and seven, part of the ensemble) in color-coordinated outfits were subheads like "No ironing" and "No mismatching" that paid off the No-no's promise. A considerable upgrade in style and price from typical Sears offerings, Winnie became an enduring and profitable success.

Sears then asked us to name and introduce a new line of children's jeans, their unique feature a durable double-layered knee. I gave the assignment to Bill Mackle, one of my new and, formerly, disenchanted senior writers. He was shaped like a bowling ball, possessed a cackle that pierced walls and, poor guy, cursed with a very prominent case of psoriasis. He told me once that because of his looks he would "never get the big job like I had." What do you say to that? He was as smart as they come, quick witted and knowledgeable about the business. And he was pathetically right in his self-assessment. In the upper reaches of major advertising agencies there exists a tacit gentlemen's agreement; in their management meetings, it's highly unlikely one would encounter wheelchairs, black faces—or bald psoriatic scalps.

But I didn't care about, nor could I afford, movie stars. I needed copywriters and Bill was one of the best. For Sears' jeans, he coined the name "Toughskins." And came up with a classic TV demonstration that showed kids decked out in the jeans as they merrily bounded on a trampoline made of the same fabric; a prominent Toughskins logo sewn in one corner of the apparatus vibrated with every bounce. Toughskins, too, became a huge hit.

Another Sears department came a'calling with a revolutionary product at the time—a *phosphate-free* laundry detergent. Again, Mackle came through with a great idea: let's get Stewart Udall, former Secretary of the Interior under Kennedy and Johnson and a pioneering environmentalist, to serve as spokesman. It had to be the least braggadocio detergent commercial in history. Udall at a desk, the detergent box his only prop, explaining how phosphates were clogging our rivers and streams, and mentioning, as an aside, that any fees he made for doing this commercial would go to establish a scholarship fund for "Indian" students (no doubt he would've used the term "Native American" if it existed then). Udall closed with a simple statement: "Clean wash for you. Cleaner water for America." Sears was hardly a likely or convenient place to pick up a box of detergent; still it flew off the shelves.

Big as they were, Sears was not a particularly sophisticated marketer, not, say, in the way one might characterize Procter & Gamble. Which was fortunate for us since we were far from a sophisticated advertising agency. We had no floor full of researchers, analysts or—today's prerequisite for getting a foot in the door—strategic planners. The agency partners weren't ponying up for a producer; they sure as hell weren't about to pay a bunch of eggheads.

But somehow we got through the night. True, Pooh, the jeans and the detergent, all three, credit to Sears, were viable ideas. Intuitively, Sears knew these concepts were special and they were willing to back them with serious advertising dollars. Intuition drove us too. *Sans* focus groups, in-depth probes, ponderous questionnaires or commercial testing of any sort, on instinct alone we nailed all three, delivering memorable advertising that reflected the uniqueness of the products and the character of the company behind them. (There've been innumerable instances since when I've yearned for those unsophisticated days).

⁂

And now, for the antithesis of Sears—Hunt-Wesson Foods of Fullerton, California. We became one of their agencies through the munificence of their new president, Ed Gelsthorpe, whom we casually knew during his brief stint at Colgate. Without Big Ed, Hunt-Wesson never would have hired SWS. We were two time zones away and had absolutely no credentials in the rigorous world of grocery goods (my family's little store a non-qualifier). Throwing his considerable height around, I think he brought us in to make clear to his inherited staff just who was boss.

Ed's passion was new products. He was credited for the launch of the world's first roll-on deodorant (Ban) at Bristol Myers and for resuscitating Ocean Spray with Cran-Apple juice. His assignment for us: introduce the ultimate in convenience food, Hunt's Skillet Dinners.

It seemed so simple. Heat up a pound of ground beef in a skillet; dump in the contents of the box: the noodles and spices and sauce from the enclosed can; simmer for ten minutes and voila! Lasagna (sorta) or beef Stroganoff (sorta) or whatever.

Ed had no patience for minutiae. That made two of us. But oh how Ed's minions, the marketing and research people he sicced on the agency, turned his quick dinner fix into a feast of statistical facts and focus groups and testing and testing the testing.

Admittedly, our less sophisticated clients had spoiled us. The Hunt club was consumed with an incessant need for meetings and deep think over what was at its core an eighty-nine-cent box of pasta. We were undermanned and overwhelmed. And they knew it.

Seventeen hundred miles away we came up for air.

Okay, we were shoved down their throats. They would do nothing to help us look good. We'd have one shot before the long knives came out. Let's make it our best shot. I had Jerry's full support—the non-reimbursed travel expenses to Fullerton alone were costing the agency a ton.

It has never been my preference to "gang bang" an assignment, to throw it open to every live body in the place. I've always entrusted a job to one team, a copywriter and an art director. But this was our Trafalgar and it was all hands on deck. Hopefully, we'd go back out there with one idea so compelling that, no matter how deep their resentment, they would have to acquiesce.

What we came up with, in my opinion, was brilliant; they weren't commercials, they were mini-movies; warm, funny and real; and, in tone, somewhat reminiscent of the famous Alka Seltzer "spicy meat-balls" campaign five years earlier. As an example, for their Skillet Lasagna:

Italian-American man, late 20's, comes through kitchen door.
He's been away somewhere and homecoming is
complete surprise to Mama, Papa and kid sister.
Mama hollers, ***"Tony!"***
He asks, ***"What's for dinner, Ma?"***
(We've got thirty seconds here, no time for small talk.)
Mama says, ***"Lasagna. Ten minutos."***
Son responds incredulously, ***"Lasagna? Ten minutes?"***
Papa tilts down his newspaper and grunts at prodigal son.
Meanwhile, Sis is gazing admiringly at big brother.
Cut to close-ups of Mama making the stuff and short announcer
spiel. Back to wide shot of Mama showing off skillet full
of her scrambled version of the traditionally layered dish.
"Lasagna!" *she proudly exclaims.*
Son's not so sure. ***"Lasagna?"*** *he asks.*
Papa in undershirt gives one-word command: ***"Mangiare!"***
Mama and Sis await Tony's first taste.
Obligatory bite and smiles all around.

Gelsthorpe popped his head into our meeting, said he'd been double-booked and couldn't stay but was sure SWS would be delivering the goods. One of the agency partners, Lee Walters, did the set-up as convincingly as he could considering he was far from sold on the work. And then I presented the storyboards, the one for Skillet Lasagna and two more of similar ilk for their other "flavors" (their term). Clearly, the quantity and content was not what they expected, even from us.

Hemming and hawing. Hmmm, we're accustomed to seeing a wider range of work from our agencies. Usually five, six campaigns. Then we cull those down to three that we put into diagnostic storyboard testing. (Translation: Intuition? What's that?)

Then, more huddling and finally: all right, since the agency obviously feels *that* strongly about this one campaign, we'll go directly to Phase Two and pay $25,000 for a "down and dirty" commercial. We'll insert it into a pod of other commercials and show it to focus groups. (Translation: Go hang yourselves but do it quickly.")

Using our own people as actors and a makeshift film crew, we shot a glorified home movie of the lasagna spot. It was actually pretty funny. I brought it back out to California, showed it to the team (Ed would see it later, they said), garnered some guarded grins and left it for them and their testing.

The verdict came in a few weeks later. To their begrudging surprise, people picked it out of the "pod" and really liked it. I assumed that included Gelsthorpe. Go shoot the first one for real, they said. Trying for a bigger commitment, I told them we could amortize costs by shooting all three at one time. No, let's walk before we run, they cautioned.

We awarded the spot to Joe Sedelmaier, a Chicago director known for his oddball casting, often plucking "actors" out of the lobbies of transient hotels on Skid Row. Ten years later, he gained national prominence with his Wendy's "Where's the beef?" campaign. Our commercial was right up his alley and he did a terrific job.

Naively, I couldn't wait to show it to the Hunt contingent.

This time, Gelsthorpe was in attendance and all ears (I use that term advisedly; he had the longest, largest ears I've ever seen on a human being). Behind the glass, the projectionist, a young pimply-faced guy, ran the film for the crowd in the darkened screening room. Had this been a sit-com they, justifiably, would have cranked up the laugh track at least three times during our thirty-second movie. Here, however, there was icy silence. I glanced back at the projectionist to motion him to rerun it. But he was momentarily missing in action. Laughing so hard, he had fallen off his stool.

"Would you like to see it again," I masochistically asked the room at large.

"No," Gelsthorpe barked out of the dark, "it's not funny."

This was craziness. I had nursed the commercial through all the post-production steps: editing, sound, color correction, all of it. And at every step, of the dozens of third-party people who had seen it, every last one of them had laughed hysterically. There was no doubt about it; Gelsthorpe's minions had gotten to him.

"Jeez, I dunno, Ed," I parried. "Your projectionist (the market for this dubious dinner) was cracking up back there."

"I'm the fucking president of this company, not him," he shouted. "And I say it's not funny."

Soon thereafter, for those who remember, another, more accommodating advertising agency found Hunt's comfort and taste level—the star of their commercials, a lame-brained talking skillet.

⟡

FOR REASONS NEVER EXPLAINED TO us, in the early seventies, Andy Granatelli decided to uproot his northwest suburban headquarters and move the entire operation to Ft. Lauderdale. Perhaps he wanted to be closer to his new-found appreciation of NASCAR, or Florida offered enticing tax incentives, or he just wanted to live in a sumptuous mansion across the Intercoastal Waterway from Ray Kroc's winter estate where he and his wife Dolly could take part in the tony social scene down there.

Whatever his reason, SWS had to respond in kind. We opened a small service office there, Bill Lowney in charge, which meant more travel for me, more overhead for the agency. It behooved us to pick up additional business in South Florida, a land devoid of smokestacks, to help amortize our costs. The traveling squad, comprised of me, sometimes Stern and others, stayed at the tallest building in Ft. Lauderdale, the Pier 66 Hotel owned then by Phillips Petroleum, purveyors of Phillips 66 gasoline. Getting chummy with the general manager of the hotel, one thing led to another, and we soon had Pier 66 as an account. Besides great views of the harbor and the constant flow of massive cruise liners, the hotel boasted a revolving rooftop cocktail lounge. The G.M.'s goal was to make that bar, in a town full of watering holes, *The* meet market of choice.

At the opposite side of the country, in Burbank, California, while out there on shoots, I had become a frequenter of a place called the China Doll, an incongruous spot serving mediocre Chinese food to the mellow sounds of Bobby Troup's jazz trio. I'd sat around Bobby's piano enough that we were on a first-name basis and, on my next trip out, I hit him up for a favor.

Besides writing "Get Your Kicks on Route 66" while driving cross-country with his first wife, Bobby's other claim to fame was his second wife, Julie London. I loved her. Formerly married to *Dragnet*'s Jack Webb, she had a voluptuous figure and a smoky sexy voice to match. Even I could dance to her "Cry Me a River." She had an advertising connection, too. Leo Burnett, before they invented the iconic smoking cowboys, hired Julie to intone the memorable "You get a lot to like with a Marlboro, filter, flavor, flip-top box."

I talked to Bobby on a break at the China Doll. Would his trio record a special version of his big hit, substituting "at Pier 66" for "on Route 66" along with some other parody lyrics? I caught him at a propitious moment—a year before he and Julie were cast by none other than producer Jack Webb to co-star in a TV series called *Emergency!* At the time he needed the money, such as it was, and the resulting radio jingle he sang became a major commercial hit in South Florida. The rooftop bar, now throbbing with action, even concocted a potent Long Island tea–type drink served in a souvenir cyclone mug. The bar call was "Give us two Kicks."

I had his home number and one day needed to talk to him about renewing the rights to his song for a second year. Who answers the phone but Julie London. "Helllll-oh," she purred, sending my heart racing. "Is Bobby there?" I stuttered. "Yehhhs," she purred again. And then, transformed into a mere mortal housewife, Julie London, my dream woman and fellow filter-tip smoker, shrieked at the top of her formidable lungs, "BOBBY! TELEPHONE!" and with that yelp went my fantasy forevermore deflated.

⁂

Lowney got a call one day from a Ft. Lauderdale company called Aloe Crème Laboratories. They were seeking advertising help. I happened to be down there so Bill and I went out to meet with the founder, Dr. Rodney Stockton, an eccentric self-described scientist with a head of wild white hair.

At the time, I had never heard of aloe vera, but Dr. Stockton had already turned that nasty-looking succulent into a nice little business (there were pots of them all around his office). Living in the land of perpetual sunshine, he had discovered the benefits of the plant's extract as a healing ingredient in various tanning products. The one he really had heart for was Aloe After Tan, a lotion, he warranted, that would prolong the duration of a suntan.

He didn't have a big ad budget, but Bill and I liked the concept and agreed to do some small-space newspaper and in-store display materials for him.

I had the idea driving back to our office. "Brilliant," my sounding board (and biggest fan) Bill exclaimed. It was inspired by a phenomenon I'd observed repeatedly in Chicago: it's dead of winter and a young lady returns from her Florida vacation; she now possesses a gorgeous suntan and to make sure everyone notices and comments on it she shows up at the office dressed, no matter the seasonal appropriateness, all in white; she basks in her fellow workers' envy. Back then, Ft. Lauderdale was "Where the Boys Are," and thousands of Northern young ladies baked on the beaches down there. The small campaign would run in Florida to reach the sun-worshippers before they returned home.

The visual was simple. Three young ladies at the water cooler. One has a beautiful tan; the other two, pale as ghosts, are glaring at her. The headline promised "They'll hate you back home a lot longer."

We brought the layouts to the client on my next trip down. Doctor Stockton understood how this invidious idea would stand out from his big-name competitors all of whom took the standard cosmeticky approach. One thing bothered him, good Southern Baptist that he was.

"'Hate' is a terrible thing," he said running a hand through his shock of hair. "Can you change it to 'loathe'?" Bill, closer to Stockton's age, interceded. He counseled the client that "hate" was part of the vernacular of young people. They tossed it around like popcorn. It didn't have a sinister connotation; if anything, "loathe" would stand out like a very sore thumb (not to mention what it would do to my headline).

Stockton backed off but he did turn to me and say, "If we get angry letters, you have to answer them." Fair enough.

The campaign was a huge success, so much so the company, for the first time, gained distribution in Northern Florida and surrounding states. But there were letters, tons of them, all saying the same thing, all postmarked from the Boston area. Some organization, perhaps a precursor to NOW, had organized the letter-writing campaign. Their objection? The ad was promulgating hatred amongst the sisterhood. My polite retort, which Stockton approved, was that every other suntan product featured bikini-clad women in provocative poses. We, alone, were taking the high road. I sent it only to the woman identified in her letter as president of the group. The client never heard another word from them.

⁂

BACK HOME WE HAD WON several local but high-profile accounts that would help bolster our Chicago presence.

One was the CTA, the Chicago Transit Authority (successor to the Chicago Motor Coach Company my father had driven for twenty-five years earlier). Wracked by public dissension over recent fare hikes, they wanted to put out a "feel good" message about their service to the community. We delivered for them on billboards, radio and the sides of their buses; ridership increased; and, along the way, we won a bunch of creative awards for our work.

Eighteen months into the relationship we received an unexpected document, an RFP, a Request for Proposal, meaning somebody—namely Mayor Richard Daley, the "Boss," who had been buttonholed by political cronies who happened to own an advertising agency—wants the CTA to take a good hard look at their current "vendor," us.

We smelled a rat, actually three rats, an agency with a name that sounded like a Chicago political ticket—Weber, Cohen & Riley; their clout solely based on the fact that Riley always marched shoulder-to-shoulder with Hizzoner in the St. Paddy's Day parade.

Our sympathetic client contact gave us the heads-up: the selection process was careening out of his control. The CTA board was comprised of fifteen dollar-a-year appointees. He figured we had seven votes and that Daley's contingent of seven would go the other way. What about the fifteenth member? I asked. That's Ernie Banks, the obligatory black board member, he said, and he's off playing baseball and has never come to a meeting. Why don't you replace him with somebody who'll show up and maybe vote our way? I suggested. "What!" he blurted. "And end up with some uppity nigger on the board!"

As the client predicted, the vote went seven-seven. The tiebreaker came down to each agency's financial requirements. We merely asked for what the RFP had included as a budget number. But, this being Chicago, our competitor had been given an RFP specifying a different and slightly lower number. Fast on the take, they incorporated that low ball into their proposal and were handed the account.

I wrote a scathing, tell-all letter to the crusading Mike Royko, then Chicago's most influential newspaper columnist. I titled it "You can't fight City Hall" and knew he would bite. Before mailing it, I showed the letter to Jerry who said it was honest and well written and then unceremoniously tore it into quarters. "Do you want every goddamn department in the city marching in here with inspectors and tax assessors?" I guessed not.

⁂

THE OLDSMOBILE DEALERS OF CHICAGOLAND was the other local account we landed. As a group, they suffered moniker envy and yearned for an ad campaign to counteract the Plymouth dealers' long-running "Men in the White Hats" campaign.

We latched on to a theme line that, in one breath, not only out-promised the Plymouth guys in terms of courteous customer treatment but unmistakably incorporated their product name as well. And you could sing it:

We're the Gallant Men of Olds
We're brave and kind and good
We believe in baseball and the flag
We believe in motherhood
(Very big on motherhood!)
We believe that there's a Rocket
Priced for every pocket
We're the Gallant Men of Olds

Early on, we'd met with the chairman of the association who had given us the challenging assignment. He was a man's man and a golf buddy of Stern's, though what brought him to SWS, he said, was our experience with Suzuki and STP that he could merchandise to his fellow dealers. Had I encountered the entire group, as I did the day we presented the final campaign to them, it is doubtful the term "gallant" would have crept into our lyric. They were an ornery lot of self-made millionaires. From their questions about financial remuneration I had a hunch half of them had a brother-in-law who owned some kind of cut-rate ad agency. They were, well, car dealers.

Be that as it may, by secret ballot, they bought our act. They particularly loved the cartoony logo Sol conjured up for them: three guys side-by-side in business suits accessorized *à la* Musketeers—flouncy velvet hats and soaring feathers, draping capes, swashbuckling boots. And, at each of their sides, what else but a cutlass? Take that, White Hat boys.

We had fun with the campaign and people responded. Incredibly, given their price range, Oldsmobile soon became Chicagoland's best-selling car.

The Gallant Men decided as a group to offer an appealing price on a stripped-down Cutlass. To promote it on television, we suspended a mock-up of the car from a helicopter and had it flown over a fallow farm field out near O'Hare. At a point, the car would be released and float to earth as an announcer exclaimed, "Talk about a windfall!" Today, computers would be tasked to produce this stunt. Then, it was for real, one take, three cameras with varying lenses and speeds were spread around the field's perimeter to ensure we got the footage we needed to dramatize the fall and stretch its length to thirty seconds.

Except the location scout had not noticed that the low brick building just beyond our landing site was an elementary school. And just as the chopper approached for the dramatic drop, school let out. I could see kids attracted by the whirlybird and dangling car clambering over the farm fence and running toward us. Visions of children planted into the rich Illinois loam. Along with my career.

I screamed at the director, whose attention and eye were glued to the viewfinder of his camera pointing skyward, to wave off the drop. Thank God, his walkie-talkie worked. The pilot moved over a nearby field until we could corral the kids and allow them to watch from a safe distance. Finally, came the free fall, and as if piloted itself, the car made a perfect four-wheel landing. No problemo.

Another time, we brought the dealer group an idea for a special edition 88 made just for Chicago. In their honor we named it the GMO. They loved the idea and joined in the fun by agreeing on a custom pale purple paint job (their choice, not ours). We suggested it be distinctively badged with two chrome logos; on the trunk, a version of our Three Musketeers design, and above the driver's side wheel well, the letters GMO. To talk Oldsmobile into manufacturing the vehicle, the officers of the dealer group, along with Stern and me, went over to Lansing, Michigan for a meeting.

I couldn't believe it. We entered an enormous conference room where already seated along the forty-foot burled oak table were at least two dozen executives all in dark suits, white shirts and somber ties. (I had on a striped shirt and felt like a convict.) It appeared that nobody at Oldsmobile above the rank of shop foreman had anything better to do that morning.

Chicago being their best market, one would think this modest production request would be a slam dunk. But the Detroit mentality being what it was (and is still), the meeting droned on for hours—including a lengthy debate as to whether or not the U.A.W. would allow its workers to install our two special chrome logos—before they granted our wish. At one point, I overheard two of the Olds execs trying to identify a guy they didn't recognize at the other end of the table. One of them pulled a folded organizational chart out of his suit jacket. He ran a finger down the columns of names and ranks and finally made the I.D.—that's Chuck Johnson, assistant to the sales manager of the Upper Midwest zone; he's ol' Charley's son. The other exec nodded approvingly. Nepotism was alive and well in Lansing.

I vividly recall the drizzly day we shot the commercial introducing the GMO. A simple enough idea. The car, its color actually looking half decent diffused by raindrops, had been loaded on a barge pushed by a tugboat. It was coming from the east symbolizing Lansing and fast approaching the famous Michigan Avenue Bridge over the Chicago River. Now would come the money shot—on cue, the bridge's double leaves would slowly rise to symbolize a great city's welcome with open arms.

I knew the film company had reached a financial understanding with the bridge tender up in the tower. But here comes the barge and the bridge ain't budging. It turned out no one thought to grease the bridge tender's boss back at City Hall and, once he got wind of it, he wasn't about to tie up traffic for a stupid car commercial, especially given the bird's eye view both the *Tribune* and *Sun-Times* had of that bridge. Fortunately, we, too, had a bird's eye view, a camera strategically installed at the top of the 333 building directly behind the tower. That camera kept rolling, peering down as unknowing pedestrians and their big black umbrellas floated across the bridge's wet walkway—an accidental effect right out of a British spy thriller—while below, bow poking out, the barge and its glistening cargo made its grand entrance.

Each Olds dealer was allotted ten GMO's. They sold all of them at full mark-up.

One of those dealers, a good guy named Ray Scarpelli, asked me to interview his nephew Bob, just graduated from college. I liked him right off the bat, especially since I doubled as pitcher for our agency softball team and Bob mentioned he was a stellar shortstop.

He wasn't kidding. With him sealing the middle, the next season little SWS beat all comers including the giants to win the ad agency city championship. I still have the last game ball. Inscribed with a Pentel it says "SWS 23—FCB 6."

Bob was a talented writer, too. Funny punch lines poured out of him. Client uncle or not, I thought he had great potential at the agency. That is until several ungallant malcontents with their own agenda managed to gain leadership of the dealer association and SWS became their first political casualty. It was cold-blooded and undeserved and I took out my anger on Bob—and his uncle who couldn't plug the dike—and let him go. (I made amends to him a few years later when I moved to Needham. Today Bob is Chief Creative Officer, Worldwide of what is now called DDB. I doubt he has the energy to run the bases anymore.)

Win Some, Lose Some

In early 1976, SWS had an opportunity to go global, if Costa Rica qualifies. I bumped into an acquaintance at the Knight Cap who had left the ad biz to develop and run a fishing lodge on the *Golfo de Nicoya*, the bountiful waters off the country's west coast.

He told me one of his guests down there, Rodrigo Odio, was Director of the Central Bank as well as head of their Department of Tourism, and that he had urged *Señor* Odio to open the coffers and begin promoting the country to Americans as a desirable destination, which, not so incidentally, might help lure more fishermen. When he returned to Costa Rica he came through. He had arranged a meeting for Jerry and me with the Director in San Jose. We had the inside track, my old drinking buddy said; there were no other agencies involved.

Off we flew to the tropical paradise. A car picked us up the next morning and drove us to a slightly tattered government building close by the Presidential Palace. We were ushered in to Odio's incongruously lavish office, an expanse of windows surrounded by three walls of floor-to-ceiling mirrors. It was a bright and sunny day. The room was afire with glare and all three of us sat through the meeting wearing our sunglasses.

He was a man of short, stocky stature, his hair slicked back with the aid of pomade, and his English was perfect. The office had a semblance of air conditioning but it was over ninety outside; still Odio's double-breasted suit jacket was snugly buttoned. We gave him a brief review of our credentials. He nodded occasionally but seemed more engrossed with his own reflection in the myriad of mirrors.

The Director recited the copy points of his country—its unspoiled jungle and beaches; the lowest crime rate and highest literacy rate in Central America; the fact that they had more teachers than militia. (He did not mention they had more hookers than teachers; I figured the fishermen would find that out for themselves.)

He told us he could allocate a million dollars U.S. to the project. Jerry reminded him that our fee of fifteen percent would come out of that amount. Odio understood. I chimed in saying at that budget level we could not blanket America with advertising but that we would come back by the end of January with ideas and a plan to target a smaller though highly receptive audience. I already had in mind who that audience would be.

On the dragged-out flight back—from San Jose to Belize to Miami to Chicago—I gave Jerry my thoughts. It so happened that just a month earlier Mexico had cast a vote in the U.N. denouncing Zionism as racist. American Jewry responded by organizing a much-publicized boycott of Mexican tourism. I thought we could make a case for Costa Rica as an attractive travel alternative targeting Jews in the three major metro markets. Jerry agreed but cautioned me about being overtly exclusionary. Gentiles travel, too, he observed.

I had the slogan by the time we hit O'Hare. "Next year, Costa Rica!" Without pounding salt, it would resonate with Jews familiar with the shibboleth "Next year, Jerusalem" and would be seen by others as nothing more than a novel travel suggestion.

We put together upbeat, colorful ads, the informative copy tagged with the line, designed for the Sunday supplements of the *N.Y. Times*, *Chicago Tribune* and *L.A. Times*. And wrote radio commercials reinforcing the campaign. We thought a perfect radio spokesman would be Alan King, a subtly Jewish comedian with universal appeal, and got a receptive go-ahead from his agent.

Flying back down there, I felt strongly that this work, despite the limited budget, would make a big splash. And *Señor* Peacock agreed. He seemed as pleased with it as he did his own mirror image. We had a deal. Could we begin right away to still catch the travel season? he asked. Radio, yes, I said. Newspaper would come as soon as possible. Momentary jubilation all around.

Then he looked directly at Jerry and asked, "Did I mention my brother-in-law?"

Puzzled, Jerry responded, "Uh, no. What about him?"

"He has an advertising agency here in San Jose."

"Uh, huh."

"Because you're an American company, we will be required to... what's the word?...funnel, funnel the money through a Costa Rican company, in this case my brother-in-law's agency."

Jerry was gritting his teeth, a telltale sign. "Whatever you say, *Señor* Odio. What's that mean as far as we're concerned?"

"It means for his services, funneling the money to you in America, he will retain half your fee."

It looked like Jerry was going to lunge over the Director's big clean desk to maybe strangle him. But Jerry had seen what I'd seen—the reputed handful of militia the country possessed all, it seemed, stationed within shouting distance of the Director. We silently gathered up our materials and departed. No handshakes. No *hasta luego*'s.

Going through the interminable departure procedures—at the end of one line a guy applied an official stamp to our passports; as we baby-stepped down the next line, a woman waited to rubber stamp that stamp and so on—we kept looking back half expecting to be arrested for insolence.

We said nothing to each other about the meeting until the plane made its first stop in Belize. Then Jerry began rehearsing his imitation of *Señor* Director. It would take the curse off our report to the troops back at the office. And who knew, but two years later when Odio was elected *El Presidente* of Costa Rica, a country then still surviving without advertising support, perhaps Jerry would be invited down to entertain at the inauguration.

Questioning Myself

From the way you started out—four months at the department store, couple of years at Sears—it looked like you were tracking to become one of those infamous job-hoppers. Now you've stayed at SWS more than a decade. What changed?

For most of those years I was the boss, other than Jerry, who treated me like an adopted son. He almost always backed me especially when there were confrontations with account guys including his two partners, which became one partner when Marty Simmons passed away suddenly. And interviewing so many job applicants over the years, I heard enough horror stories about other agencies to know the grass wasn't any greener down the street. I liked what I was doing and as long as Jerry was running the show, I felt completely secure, free to push for better creative, free to make mistakes, too.

C'mon, there had to be something you hated.

Mondays.

You didn't look forward to coming to work on Mondays?

Never felt that way. It was just that it was always on a Monday, when one of my beloved staff, after hand wringing all weekend with family and peers, would come into my office first thing and resign. The moment I saw them, I knew.

So your department had a revolving door?

Not rampant. But I did have a knack for finding good people with a lot of potential. And a lot of them realized that potential at the agency, put their reel and print samples together and either were recruited by some big agency, usually Burnett or Needham, or they shopped it themselves. I wasn't paying them all that much. Hell, *I* wasn't making all that much!

Did you attempt to keep them?

That was one area where Jerry put his foot down. He was deeply opposed to chasing people with counteroffers even though my long tenure there was the result of exactly that. All I could do, particularly when they told me how much more they would be making, was wish them well.

So you were manager of the farm team for the big league guys. That make you bitter?

Bittersweet's more like it. And in a perverse way, I took it as a compliment. I don't recall anyone leaving for a job at a third-rate agency. We had to be doing something right. The samples that got them that new job were created at little ol' Stern Walters. Except Badofsky, my friend to this day. He jumped ship for a so-so agency but he turned the place around and ended up running his own small successful agency. And Klaff, also still a close friend, he left for Burnett but then quit to start a music house. He thought music was the answer to everything.

Seems like you felt the same way.

Well, you can't bore someone into buying. There has to be some entertainment value. And a hooky music track can make a big difference. Even now, look at *American Idol*. I don't care how good the singer is, if she selects a bad song, it's thumbs down. Or Olympic figure skaters. They pick a ponderous piece, they get pounded. But music's not the only solution. With the right client and product, humor works too. There was no music in the Skillet Dinner commercials (*sardonic laugh*) and look where that got us.

That's all broadcast. You haven't had much to say about print.

I love print. Personally, I got a bigger kick out of seeing an ad I wrote in the *New Yorker* than a spot on the Super Bowl.

Okay, what's the best print ad you ever wrote?

At SWS, I had two favorites. One was for Booth Fisheries. Definitely not for *New Yorker*, it ran in trade magazines directed at food retailers and restaurants. Booth wanted to say they purveyed fresh fish from all over the world. The ad was very simple. A spread of ocean water top to bottom. Just a stock photo we paid next to nothing for. The modest-sized headline, reversed in white out of the dark sea, read, "One of our seven warehouses. Partial view." I've always loved that.

The other was written for a new condo building, not particularly luxurious, but located on the ritziest street in the city. Condos hadn't come into their own back then, at least not in Chicago. People harbored suspicions about them; you know, no plot of land, assessments, owner associations, et cetera. In this building all the units were the same size, all with narrow balconies fronting the street. So above an architectural rendering of a furnished interior facing out, the headline read "Your own fifty feet on Astor Street." It gave buyers a sense of owning something more than their four walls. But condo developments are losers as clients; the better the advertising, the sooner they sell out—and the sooner they stop advertising. We only got involved because the developer was a golf buddy of Stern's. The ad ran a grand total of twice. No condo, especially without a lake view, canceled advertising faster than that one.

You've steered clear of your personal life for the last ten years. Hiding something?

(*Pause. Clears throat.*) This is a love story—about advertising. Most of that decade I was a bachelor. But yeah, I had married too young and was living the life I should've led early on.

One story I can tell did have an advertising angle. I was at a holiday party thrown by a film company and met a young lady, a part-time model, who worked at another agency in film production. Turned out she had been a recent contestant on *The Dating Game* and had been chosen by some celebrity bachelor. Except he took a pass on the prize trip. We hit it off at the party and out of nowhere she asked if I had a passport. Uh huh, I replied. Well, would you like to go all-expenses-paid with me and the chaperone from the show on the S.S. *Michaelangelo* to Naples, then on to Rome for four days? It was first class all the way. I had to rent a tux to wear each night at dinner.

I even got chummy with Sidney Lumet. He was off to Italy to make a movie and his wife hated flying. I think she had a change of heart by the end of the voyage. Early February on the North Atlantic? We ran into monster waves. My "date" and the chaperone were seasick most of the trip. Still, back home, I was the envy of a lot of my friends.

Wild bachelor, huh?

Not quite. I was also a pretty responsible weekend father. I learned there are only so many museums you can revisit in the dead of Chicago winter.

As I said before, I ended up in an apartment right across from the office. And, in time, fell in love and married the girl next door, well, three doors down the hall. At the time, Lillian was a flight attendant for Eastern, away a lot, so jumping in again wasn't a match cut from my space to marriage, more like a slow dissolve. She was Chinese, not long removed from Hong Kong, and came from a large family. And was great with my sons. And she is to this day. A lot of women I had dated resented the kids' intrusion. That I couldn't abide. The boys and I spent many long weekends flying on Lil's trips to San Juan and other islands down there.

So you settled down? The wife, the kids, the steady job...

Job-wise I was content, maybe too much so—the steady paycheck, the security, a pittance of a profit-sharing plan. But I really hadn't saved a dime. My friend Mike Miller, who had left to go into banking and knew what role I played at SWS—and far more than I about financial stuff—he urged me to push for equity in the agency. That concept, in my head, was right up there with advanced algebra.

They were taking advantage of you?

Maybe. But I'd never given any thought to agency ownership. It just seemed restrictive. I guess I always figured, one day, like so many of my staff, I'd move on. But married again and knowing I couldn't get away with my shabby-not-chic furnishings and apartment, Mike was right; I needed to get smart with Stern about the future.

You broached the subject?

Yeah, and of all places, I hit him up in the revolving bar at Pier 66—after a couple of "Kicks." He reacted like a cornered raccoon. It was a sore subject, for sure. Today I know how complicated equity participation can be. Then, all I knew was the agency had grown five-fold in my ten years, had moved three times to accommodate the growth, and the only extraordinary thing I had to show for it was the car the agency leased for me, a Cutlass Supreme with a four-speed Hurst stick shift.

What'd he say?

What anyone in a similar position—and no good answers—would say: he'd discuss it with his partner. And oh, in the meanwhile do him a favor. Find a place for the daughter of another of his country club buddies. A good kid. Wants to be a copywriter. Maybe you can train her. Incidentally, my golf cleats had never set foot in that club of his.

So...

So I went about my business. That friend's daughter, I could tell right away, was a spoiled suburban brat, clearly being pushed by her father to "do something" with her English degree. I had the feeling she acceded because Gucci, Pucci and Saks were walking distance from our office.

I was smart enough to convince Stern we should bring her on freelance, not hire her full time. I gave her the easiest job in the house, a thirty-second radio commercial for Le Creuset cookware and a week to do it. I'd written the slogan for them several years earlier—"Les pots and pans de France." All she had to do was fill in the blanks, something anyone in the department could've knocked out in twenty minutes.

The desk in my office was situated so I could see down the hallway. Came the appointed hour, right before lunch, and she is tiptoeing past my door, no doubt heading out for some serious noontime shopping.

"Celeste," I called out, "aren't you forgetting something?"

She turned back to my doorway and uttered the most honest words in the history of advertising: "I couldn't think of anything."

I beckoned her into my office and gently led her to my limited view of the Magnificent Mile. "Celeste, see all those people down there? They can't think of anything either. But they don't work here. And now, neither do you."

Sounds like a shot across Stern's bow.

It was. The country club thing irked me. And he'd had plenty of time to "discuss" my request with Lee Walters.

He ever get back to you?

Months later. He and Walters sat me down. Very business-like, Jerry told me I would have the opportunity to buy, I forget how many shares, at a price equivalent to one-and-a-half times book value. I guess I should've known there'd be a "buy" part though, in truth, I thought they'd just *give* me a token amount. They knew I had no spare cash. But the "one-and-a-half" part, that pissed me off. What's the "half" for? I asked. Walters was passive. But Jerry's face turned red. "That's for the partners, us, for all our years here," he said, teeth clenched. I told them I'd think about it.

I sought out Mike. He said they were "bushing" me, whatever that meant. But as time went on I found out they had something up their sleeves. They'd been negotiating a merger with an old-line agency in town and maybe they'd made it hard for me because another stockholder would just muddy up the deal.

Was your agency hurting?

No, not ours. Earle Ludgin, that was the name of the other agency and its owner. I didn't know their situation but I guess they represented a quick way for SWS to grow. Ludgin was retiring so he wouldn't be in Stern's hair. He was a well-known art collector in Chicago and, it turned out, much of his collection would travel on permanent loan with the merged staff to our place. Matisse, Degas, whatever; Jerry said I could have, after him, the pick of the litter for my office. When the deal was close to a *fait accompli* Jerry gave me the final details. The new name would be Stern Walters–Earle Ludgin, SWEL for short. Horrible, I thought. And my job was not in jeopardy; in fact Ludgin had no creative director at all, which struck me as very odd. Jerry arranged a lunch, just me and the newest members of my creative department, such as they were, a half-dozen people. To get acquainted, he said.

How'd it go?

Ah, that question again. They were the most beaten-down bunch of hacks imaginable. Poor saps told me why they didn't have a creative director: because each account man served that function on his own hip-pocket accounts. My lunch mates were really looking forward *finally* to having someone—me—fight their battles for them. SWEL, my ass! Yea, when I started at SWS, there was a little of that old-school crap, but nothing close to what I was hearing now. I'd be put in the position of re-educating a new litter of antagonistic and defensive account guys I could picture sight unseen. And I knew I had no stomach for the turf wars sure to come.

What did you do about it?

I returned a phone call I'd been avoiding from some guy at Needham.

The Majors

My office door closed, I chain smoked three Kools before picking up the phone. I had a premonition something significant was about to happen; I didn't think they wanted to sign me as a softball pitcher.

There was no big agency runaround. Jack Hetherington immediately took my call. He introduced himself as V.P. of something or other, then, in a candid way I later discovered was his trademark, he said his real job was hire-and-hatchet-man for Keith Reinhard, Creative Director of Needham, Harper & Steers. "As you may know," he said, "a number of your people now work for us. Keith thinks the world of those people and is well aware you nurtured them. He'd like to meet with you about an opening here as Senior V.P. and Group Creative Director." Just like that.

"I don't even have a résumé, Jack," I said trying to downplay the feelings of fortuity and guilt clanging away in my gut.

"No problem," he assured me, "Keith's done his homework."

Given all my "people" running around Needham, we agreed I couldn't show up there for an interview. We would meet clandestinely in a suite at the Hyatt just across the river from their offices in the Equitable Building.

When Reinhard opened the door I smelled smoke. A compatriot! I knew I could muddle through this meeting. And his warm Midwestern greeting gave me more comfort. I expected slick and

My mentor Keith Reinhard sharing wisdom, 1980

flashy. He was anything but, his lean frame moving fluidly in a dark casual suit. He exuded confidence leavened by a humility sprung from his small-town Mennonite roots I learned about as we swapped life stories. Were I a client, I knew I'd feel secure about my advertising with him at the helm.

The room had been set up for a video presentation and like any ad guy he introduced his agency by showing me a reel of their commercials. I'd seen every one of those spots on air, all from big name clients and mostly major productions. I gulped the first time he paused the machine assuming he would ask for my critique. Instead, he made me feel like an insider, like family just sitting on the couch watching TV. He handled all the commentary (better him than me), along the way candidly calling a number of the spots "turkeys" though in some cases I thought he was being a little hard on himself. When the show ended, he said his goal was to have no more turkeys coming out of Needham and he thought I could help him achieve that objective.

He had nice things to say about my agency's work (he never asked about my "reel," which had its share of cats and dogs) and complimented my eye for the talent now working for him at Needham.

He explained the job. I would be splitting the client load as one of two Group Creative Directors. I'd be responsible for adult and teen McDonald's, State Farm, Morton Salt, Wrigley Spearmint Gum, their Campbell business consisting of SpaghettiOs, V-8 juice and new products, a portion of General Mills, namely Bisquick and Hamburger Helper (Hunt's Skillet dinners all over again!), Johnson Wax's Edge shaving gel and Armour-Dial's Dial soap. I could only guess how much those blue chip clients represented in billings. To handle all of it, there would be forty-five staff members in my group. At SWS, my department was a fourth that size.

While it was on *my* mind, at no time did he broach the tawdry subject of remuneration. In *his* mind, I gathered, he had found his man and details like money would be left in the hands of Hetherington.

Did I have any questions? he asked. There was one nagging at me even as I had walked to the hotel. Back when I'd met with Morris Jacobs' son who sent me on to Goldblatt's, I remembered he gave me an unsolicited rundown on agencies I should steer clear of, the "anti-Semites," he called them. And Needham was front and center on his list.

Cornering someone as classy as Keith felt smarmy, but I was compelled to bring up the subject. I think he had anticipated my concern. He inhaled deeply and then in his soft-spoken way admitted the accusation was unfortunately true—twenty years ago when the agency was called Needham Louis & Brorby. My fellow Group Creative Director, Joel Hochberg, whom he wanted me to meet and who would corroborate his answer, was Jewish and, more telling, so was Keith's fiancée, Rose-Lee Simon, a senior account executive at the agency. And there were many others. Enough said.

Like Columbo, I had one more thing. Was there anything else he expected of me? He took another puff and said, "Yes, I want you to help me become president." I already had decided he was the closest to Presidential timbre of anyone I'd ever met, a mix of Lincoln, Carter and a dollop of ol' Harry. He saw my quizzical look. "Of the agency," he continued. "I'd like that challenge one day." Love him as I did, expressions of that weightiness would never flow from Jerry Stern's lips. I nodded my understanding.

Think about it, he said. And, almost bashfully, be sure to talk to Jack about the "package." He was certain I'd find it fair. And there'd be a few other management people he'd want me to meet *after* I reached a decision, but those were just courtesy calls. President not yet, Keith was clearly in charge.

We left the room as it was. Someone would be by to pick up the equipment, he said. In the hallway, when an elevator arrived, he motioned for me to take it. He knew the spy drill and said he'd catch the next one down.

Crossing back over the bridge I looked up at the Equitable and tried to count to thirty-four, the floor where Keith mentioned my corner office would be located. I imagined gazing out at the gleaming Wrigley Building and the river flowing west through the booming new downtown. There could be no better vantage point in the city. Just hours ago the prospect of SWEL had me as down as I'd ever been in my career. And now that view on high was mine for the asking.

⁂

THE "PACKAGE" WAS MORE THAN fair, more than my father and his two brothers in toto ever dreamed of making in a year. And the lunch with Hochberg, the friendliest New Yorker I'd ever encountered, was completely reassuring.

Now for the gut-wrenching part: telling Jerry.

I thought I could put lipstick on my parting shot by offering up a replacement I knew Jerry respected. Lane Larrison had left SWS to start his own agency, which I heard wasn't going well. I called Lane, confided in him about my Needham offer and asked if I could throw his hat into the ring when I spoke to the partners.

He was ready and more than amenable. That would make things much easier for me. And, he was a perfect choice.

The confrontation with Jerry and Lee became, instead, a love fest. For one thing, they were preoccupied with the Ludgin merger and the last-minute hiccups that always accompany the melding of agency cultures (if culture described Ludgin's operation). And handing them Larrison on a silver platter went over even better than I'd hoped. New agency name. New agency look. New agency creative director (devoid of the animus they knew I was bearing). It made sense. And, in truth, especially for Jerry, I think they felt a certain pride hearing that one of *theirs* had been anointed to such an exalted position by an agency as prestigious as Needham. (Until he died in 2000, Jerry Stern remained my pen pal, father confessor and one-man admiration society.)

⁂

October 1, 1976. Hetherington said he'd be back in an hour to walk me around to meet my new staff and then take me to lunch across Michigan Avenue and down a flight of stairs to Riccardo's. Meanwhile, like the first day at school, I was setting up my desk, unpacking the cartons of keepsakes Needham had graciously arranged to pick up and deliver to my new digs. I saved my Royal for last. When I hefted it out, something new had been added—a small engraved copper plaque affixed to the casing above the keys. "From your staff at Stern Walters & Simmons…Good-bye Mr. Quips," it read. I dabbed at my eyes with a shirtsleeve; it had to be the sun glaring off the river on that crisp Friday morning.

Where was Dale Carnegie when I needed him? Other than the few I bumped into from SWS days—Susan Downs, Jim Retzer, Laura Rudman—the assault of new names and faces, welcoming though they were, was overwhelming. Jack warranted that I'd get to know them all "really well" soon enough.

To wit, Neal Vanover, a few doors down. An associate creative director on McDonald's, he was rattling around his office piled everywhere with storyboards looking for one in particular he wanted to show me. It was the leadoff commercial for a new campaign he had conjured up built around the notion of a "Big Mac Attack." (The line would soon become famous and often emulated.) He had an infectious laugh that put Mackle's cackle to shame as he explained the "legs" of the idea. He and Jack agreed I should attend the big presentation a week away out in Oak Brook.

At the last of our office stops, three guys and a young lady were sitting cross-legged on the carpet poring over storyboards strewn between them. The oldest jumped up, a wiry guy my age with a harried look. Associate Creative Director Dick Corrigan eagerly shook my hand. "Boy, are we glad to see you," he said. "We're scratchin' our asses over State Farm." I knew that account was bigger than all of SWS's clients combined. Suggesting we could get together after lunch, I wondered what miracle Corrigan expected of me.

Walking over to Riccardo's, Jack explained why the panic. My predecessor, Dan Nichols, had left rather suddenly to launch a commercial directing career in L.A. And Keith had taken his sweet and methodical time finding a replacement. My creative group had been operating virtually rudderless for months. Keith had a plateful and was not always accessible for every little crisis (as I would now be).

Jack, who'd began his career in New York and knew all the haunts my brief boss Clark knew, held court at "Ric's" in a sizable side booth. Several of his cronies from other agencies slid in to meet and congratulate me. At a similar booth in the back of the bar area, the newspaper guys I knew only by sight held sway: Ebert, Royko and Terkel among others. There was more drinking going on in the place at lunch hour than I'd ever seen this side of Manhattan; O'Connell's, my old spot three blocks north, didn't even have a liquor license. If Ric's was going to be the routine, I'd have to watch myself.

Back in the Equitable lobby, we bumped into one of the management guys Keith had wanted me to meet. Jack Copher was pushing sixty, his gray hair slicked back banker's style. "Glad to have you aboard," he said sincerely. Then, directing his words to Hetherington, the assignment sheriff, he mentioned that while Kraft was one of Hochberg's ongoing accounts and he was doing a great job, the client had a new product they wanted us to handle, and since Larry's the new guy, Copher thought it was time to show a new face to Kraft and maybe Larry could come out to Northbrook Tuesday for the "cutting" (a term I'd learned during the Hunt's fiasco that meant an orientation meeting at a client's test kitchen where the agency had a chance to taste whatever it was they had cooked up).

Here I am with the firm all of five hours and they're hanging more iron on my barbell.

CORRIGAN WAS WAITING OUTSIDE MY office schmoozing with my new secretary Carol, a handful of those storyboards under his arm. His dilemma was endemic to the ad biz—somebody at State Farm had grown tired of their current advertising, a campaign that featured real State Farm insurance agents behind their desks describing their personalized service. He and his team had been tearing their hair out trying to top it. From afar, I had admired those commercials; they had an honesty about them and put a real live face on the company and their "good neighbor" agents' ubiquitous storefront locations. I didn't know the politics but the new ideas Dick showed me, which were not too shabby, seemed absolutely premature.

Back on STP, I had managed to talk Granatelli into doing a series of testimonials featuring "real" people—folks who had written love letters to him about their positive experiences with the product. He resisted at first since he would not be starring in the commercials but finally gave in—Studebaker management zinging him about the "cult of the personality" may have helped—and we shot all sorts of STP fans, from a volunteer fireman who counted on his car to get to burning buildings, to an old geezer who claimed to have put more than 300,000 miles on his Chevy without any engine repairs thanks to STP Oil Treatment. It was dicey working with amateurs but the spots did add dimension to the campaign.

Talking to Corrigan, I thought adding a little texture to his State Farm campaign might alleviate the client's fatigue factor. Perhaps include real policyholders in the equation interacting with the agents; maybe take the agent away from his desk out to the scene of an accident. Whatever. But let's fight hard to keep intact the essence of the campaign and not present newly minted and unnecessary alternatives.

Fortunately, Reinhard and State Farm went back a long way. He began his career working on promotional materials for them in Bloomington, Illinois. They eventually sent him up with their blessings to be hired by their agency, the former Needham, Louis and Brorby. A few weeks after my meeting with Corrigan—and with Keith's full support—State Farm embraced the nuanced campaign.

IT WASN'T A *BRIS* BUT we were there in the Kraft kitchen witnessing a "cutting." Eight of us from Needham—a number Stern would've thought excessive—stood at ease as two middle-aged ladies in white, a nutritionist and a home economist, extolled the wonders of what they had wrought. "The world's first successful combination of peanut butter *and* jelly," the home ec proudly proclaimed. It *was* somewhat mesmerizing, the swirls of tan and purple we could see through the large glass beaker on the pristine countertop separating the ladies from our gang of eight. I began to imagine the hypnotic commercial we might do.

At that moment, Jack Copher, who was standing next to me, leaned closer. "Your fly's open," he whispered.

It was just my third day on the job so I thought perhaps this was his idea of a hazing gag. But sneaking a peek, alas, I'm not open, I'm *wide* open.

I'd been concentrating on the Kraft ladies. Now I was positive they'd been concentrating on me.

Turning away from the counter for a moment I feigned a cough then grabbed at my zipper tab in one deft upward motion.

As it happened, the vertiginous product never made it past the taste tests with kids. They either preferred their pb&j neat, slathered on separately or, for a surprising percentage, without the jelly part at all.

So my Kraft assignment died at birth.

Around Needham though, the story of my first client encounter lived on for years just below the belt.

Under the Golden Arches

My five years at Needham Chicago passed in a blur. There were flights to Philly, then across the Delaware to Campbell's in Camden; to Phoenix for Dial; to Minneapolis for General Mills; to both coasts for various shoots. There were drives to Racine for Johnson Wax; to Bloomington for State Farm; and most of all, to Oak Brook—except for a time when I was asked off the account—for McDonald's.

McDonald's was a full-time job for a third of my staff and, by osmosis, for me. I began to measure out my life in Shamrock Shakes. Every year the client, to assuage its thousands of demanding owner-operators, would ask us to come up with a new commercial to promote the green-dyed concoction that ran for just the week preceding St. Patrick's Day. To keep the creative fresh—the agency already had done leprechauns to death—over the years I tried to spread the project around. It wasn't easy though, more a game of hide-and-seek; my staff would dive under their desks when they saw me walking the halls, that daunting assignment in hand.

I did ride into McDonald's on a good day thanks to the glowing reception Vanover's "Big Mac Attack" received, so my own acceptance in Oak Brook had a solid start. Those were still the days when McDonald's took the high road, when their advertising strove for an emotional connection, when nary a word was spent on price promotions. Shamrock Shakes aside it was, *begorra*, a plum account.

Like most clients though, McDonald's was insatiable. Once the Big Mac push had run its course, they hungered for something just as good on the subject of French fries, their other star seller. Fortunately, I had two stars of my own, Joey Cummings and Lee Gleason, ready for the challenge.

Joey, the writer, was a petite but feisty Southern lady who came to Needham from Burnett where she had coined the "finger lickin' good" line for KFC. Lee, the art director, was her polar opposite, the tallest creative I've ever known, an even-keeled Northwest Side Chicago guy with a great grasp of middle American sensibilities. Together, they came up with a concept built around the line "Keep your eyes on your fries," a humorous primer on how to fend off all those fry swipers out there, the perfect premise for McDonald's most irresistible product.

I think I signed a non-disclosure at the time, so I can't give specifics now, but I did learn why their French fries are so tempting. The magic was revealed while on a whirlwind tour of McDonald's vendors, a mission to uncover interesting "nuggets" we could incorporate into an upcoming campaign aimed at reinforcing quality perceptions.

Traveling with several McDonald's marketing people, a number of us began the tour by visiting an immaculate meatpacking plant in Chicago. We watched as cylinders full of bright red hunks of beef and far lesser amounts of gleaming white fat were fed into a massive stainless steel contraption out of which came an endless procession of flash-frozen hamburger patties untouched by human hands.

We then climbed into a McDonald's jet heading for two far-flung suppliers. First stop, Gorton's of Gloucester, Massachusetts, where burly men wearing rubber aprons and galoshes wrestled jumbo cod straight off Atlantic Ocean trawlers. Not quite as mechanized as the burger plant, scores of hand-held flashing knives were at work trimming the cod down to manageable blocks ready to be sliced, breaded, frozen and shipped off as Filet-o-Fish patties (still my personal McDonald's favorite).

Back aboard, we headed for Idaho, home of J.R. Simplot's potato dynasty. Ol' J.R. had to be the wealthiest man in the state (the word was the reigning Miss Idaho was always one of his house guests). His mile-long processing plants—at the time there were seven of them scattered around Idaho—cranked out flash frozen French fries every day but Christmas for virtually every major fast food company, most of all, for McDonald's.

At one end of the facility we visited near Boise, a five-story mountain of beautiful Burbank potatoes stood outside in the high dry air. Before Simplot was through, there'd be nothing left of them.

The potatoes were loaded into a wide trough of fast flowing water that carried them through the process. Mechanically peeled and sliced, they then passed the inspection of a long line of Native American women standing to either side of the trough; by hand they pulled off potential fries blemished in any way (these along with the peels and remnants from the slicer ended up as feed for Simplot's cattle, scores of them roaming in fenced-in pastures lining both sides of the facility).

Now the inspected slices rushed toward a Y in the watery conveyor, half heading one way to be parboiled, frozen and boxed up for Burger King, Wendy's et al.; the other half, McDonald's half, receiving special—and top secret—treatment in the parboiling phase. At the finish line, we witnessed a virtual Niagara of fries tumbling out of the enormous freezer, then immediately boxed and sent on their way.

(FYI—even the water used to propel the potatoes did not go to waste. Simplot distills out of it a milky substance leached along the trip from which they made a variety of starch products. All part of a nice little business.)

What we made out of that trip was a series of commercials extolling the virtues of their high-quality ingredients framed by simple, heart-warming stories only McDonald's could tell. One was based on an actual experience I'd had when one of my boys returned from his first summer camp:

Mom and Dad waiting anxiously alongside other parents. Bus pulls up. Unkempt kids pile out. Mom and Dad rush to hug cute ten-year-old daughter. After greeting, first words out of her mouth—"Can we go to McDonald's?" Cut to close up of French fries cooking as announcer praises Burbank potatoes. Cut back to bite-and-smile three-shot. Amidst the aseptic setting of red, white and gold Formica-lined restaurant, girl looks up at parents and ingenuously says, "I'm glad to be home."

⁂

BREAKFAST AT MCDONALD'S. IT SEEMS so obvious and commonplace today but as late as 1977, during my time on the account, the restaurants didn't open their doors before 11 a.m. That is, until an enterprising operator in Santa Barbara came up with a big idea: a breakfast-y sort of egg sandwich—neat and round thanks to the metal egg ring he designed—that could be cooked on the good old burger grill. He called it an Egg McMuffin and, at his store, it was a roaring opening-hour favorite. Oak Brook got wind of it and the light went on. The restaurants are just sitting there; why not open for breakfast?

The task was served up to my group: alter the mindset of millions of Americans, all with their favorite and familiar morning stop; create a new "meal occasion" for McDonald's, the 7 a.m. to 11 a.m. time slot; and, whatever you come up with, make damn sure the folks know those ain't powdered eggs we're breaking!

As it happened, the team I assigned to the breakfast project included a junior copywriter named Jim Glover, the only African-American in the entire creative department.

For some inexplicable reason, the clarion call from the creative side of the agency business has rarely tempted African-Americans. Of the countless job interviews I've conducted, I can tick off on one hand the number of black applicants. The industry tries—it certainly has been cajoled—to do something about the imbalance: job fairs, school tours, minority scholarships and intern programs.

To this day, by any statistical measure, the outreaching efforts of general market ad agencies have accomplished next to nothing.

Jim was the exception, a young man raised in Harlem; his only previous credential was, in fact, a minority intern program at Y&R in New York. Still, he was as green as he was black. Hetherington, who had handed me a very strong staff of professionals on a silver platter, spoke about Glover at lunch my first day on the job. He said Glover would be "my project." I knew what he meant. I was sure Reinhard had made some sort of commitment and was counting on me to nurture Jim along.

The guy did have potential. For one thing, he was very musical. Once, he came into my office seeking approval on a magazine ad. He was carrying a boom box. I thought maybe he was tossing in a radio idea as a Lucky Strike extra. No, he said flipping the stereo on to Ahmad Jamal's "Poinciana," he just wanted me in a mellow frame of mind when I assessed his print ad copy. I bought it.

I liked Jim. I never knew what he'd come up with next. He was my alien son and the most interesting character in a creative group crammed with characters. About business, he was woefully naïve; as for street smarts, he had an advanced degree. Hetherington came by one day with Glover's expense account. Jim had been in New York covering a "table top" shoot on 23rd Street, a cab ride away from his hotel but, for some reason, had put in for a rental car. Company policy, Jack said, was that nobody rents a car in New York particularly for a shoot in Manhattan. Jack told me to inform Jim it was no dice on the $200 expense.

After giving Jim the bad news I asked him why he had gone to Avis. "Well, y'know, Larry, it was my first trip back there. I just wanted to get me a big white Lincoln, drive it up to Harlem and stick my arm out the window so I could wave at my ol' homies."

Endearing, I thought; but rules are rules, I said. He reached into his inside jacket pocket and pulled out an official looking piece of paper. "Then I guess you ain't gonna pay this towin' ticket, either." He guessed right though for a heartbeat I did consider covering it.

Finally, the team assigned to the breakfast project, Jim included, came in to show me their rough ideas. Jim was last at bat. From the halting way he presented his idea, I'm not sure he knew how brilliant it was. Built around our jingle *du jour*, "Nobody can do it like McDonald's can," Jim had written soulful new lyrics to accompany a stylized visual treatment. In part:

Nobody rises up in the morning like McDonald's can
Visual: sunrise over Golden Arches sign
At the crack of dawn
Visual: fresh egg breaking
Hot coffee's on
Visual: steaming coffee pour
It's a glorious day all over the land.
Visual: happy customers gobbling up breakfast

For Jim, and Needham for that matter, I was overjoyed. In a few artful words, he had covered all the bases: the fresh eggs, the coffee, the store, the potential impact on America's breakfast habits. Then, as a capper, in his naïve, street smart way he added, "I think we ought'a get Richie Havens to sing it."

I gulped. First of all, McDonald's had never resorted to celebrity singers (Barry Manilow wasn't famous when he penned and sang "You deserve a break today" ten years earlier). And secondly, would McDonald's buy into the crown prince of Woodstock and all his sordid sidebars? With Reinhard's endorsement, we went for it.

Long story short, Havens and his agent agreed to do a "demo" track based on Jim's lyrics. Fortunately, in McDonald's managerial ranks there were several one-time flower children. "Freedom" still stirred them. The breakfast concept, presented via Rockwellian storyboard frames and Havens' emotive track was approved in Oak Brook by standing ovation. (Today, despite the clamor of nutritionistas, McDonald's accounts for more than a fourth of all out-of-home breakfasts served in America.)

McDONALD'S OWN TEST KITCHEN CAME up with an idea not quite in the league with the Egg McMuffin. Someone must've fallen in love with pressed duck, the made-in-America entrée one finds on menus in old-fashioned round-eye Chinese restaurants right next to the egg foo young. In McDonald's case, it was pressed chicken, formed into a patty, deep-fried and put in a hamburger bun. The working name for this new—and absolutely awful—creation was Chicken McSandwich. Our job was to develop commercials McDonald's initially would run in several test markets (unlike the all-out national introduction of breakfast, there was enough skepticism in Oak Brook about this sandwich that they wisely decided to walk before they ran with it).

Probably because it was an opportunity for McDonald's to finally add a chicken item to the menu board, Paul Schrage, head of marketing—an affable fellow, a great audience and a man normally gifted with laser-like judgment—was determined to make a success of this Chicken McSandwich.

We had no problem selling him the storyboards. The problem was in the execution, specifically the close-up product shot. The sandwich had none of the appeal of a meaty Big Mac stack or the warm golden glow of an Egg McMuffin. And the patty itself was no more photogenic than it was palatable. We chose America's pre-eminent food cinematographer to cover the insert shots and edited his best efforts into the people part of the spots. When I showed the cuts to Reinhard, he thought what I thought, the product didn't look very appetizing. Anticipating issues, he joined the presentation posse on the ride to Oak Brook.

Schrage had me run the spots several times. Something about his newborn's picture was bothering him. "The patty looks like a hockey puck," he pronounced. I shouldn't have but I bristled back, "We hired the best guy to shoot the thing, Paul. He tried every trick in the book. It *is* a hockey puck!"

I thought I had earned some chits with Paul. Seemingly not. He fired back, glaring through me at Keith, "Well maybe we can find another agency that can make it look good."

Reinhard, well aware that McDonald's was one of the biggest advertisers in the country, stood in the way of the bullets. "Paul, we'll reshoot with a different director at our cost," he said in his low-key reassuring manner. Keith was a magician with clients; Schrage seemed momentarily pacified.

The next morning I learned from Keith that not all client decisions are expressed in open meetings and that I now was saddled with an additional title: *persona non grata* at McDonald's.

I figured I was toast. But Keith, bless his heart, told me that Paul occasionally displayed a short fuse and that I should lay low for a while, keep doing my job, and just send the associate creative directors out to Oak Brook until Paul simmered down.

At no small cost my guys reshot the patty. Its stripes however didn't change. But Paul, no doubt resigned to the fact that he'd fathered an ugly baby, accepted the results. It turned out none of it mattered. In the test markets, folks did not come back for seconds. (Ironically, several years later, the same basic ingredient—shredded chicken parts—now formed into bite-sized deep-fried balls and christened Chicken McNuggets, became a mainstay money maker for McDonald's.)

Meanwhile, I'm a pariah on Needham's flagship account. Keith's loyalty would only go so far. Others in top management at the agency were, I was certain, urging him to bounce me and my big mouth. I loved my job and was extremely disappointed in myself. I had to do something to get back into Schrage's good graces.

*

It was November, 1980. Ronald Reagan had just defeated Jimmy Carter. Rumors were swirling that as some sort of goodwill gesture the Iranians were planning to release their American hostages—held captive now for a year in the U.S. Embassy in Tehran—around the time of Reagan's inauguration.

Maybe Mayor Puckett was sitting on my shoulder whispering in my ear, but I had an epiphany: wouldn't it be appropriate for an all-American company like McDonald's to welcome home the hostages when and if?

I worked up a storyboard, simple and understated:

Morning outside a McDonald's.
Counter kid comes out to raise the American
flag, a ritual at every store.
Sound of creaking pulley and flapping as
flag rises, back lit and majestic.
Counter kid secures rope, turns to go back inside.
He reconsiders.
Turns back toward pole, looks up, and resolutely salutes flag.
Announcer: McDonald's joins all Americans
in this joyous welcome home.

Keith was ecstatic. He said he would take the idea to Schrage and give credit where it was due. He knew Schrage would buy it. I think he was as much concerned about my fate as he was the hostages'.

Schrage did buy it and was certain the franchisees would take great pride in seeing it run. Given the uncertainty of the outcome in Iran, Paul told Keith I should personally produce it with a director we could trust working with a limited film crew sworn to secrecy at an inconspicuous location. He even suggested the store, on the outskirts of Santa Barbara, which happened to have a postcard mountainous backdrop. Paul had it right. We finish the spot, put it in the can, keep the lid on tight until, as it were, we see the whites of the hostages' eyes.

I had the perfect director in mind. Jon Yarbrough, an associate creative director I had worked with since joining Needham. He had recently left the agency to start his own film production company in Los Angeles. While still with us, Jon had directed a terrific McDonald's commercial starring, for the first time on American television, a Canadian teen named Michael J. Fox. Schrage admired Jon's talent as much as I did and applauded the choice. And Jon delivered a poignant and decidedly un-commercial commercial.

Except for a blurb buried in a *Sun-Times* marketing column alluding to some mystery surrounding a new McDonald's commercial—my guess was an assistant editor working on the project's post-production had had one too many at Riccardo's—there were no leaks.

The rest, of course, is happy history. The hostages, all fifty-two still being held, arrived home safe and sound. After counting to ten, we ran the spot for several days. As Schrage predicted, the franchisees, hearing plaudits from their customers, were proud of their role.

And, praise be! Back in Oak Brook I, too, was welcomed home.

The Beer Baron

Despite its inherent anxieties, advertising is not a death-defying occupation, not, say, like mining coal or felling trees. So why do I find myself with two other frightened passengers on a Friday at three in the morning in the back of a limousine, the driver unable to hold a straight course against the blast of an unrelenting ice storm? And why are we on the desolate, wind-swept I-55 following the same path I took many times before on old Route 66—but never like this!—trying to reach St. Louis by dawn? And, seated between Keith Reinhard and me, why is Susan Downs, one of my most levelheaded associate creative directors, digging so hard into my left forearm with every unnerving swerve of the limo?

Why?

⁂

August Adolphus Busch III, like Andy Granatelli before him, trusted his own intuition. When he became disenchanted with the advertising for his eponymous Busch Beer, he watched a little television and then reputedly told Mike Roarty, his director of marketing, to "get hold of the guys who do McDonald's."

The brand was Anheuser-Busch's smallest though, after Keith took Roarty's call, we all saw Busch as a big fat foot in the door of an advertising colossus. We would compete with their current agency, an old-line St. Louis firm. As St. Louis royalty, the Busch family had always shown loyalty to local vendors. And, as intense an account as A-B no doubt was, having their agencies down the street at their beck and call might've contributed to their allegiance. It's likely we were the first outsider they'd ever considered and there was no guarantee they would, in the end, cross the Mississippi to hire us.

While geography wasn't in our favor, we believed we had the firepower to unseat the incumbent.

Busch was priced at the low end of the spectrum right there with Pabst and Old Style. Our research department identified the target as a "reparative drinker," the blue collar guy who rewards himself after an honest day's labor by cracking open a can of beer at home or calling for a bottle at his local saloon.

Susan and, at the time, her art director partner Jon Yarbrough, created a very smart campaign that, at once, appealed to the reparative's need for reward while connecting mnemonically to the Busch Beer label, a design prominently depicting a range of mountains. (Last we looked, St. Louis was as flat as Chicago. To us, mountains seemed to be the province of rival Colorado-brewed Coors, probably the reason A.A.B. III had chosen them in the first place. But there they were.)

"Head for the mountains," Susan and Jon's exhortation, was a great way to say it on every level, made even more manly and memorable when spoken and sung by Hoyt Axton, a country-western star with a basso profundo twang.

Then, thanks to Keith, came the clincher. At the moment of the obligatory pop-top can opening in the commercial, he suggested, why not an unexpected sound effect to accompany the action—an elongated, resonant "Buschhhhhhhh!" August would have to love that.

There was no doubt in any of our minds. We would win the business. All that remained was to spend the next two days tidying up the presentation, get on a plane Thursday evening arriving in time for dinner down there and a good night's sleep, then knock them for a loop Friday morning at nine bells. It was a sensible plan—that is until the call late Thursday afternoon from our travel agent: a big storm has just moved in from the north; they've closed O'Hare 'til tomorrow morning.

Were Anheuser-Busch already a client, a simple and reasonable request to delay the meeting would have been granted. But that wasn't the case. We could not allow distance to affect their impression of us, or the outcome. Without hesitation Keith said that we would just get a limo and drive down there. Blair Vedder, head of the office, was on tap to join in the presentation. We all thought Blair's forceful, gregarious style would add to our arsenal. But told of the change in travel arrangements, he balked. "I'm way past all-nighters," he said gruffly. Old sailor that he was, he predicted the storm would pass. He'd get out first thing in the morning, he said, and meet us at the hotel for breakfast.

Back when, even on good old Route 66 driving my clunker to Mizzou, the leg to St. Louis normally took less than five hours. On this horrific night, we were quaking in that limo for more than twice that. When we finally reached the hotel at 7:30 a.m., we agreed to go to our rooms, freshen up as best we could, grab some coffee and head for A-B's nearby headquarters. Then who greets us, fresh and clean-shaven, his mane of white hair perfectly coifed, his grin lighting up the lobby? Of course, the bossman. "You people look like hell," Blair said. "What took you so long?"

A few months after we won the account the annual Anheuser-Busch sales convention was held at the Fairmont in San Francisco. August spared no expense softening up his distributors. A long line of sports celebrities were introduced on stage, Tony Bennett sang his love song to S.F., and just when you thought you'd seen it all, Bob Hope strolled out to do twenty minutes.

With nothing really new on the Budweiser or Michelob front, the "Mountains" campaign for Busch became the focus of the business portion of the show. One of the commercials was what the brewery referred to as a "quality" message, that is, a beer-centric spot long on languid pours and creamy heads and hops but devoid of people, akin in spirit to their ubiquitous Budweiser Clydesdale commercials.

Naturally, in our rendition, we headed for the mountains:

Music begins over
a gurgling mountain brook fringed by winter's last gasp of ice.
The crystal clear water cascades over boulders.
Match dissolve to golden beer pouring into clear and masculine mug.
Cut to wide shot of mountain slope and surrounding forest.
Cut to Busch beer can, label design facing camera, as hand pops top:
Buschhhhhh!
Cut to chipmunk. Startled by sound, it sits up, curious.
Hoyt Axton delivers short spiel
over medium beauty shot of brook.
Music and Axton conclude with
"Head for the mountains!"

We had created a new world for Busch Beer, artificial though it was considering the fact that the brew's main ingredient came from the flatlands—purified Mississippi River water. From beginning to end, the spot was far more symbolic and subtle than the millionaires in the audience were used to. But they seemed to appreciate the touch of class it brought to their bargain brand. With the loud applause, Needham's table of ten began breathing again.

Over dinner, I noticed August making the rounds. A man of average size and appearance; if you didn't know who he was you would never cast him as America's uncontested beer baron. His complexion was ruddy, no doubt the result of his avid duck hunting. We'd heard that his estate, located on a triangular tract of land formed where the Missouri and Mississippi converged north of town, was a major flyway for migrating fowl—he could go out to his back forty and shoot skeet with live birds. I watched him move quickly from table to table, everyone rising at his approach. The distributors knew who he was.

Our table, off in a far corner of the ballroom, was his last stop. He was smiling, a good sign. There were handshakes all around and pats on the back for those of us he recognized as the "creative guys," including Susan. "Not too shabby, not too shabby," he said repeatedly. But then, as he turned to leave, he dropped a live grenade on our table, an inexplicable four-word critique: "It needs more rocks." And with that, he was gone.

None of us were sure we'd heard right. The creek was splattered with rocks. The mountainsides above were jagged with rocks. We had no idea what A.A.B. III was talking about.

Later, over drinks in the Fairmont lobby, it was left for Mike Roarty to interpret his boss. August had told him moments before that he no longer liked the chipmunk. Perhaps on his rounds of the tables a distributor had questioned the rodent's masculinity. "More rocks means more *cojones*," Mike said. "August loves the idea of an animal rising up to the Buschhhhhh sound, he just thinks it should be a much bigger animal. A big black stallion is what he wants to see there."

New to August and the account, I wasn't sure how to play this absurdity. "Mike, would horses hang out halfway up a mountain?" I innocently asked. Roarty was a legend in the industry, a true "beer guy," loved by the distributors and August's right-hand man, a well-paid position he clearly intended to keep.

"Yea, I mentioned that," he said somewhat embarrassed, "but August just reminded me that there was no telling where a horny ass mustang might end up." I knew where our cute little chipmunk just ended up—on the cutting room floor.

A film crew was sent back to the location in the Rockies, stallion in tow, one trained to rise up on command. Non sequitur though it was, in the abstract the shot was dynamic and powerful. We cut it into the spot and took the revision down for August's okay.

Hunter and, now we learn, horseman as well, August reacted badly. "That horse's been gelded. Get one that's really hung." He stormed out of the conference room. Shades of Schrage and the infamous chicken patty!

Describing the new specifications to the film company was delicate. Fortunately, for a gig, most of them will try anything. They went back up to the mountain now hauling a Thoroughbred stud, seventeen hands high, and reshot the scene.

When the stallion rose up on the conference room TV monitor, gleaming black and beautifully side lit to accentuate his belly and beyond, August clapped his hands in glee and shouted, "Now *those* are rocks!" And this time he left the room happy and satiated.

⁂

Well ensconced now as a minor member of the A-B family, Keith, the account director Ron Bess and I were asked by Roarty to come down for a highly confidential meeting. The subject was something the brewery had been avoiding for years—a response to the inroads being made by Miller Lite.

That brand had taken off thanks in large part to their clever "Great taste; Less filling" TV debates between over-the-hill athletes (a slick end-around government guidelines forbidding the use of active sports celebrities in beer commercials).

According to Mike, August and his brewmasters were being dragged into the fray by distributors clamoring for a serious answer to this upstart—not something tepid like Busch Light or Michelob Light—the answer had to be Budweiser Light. No question there had been teeth gnashing and hair pulling over such a monumental decision. Budweiser was the King of Beers, fondly referred to at the brewery as "Big Red." Watering it down, even as a simple line extension, because of archrival Miller was an admission of vulnerability for a brewer with such a long and proud family history. It was also risky business; Mike mentioned "cannibalization," the fear of cutting into Big Red's sales, over and over. But despite all that, the decision had been made.

And while everyone involved with marketing thought we deserved the assignment based on our Busch work, it couldn't just be handed to us, Mike said. There was the reality of D'Arcy, the Budweiser ad agency for decades. And the fact that their St. Louis office was headed by a man—a lucky man—who'd married into the Busch family.

A-B had decided to conduct a competition, D'Arcy versus Needham. The ground rules were eminently fair. Each agency would come up with an approved campaign and be given an identically hefty production and media budget; each agency would run their campaign in a different set of test markets, the sets consisting of a small, medium and large market. The winner would be based solely on comparable sales. None of us had ever heard of a selection process so politically correct. Or as costly. But we liked our chances.

I gave this important assignment to a strong team—beer drinkers all—headed up by an erudite writer named John Welch and his new art director sidekick Lee Gleason of French fry fame. Theirs was not an easy task. The campaign would have to differentiate Budweiser Light (the name was shortened to Bud Light four years hence) from the somewhat frivolous image of Miller Lite and at the same time stand alone and separate from Big Red. It was early summer of 1981; they had a month to work with.

I'd swing by Welch's office (normally butting in was not my style) to check on their progress. "Not yet, Boss. But we're getting there." Cool. Meanwhile understandable pressure was coming my way from the Needham powers-that-be.

Needham was a far cry from SWS when it came to top-down direction. At SWS, I'd stroll into Stern's office, really a courtesy call, and flash a storyboard his way. With rare exception, an occasional "gotch'a," I'd gain his approval in a matter of minutes. Needham was far more formal. Any new campaign, and certainly any new business presentation, had to pass muster at an executive management review, basically a meeting comprised of the agency graybeards—account, research and media heads. Almost always, Keith had my back in such meetings and as assuring as he was with clients, his imprimatur meant even more in these internal reviews. Yes, my creative imprint was somewhat abraded at Needham, but with the blessings of Keith and the committee of elders, at least I wasn't flying solo.

In the midst of the Budweiser Light quest, a few of us were summoned to the brewery to witness a major event. It took place in a rather small room crowded with people including Roarty and two of his marketing guys along with a handful of our D'Arcy adversaries. August in shirtsleeves and his brewmaster in a long white lab coat were standing behind a table where sat three frosty pitchers of beer and a like number of glass mugs.

August held court. The brewmaster had conjured up three versions of Budweiser Light, he explained. (They looked identical.) August, and August alone, would sample each of the versions. There was a lot riding on this moment for the brewery and both ad agencies. I, for one, hoped August would taste something he and the rest of America would like.

Now the man in the white coat ceremoniously hoisted pitcher one, carefully filling a mug. August examined the frothy head, deftly swirled the brew, like an oenophile, then took in the aroma before savoring the contents. The process was repeated twice more. He sipped water to clear his palate between each savor. After sampling all three, without hesitation, he pointed at the middle pitcher. "This one," he said decisively. Then, like F.D.R. grilling Oppenheimer on the inner workings of the atom bomb, August turned to the brewmaster and asked straight-faced, "You wrote down the formula, right?" No one in the room knew whether he was kidding or not.

⁂

FINALLY, THE BUDWEISER LIGHT TEAM brought in their ideas. They had a pile of them. One instantly struck me as a grand slam home run:

"Bring out your best."

Their TV concept centered around the determination of athletes—a four-man rowing team; a 4x100 meter relay team, a minor league baseball team—and the camaraderie they share after a victory toasting, natch, their Budweiser Lights. Given the guidelines, the cast would consist of unknown college athletes. To build the drama and nail the theme line we turned to my old friend Gary Klaff who came up with a rousing anthem.

There is a bit of voodoo employed in the ad business to simulate a style and tone for a commercial-to-be. It's called a "steal-a-matic" and it helps a client get the idea. Film clips garnered from various sources—movies, television, even other commercials—are strung together and edited to a music track. For the presentation to Anheuser-Busch, we culled recent Olympic TV coverage including footage from the 1980 winter games held the previous year. Klaff produced a two-minute version of his anthem, a raspy male singer belting out a steadily intensifying "Bring out your best...Budweiser Light!" As a crescendo to our steal-a-matic video, we closed with scenes from the U.S. hockey team's Cinderella victory over the Soviet Union, the so-called "Miracle on Ice," a singular Cold War moment still pulsing at the time through the arteries of every red-blooded American.

Mike Eruzione's game-winning goal, the furious and vain last-ditch attack by the Russians, the exultation of the underdogs at the final buzzer, the Stars and Stripes skated around the arena—all cut to the insistent strains of "Bring out your best"—had a palpable effect on everyone in A-B's conference room, most of all, thankfully, on August.

He gave it what we now knew to be his supreme compliment: "Not too shabby," he exclaimed. And followed that up with an astute question directed my way. "That's once-in-a-lifetime stuff you put in there. Can you get that kind of impact shooting your storyboards, just with those rowers and runners?"

"We'll bring out our best, August," I answered honestly.

⁂

WHEN WE PRESENTED CASTING TAPES to Mike Roarty for the relay team commercial, we recommended four black runners, all gifted college athletes. Mike took exception. "Why can't there be any white guys on the team?" he asked no doubt thinking about A-B's southern distributors.

"There hasn't been a great relay team with any white guys in decades, Mike," I said.

"The East Germans got 'em," he shot back a tad red-faced.

As filmed, a black runner ran the first lap, then passed the baton without mishap to a white runner who passed it to another white runner who passed it, for the anchor lap, to another black runner, swiftest of them all. And the compromised casting did not hurt the team. In our commercial, they won the race handily.

As for winning this potentially huge account, the methodical client was giving their in-market sales contest a fair shake. Yea or nay, it would be months of nail biting, around the end of January, before we heard the word.

The Brass Ring

It is said that cleanliness is next to godliness. In my case, convenience takes a close second. Which made Wrigley the most divine account in my group. I could almost touch their famous building out my office window. Even lugging a black bag full of storyboards, the elapsed time to Bill Wrigley's reception area—including the fifty-yard dash across Michigan Avenue—was a matter of minutes.

But at this moment on Wrigley's behalf I am in the seventh hour of a thirteen-hour flight to New Zealand. My travel companion is an agency elder, Jim Fasules, account director on the Wrigley business, a loquacious Greek-American, a sweet guy and close friend of both Blair Vedder and Paul Harper, chairman of Needham Harper & Steers.

Neither Jim nor I planned or needed to be doing this. The Spearmint shoot down there was way over our heads—literally. There were two spots in the package, both taking full advantage of the incredibly diverse New Zealand scenery, both starring a photogenic and (hopefully) skilled hang glider pilot. In the first, we'd open with him perched on a snowy ridge near the summit of Mt. Cook. A few days later, and only fifty helicopter miles away, he'd be airlifted onto one of the verdant peaks forming the fjord at Milford Sound. From both lofty locations, he follows the same scenario:

Close up of young man wearing helmet.
Unwraps stick of Spearmint and inserts gum in mouth.
Puts wrapper and foil in vest pocket
(an environmentally-conscious step requested by Mr. Bill himself).
Camera zooms back to reveal magnificent background
as pilot soars off on seemingly endless flight.
Air-to-air shot of hang glider moving left to right.
Red glider sail strapped to pilot's back
dissolves into red arrow on Spearmint pack.
Announcer: The flavor lasts a long, long time.

The harrowing logistics were in the capable hands of a documentary film crew known for their derring-do productions, and was being covered by the campaign's creators, Gary Yoshida and Dexter Poole, one of Needham's and my brightest young teams. (Gary was a particular favorite of mine, easily the most talented—and taciturn—art director I've ever known. He would sit through an agency rehearsal without uttering a word then, in the ensuing client meeting, present in a confident, low-key way one of his brilliant storyboards, his sphinx-like mystique utterly mesmerizing them. Once, on a shoot in Hawaii with a free morning to kill, we decided to visit the memorial at Pearl Harbor. Black and white photographs lined the walls of the waiting area. Along with the expected shots of the fleet's destruction, I was surprised to see on display a group of photos taken at the notorious California internment camps. Gary stared at them without comment. Finally I asked if he knew of anyone in those camps. "My parents and older brother. They spent three years in there," he stoically answered pointing at one of the photos. The line moved forward.)

As for this trip, the truth is I talked Fasules into taking it at the last minute. We would get to the South Island just in time to stand around on a creaking glacier watching the action on Mt. Cook—the same place Hillary chose to rehearse his storied ascent of Everest—via high-powered binoculars. That would be the extent of our contribution.

I did not seek travel approval from Keith or Jack. Jim's initials were enough to authorize the pricey airfares. I did slip a note under Keith's office door explaining my sudden departure, something along the borrowed lines of "Why am I going? Because it's there." On reading it the next morning, he would know as well as I did that that was not the case.

⁂

WE'D BEEN ON A ROLL. *AdAge* had recently named Needham "Agency of the Year." Business was booming on all fronts and we'd heard enough scuttlebutt concerning early sales results out of St. Louis to feel even more optimistic about landing Budweiser Light. (D'Arcy, we learned, had even tried to replace in midstream the lead singer in their commercials with our guy. He turned them down.) Because Needham's employee count had grown with the increased billings, we were running out of space. A move was in the offing to larger quarters in a high-rise just completed across the river.

One evening, out of the blue, my wife told me she'd like to see the new offices, something I hadn't had time even to think about. Okay, I said, maybe we can go this weekend when the construction crews won't be working. The office manager made the arrangements for Sunday morning. A guard would give us hardhats and escort us to the Needham floors. She lent me a copy of her space planner's schematic to help us find our way.

Stepping around stacks of virgin drywall, I took Lillian to the northwest corner of the creative department where I knew my new office was located. Blue tape on the concrete floor delineated how much of the corner would be mine. Sizable, I thought, and the panorama—framed to the west by the new Sears Tower and to the north by the crisscrossed beams of the Hancock Building—was even more spectacular than what I currently enjoyed. From here, the sunsets would not be too shabby. (Oops! Sorry August.) Lillian seemed duly impressed.

On the southeast corner of the floor plan she saw Hochberg's name. "Let's check out Joel's view," she said really enjoying everything about this first-hand peek.

We made our way through the construction detritus to the opposite end of the 24th floor. He, too, had a magnificent vista: Grant Park, the lake, and gleaming white off in the distance, the Field Museum, Adler Planetarium and Shedd Aquarium.

I wondered if my wife noticed what I did—the blue tape indicating Joel's corridor wall. It was twice the length of mine. "Doesn't it look like his office is a lot bigger?" She had an eye for that sort of thing. "They probably just forgot to lay down the tape for the wall separating his office from his next door neighbor's," I said, suspecting something very different and feeling a knot suddenly form in my intestinal tract.

⁂

I called on Keith first thing Monday morning. He knew we'd toured the new building.

"What'd you think?" he asked somewhat cautiously.

"I think there's something you haven't told me, Keith."

Then came the news he said he'd been reticent to reveal: that concurrent with the office move, he would attain his goal; that thanks to the help of people like me he would be named president of the Chicago office; that Joel would replace him as chief creative officer. Ka-boom!

I interrupted. "What's wrong with the way it is? Joel oversees half the accounts, I the other half. We still report to you."

There had to be someone at the top of the creative pyramid, the spokesman for our product, he explained. The agency would bring in a new group creative director to take on Joel's accounts.

Joel had become a friend of mine. He is to this day. We had our separate silos at the agency and had functioned collegially without the backstabbing infamous at other agencies where multiple groups vied for creative kudos like, say, down the street at Leo Burnett. Still, was there an unspoken competitiveness between our creative groups? And between Joel and me? Of course. Did Hemingway love everything Faulkner wrote? Did Braque swoon over every Picasso painting? It might have been the client cards I'd been dealt but I knew for certain the work coming out of my group was the agency's best. And my staff knew that as well.

"Okay, Keith. Why Joel?"

Like a scout, Keith was always prepared. I'd seen him at a loss for words only once. I happened to be chatting with him and his new wife Rose-Lee at a Needham Christmas party when an inebriated woman who worked in the mailroom wobbled over to confront the two of them. I knew her, a fellow Southsider; she liked me; I was not a target.

"Well if it isn't the Prince and Princess of Needham, Harper and Steers," she slurred quite loudly. "I've been delivering your mail for ten years and you don't even know my fucking name." Whew, here comes another agency Christmas party casualty.

But Keith didn't blanch. He acknowledged the truth of her accusation and apologized, then calmly asked what her name was. I led her back to her lady friends.

Several weeks later, the Reinhards were hosting a cocktail party in their condo high above Water Tower Place. At one point, I needed to use the powder room. It was occupied so, requiring immediate relief, I eased into their master bedroom. On the counter next to the commode were stacks of 3x5 cards. Printed on each was a small photo of an employee along with a name and job title. Obviously Keith was putting his time in there to good use, committing to memory the names and faces of every last person in the agency.

As for "Why Joel?" he was prepared with an answer. "We all have three publics," he said ticking them off on his fingers, "our people, our top management and, most of all, our clients."

I could tell where this was going. I'd probably get the nod on the people part. Jump ball concerning top management. But clients? Joel wins for sure. He *was* far more gregarious, flat out friendlier, and more willing to cultivate business relationships outside the chalk lines of the work itself. I understood the logic but...

"No offense, Keith. It'll be tough for me running storyboards past him. For my people too."

We both knew the irony. He had wanted me to help him become president. I hadn't hurt his chances. And now this.

"Think about it, Larry. We don't move for a couple of months," he said unruffled by my badgering. "But I'm afraid that's how it has to be."

Two days later, across the aisle from Fasules, I was seeking solace in one of Air New Zealand's cuddly sheepskin-covered seats.

⁂

JIM AND I DID HAVE a bit of work to do. Right after our return, Needham was holding an intramural gathering at, of all places, the Opryland Hotel in Nashville. Every office in the company had been asked to select what they considered their best campaign of the year and show it at the meeting. Top management in Chicago had chosen another campaign created by Yoshida and Poole, the incredibly well received launch advertising for Hubba Bubba bubblegum (yes, you heard right) and Fasules and I had been tapped to present it.

Bill Wrigley was protective of his stolid Spearmint, Doublemint and Juicy Fruit brands and had misgivings about putting his family name on a lowly bubble gum even though it was a truly innovative product—the amazing bubbles, big and bulbous as they were, would not stick to a kid's face. He placed it in Amurol, their novelty gum division, under the leadership of his nephew, A.G. Atwater.

"Mr. Bill" was inherently conservative. He sported a graying crew cut and, always, short-sleeved white shirts and tie. Perhaps it was all those long-suffering years with the Cubs, but I don't recall a real laugh ever emanating from him. A.G. was his uncle's flipside, fun loving and energetic, someone who would excel through six chukkers of polo, then mellow out in a sweaty squash match.

The first time he heard it, A.G. fell in love with "Big bubbles. No troubles," the clever line Dexter and Gary conjured up for the Hubba Bubba campaign. The commercials we presented were mini-Westerns; the hero, a John Wayne lookalike called "The Gumfighter," would take on stereotypical bad guys in a bubble blowing contest shot on location at an old west theme park outside Tucson. Naturally, at the denouement of each spot, the bad guy's black mustache becomes tangled in the web of his ordinary gum's burst bubble. Meanwhile, the sly Gumfighter effortlessly peels off his Hubba Bubba as he drawls out the slogan.

The campaign was a rip-roaring success. So much so that in the midst of the first television flight, A.G., in a panic, told us their factory could not keep up with demand. We rushed a stopgap measure into production. In the commercial, townsfolk are gathered in front of the general store clamoring for their Hubba Bubba. Out steps the Gumfighter and the mousey shopkeeper to assure the crowd that more was on the way. The shopkeeper, cowering behind our fearless hero, says "Don't worry, folks. 'Spect some soon." After A.G. authorized a second shift at the gumworks, sales again soared.

On the flight back from the safe conclusion of the Spearmint shoot we wrote our Hubba Bubba script. Sticking with the Western theme, we decided to present the campaign in crossfire fashion. Jim, the account guy, would wear a black ten-gallon hat; me, the creative guy, a white Stetson. Knowing how humorous the spots were and how well they'd play in front of a large group, even adults, we figured no matter how hokey our schtick, we'd be the hit of the show. Which turned out to be the case.

I was having so much fun swapping one-liners for the script with Fasules between Air New Zealand's free-flowing martinis, I almost forgot what awaited me back in Chicago. About Keith and the management changes, Jim was not much help. Like me, he was a friend of Joel's. And, he was a Needham lifer, a survivor of purges past. Yes, he sympathized with my dilemma but he was too much the company man to stoke my recalcitrance. Aware of my personal obligations, his grandfatherly advice was just grin and bear it.

I did have Steffan in college and Jeremy about to start; and two-year-old Daniel toddling around our new townhouse in Lincoln Park financed by the first mortgage in my life.

I also had what I thought was the best job in advertising—receptive blue chip clients; a staff never at a loss for ideas; the support of Keith and Blair, two true gentlemen I deeply respected; and the likelihood we would soon win a big fat new and newsworthy beer.

Despite all that, there remained one thing I knew I did not have—the will to grin. Or to bear it.

PAUL HARPER, A SLIGHT AND somber man in his late sixties, opened the Nashville meeting with several announcements. First, in Chicago, Keith was being promoted to president and Blair would now move up to chief operating officer under Paul. He did not elaborate on other ramifications of those changes like, for instance, my fate. He also informed the audience that the corporate name was changing from Needham Harper & Steers to Needham Harper Worldwide, which was greeted with loud applause from the worldwide participants such as there were. (At the time, the agency had only four non-U.S. affiliates.)

I felt an instant empathy for the now-discarded Mr. Steers whoever he was. Only recently I'd encountered a prior victim of the agency name-change game—Mel Brorby of former Needham Louis & Brorby fame—a gentle, age-spotted octogenarian. He was visiting our offices and had tapped politely on my open door to introduce himself, really to ask a question. Did I know what had happened to the painting that used to hang outside my office? His son was the artist.

I recalled very little of the painting other than that it was in dire need of a cleaning. Some time ago it had been removed when the agency went on an art buying kick. Now outside my office hung a strange, predominantly purplish abstraction randomly embellished by tiny flashing bulbs. One of my secretary's tasks was to turn the thing off at day's end, then flip it on the next morning.

Excusing myself I went to a phone out in the bullpen to pass the problem onto Keith. "Jesus, we put that old thing in storage. Keep him occupied 'til I can have someone go find it and hang it on a wall somewhere. I'll call you back with the new location." Keith knew how to take charge of a situation. In the awkward interim, I decided to humor Mr. Brorby with a reel of our latest commercials though I'm not sure he heard or understood any of them.

Now in Nashville, from what I could see of the attention Keith commanded, particularly from the hovering overseas attendees, the new president of the Chicago office had miles yet to climb in the agency hierarchy. Charisma aside, he *was* McDonald's in the eyes of our brethren from Munich, Auckland, Melbourne and Toronto, all of whom owed much of their bottom line to Big Mac.

Keith had orchestrated the agenda for the creative presentations. He'd saved ours for last, probably to allow the other offices their moment in the limelight before Hubba Bubba blew them away.

Needham, by and large, was comprised of a lot of smart people. Most of the presenters were, alas, far more engaging and entertaining than the work they showed that day in the Opryland auditorium.

I paid special attention when the creative director of the Los Angeles office approached the rostrum to present the latest Honda advertising. He was a thin, surprisingly young Brit, a relative newcomer to Needham, who had inherited the job in L.A. when his predecessor, Bob Cox, left to work on Ford in Detroit. I was a big admirer of the Honda campaign and knew that Cox was chiefly responsible for its elegant simplicity. I silently envied this new guy. From all I'd heard Honda was a once-in-a-lifetime client.

At the microphone, Richard Kelley had the haughty airs of an Englishman. But he was obviously finding the venue unnerving perhaps because the TV he showed—and presumably had a hand in developing—broke no new ground. And his presentation style could charitably be described as halting. Haughty and halting. A deadly combination, I thought.

As George C. Scott observed about Paul Newman's prowess with a pool cue in *The Hustler*, I turned to Fasules sitting next to me and whispered, "He's a loser." Always conciliatory, Jim agreed the guy up there did seem a tad nervous. I saw much more than that; I saw a brass ring slowly arcing towards me all the way from California. "Trust me. He's in over his head. There's no way he'll survive." I can't explain it. I didn't even know Richard Kelley. But I was never more certain about anything. "When it happens, Jim, *please* give Paul and Blair the word. I want that job."

⁂

TWO WEEKS LATER, I HAD just finished helping Jeremy lug his gear up to his dorm room at Washington U. in St. Louis. Being accepted to their School of Fine Arts was a great opportunity for Jeremy. And for me. In St. Louis as much as I was, I'd be able to stay close to my artistic wild child. In lieu of driving down in my VW Rabbit—way too small for all his stuff—I'd rented a station wagon for the round trip. My plan was to tour the art school with Jeremy, share a celebration dinner, then start the all-too-familiar drive back stopping at a motel along the way.

I checked in with my secretary late that afternoon. She was glad to hear from me (no cell phones, remember?). There was an urgent message from Blair. *Blair?* In my five years at Needham, he never once had called. She transferred me to his office. He came right on and asked when I was getting back. I told him what I was doing and that I'd be in the office the day after next. "Get rid of the rental at Lambert and catch a plane tonight—on us—there are

are plenty of flights," he said all knowing. "We need to meet first thing tomorrow."

I thought Fasules might know what was going on but I was unable to reach him. Whatever it was I'd have all night to churn over it.

Checking out the art school, I could tell by Jeremy's reaction to the facilities and the student work that he was confident he would thrive here. After the tour we said our good-byes. Dinner I had to forego. Neither of us knew it at the time but it wasn't until he graduated four years later that I saw him again in St. Louis.

Salvation

Though no fault of his own, Gerry Rubin was the agency account director on my two worst nightmares—Campbell's and Dial. Working together on those "pieces of business," Gerry's term for them (mine more scatological), schlepping storyboards to Camden or Phoenix only to have them decimated by doublethink, gallows humor kept our sanity and kinship strong.

A trip to Phoenix in the dead of Chicago's winter would have been a saving grace but, for some diabolical reason, Dial's major meetings always took place in early August. Exiting the airport in our jackets and ties, we'd be whacked by a 112-degree flatiron. Inside their downtown high-rise offices, air conditioning woefully overworked, the conference room temperature stood in the high eighties. It was almost twenty years since my hellish summer at Goldblatt's, but at least there—other than Max cooling it in his warren—we were all in it together. Here, it was Rubin and I versus them and they were invigorated in their sauna. And battle ready.

We tried to bring them new ideas to push their bar of soap. No matter how clever the concept, they insisted we include their holy mantra—"twice the active deodorant ingredient as the number two brand"—deathly prose that wrung the life out of every good idea we ever had. On the way down the elevator, drenched and defeated, Gerry would whisper, "Aren't you glad you use Dial?" And I'd finish it off with "Don't you wish everyone did?"

⁂

CAMPBELL'S WAS AN ARMED CAMP in the middle of downtrodden Camden. As a food company they had strict no-smoking rules. Inexplicably, smoking was permitted only in the employee lunchroom, the ceiling in there a deep shade of tobacco tan. As the big clock on the wall approached the end of lunch hour, I'd see grown men puffing away on not one but two cigarettes between slurps of the free soup (always some new variety they were testing, the lunchroom patrons Campbell's guinea pigs).

We had two strong campaigns—"Oh, oh SpaghettiOs" and "Wow, I could've had a V-8"—which required only occasional freshening. But we were tortured by their constant search for the next new thing: chunks of chicken in a tuna-like can; umpteen versions of V-8 including F-8, an obvious fruit variation they could never get right; and, of course, unending SpaghettiO spin-offs, a myriad of gooey pasta shapes they could cram into a can of sauce to further plump up America's youth. Trying to keep the creative department's dobber up concerning Campbell's new product quest was daunting for Rubin; the wheels he had us spin invariably ground to a halt when the taste test results came in.

One trip Gerry managed to miss was to Wilkes-Barre where Campbell's produced Recipe Dog Food. Years before I joined Needham, the agency had done an admirable job advertising Recipe employing Bud Weatherwax and his famous spokesdog Lassie. But Bud was long gone and the product—a stewy concoction of meat and vegetables not loved by all dogs—was on the wane.

Accompanied by Anne Osberg, one of Rubin's account supervisors, I traveled to the factory trying to uncover interesting nuggets we might use to reinvigorate Recipe. The factory superintendent, chief chef I suppose, greeted us enthusiastically. "You're in real luck, today," he said, "we're cooking up a batch of pork liver." I flashed on the odor of that organ. My dad occasionally brought it home from his meat counter. Grandma, who, even starving, would never eat it, happened to love our dog as much as he loved pork liver. Trusting that God was looking the other way, she would open wide the kitchen windows and cook it for Lucky in a pan used only for that purpose. Still, the smell of it lingered for days.

The Recipe chef led us into a room the size of a basketball court. In the center stood a cauldron several stories high. We followed him up the encircling steel steps, an insistent hissing sound growing louder and louder, until we reached a platform near the top bristling with gauges and valves. He pressed a pedal with his foot whereupon the enormous domed lid began to open releasing a huge steamy oppressively foul-smelling cloud smack into our faces. The chef inhaled approvingly. "That's something special, huh? Five thousand pounds of pure pork liver and other good things!" he exclaimed over the din and through the noxious vapor. I grabbed onto Anne before she backflipped down the stairs.

Later, when Gerry asked how it had gone, we told him he'd missed out on something really special.

⁂

Rubin is one of those guys who sets his watch five minutes ahead. He's never late for anything. So he was already in Blair's office when, despite a restless night, I arrived promptly at nine. Blair asked me to shut the door.

He was clearly distressed and wasted no time on small talk. There was a major problem in the Los Angeles office. Richard Kelley, who we all saw in Nashville, he noted, had managed to irreparably piss off the president of American Honda. He had brought the client an estimate for a big upcoming TV production to be shot by a British director and film company. Honda, as a "guest" in America, had a firm policy—whenever possible, they worked with American suppliers. (Top brass went so far as to eschew JAL on trips back to Tokyo; they flew United.) When the president questioned the London address on the estimate, Kelley responded that this particular director was the only one in the world qualified for the job. The president said he didn't think so. Kelley replied it was too late to change, that Needham had already forwarded a $100,000 advance to lock up this genius of a director. "Very bad business decision, Mr. Kelley," is what the president reputedly said emphasizing his feelings over what Kelley blithely, maybe haughtily, had done by pounding the conference room table three times with his fist.

Rubin was shaking his head in disbelief. He had worked in the L.A. office in the early seventies and had actually led the Needham team that pitched and won the Honda business. He knew the president well and commented that fist pounding was as uncharacteristic as it was frighteningly serious.

Blair grimaced. "That's just the half of it," he said. The head account guy on Honda, who had witnessed the ominous exchange, immediately went to Brad Roberts, head of the L.A. office and like Fasules, an old friend of Paul and Blair. Perhaps Brad felt he had discovered a rising star in Richard Kelley, perhaps he was enthralled by the ascendency of the British school of advertising. Brad told the account guy that if he had to choose between Honda and Kelley, he'd stick with Kelley. It was at that point the account guy, fearing for his own job, called Harper in New York to blow the whistle. Paul in turn called Blair in Chicago who then called Rubin and—thanks no doubt to Jim Fasules—me.

"Honda's their biggest account, right?" I asked both of them.

"Absolutely," Gerry said, still incredulous over Blair's news report. "And they'll only get bigger. They're a great company."

"Listen," Blair jumped in obviously troubled. "Paul and I've known Brad for thirty years. Something, the air out there, the water, something has gotten to him. But we can't let this thing fester."

He went on to recite the imaginary script—except for Rubin's role—I had written in Nashville. Regarding Richard Kelley, I suddenly felt guilty of telepathic wish fulfillment though, in all innocence, Blair's unprompted proposal was clearly my salvation.

He told us to talk to no one other than our wives about a move to Los Angeles. He already had arranged travel and hotel rooms in New York for the next day. Assuming all was okay on the home front, the three of us would fly out in the morning and meet with Paul off-site at his apartment to work out details of the transition. *Or coup?*

⁂

GERRY AND I WENT OFF to talk things over, appropriately at a sushi place, a good distance from the office. Since his transfer back to Chicago, he had maintained friendly contacts with a number of key people at Honda. He knew the territory. In retrospect, telling Fasules "I want that job" was nakedly naïve. Had that alone happened I would have walked into the L.A. office knowing no one, an intruder, a carpetbagger. That is, had Brad made the prudent choice of Honda over Kelley. In that case, independent cuss that he was, there is little chance he would've asked for or accepted a recommended replacement for Kelley from the bosses back East. The way fate changed my script—going West now in tandem with Rubin—was a copy revision of miraculous consequence.

He was positive his return would be well received at Honda. And he thought my past experience—working on STP, Olds and Suzuki—would be viewed favorably by Honda management, gearheads one and all. The real question marks, he figured, would rise up from the insular L.A. ad community that only recently had named Brad "Leader of the Year"; and at Needham's L.A. office where Brad, the last Gerry heard, was still well liked; and specifically in the creative department, which, according to Blair, Kelley had stocked chock full of fellow Brits. And, of course, there could be unforeseeable issues with the other L.A. clients, none of whom, Gerry admitted, he knew anything about.

In short, over the last bite of silky toro, we agreed we'd be facing issues neither of us had ever had to deal with before but, powered by Honda, we could at least hit the ground running.

Personally, there remained one more question mark: my wife. Amidst all this office intrigue, I hadn't considered for a moment her feelings on the subject. She had a gaggle of friends from her Eastern days, her now-established "play groups" for Daniel, a townhouse and neighborhood she was crazy about and an entire family in Toledo just a five-hour drive away. And, to my knowledge, there wasn't an L.A. address anywhere on her Christmas card mailing list.

She knew the situation concerning Keith and Joel and had been very worried the last three months about my unwillingness to cooperate. She knew I arrived back from St. Louis a day early and that something was brewing with Blair. But I had never brought up my Nashville revelation; at the time, it was way too farfetched.

"So Lil, I'm going to New York tomorrow."

"How long?"

"Just one night."

"What's going on?"

"Rubin and I have a meeting with Paul Harper. He wants us to move to L.A."

She was speechless. I gave her the details, those I knew, with more to follow when I got back from New York.

I tried to anticipate and ameliorate her objections by overwhelming her with my side of the story: that I always assumed I'd live out my career in Chicago, a city I loved; that I had golf buddies and poker buddies and Riccardo buddies; that Stef and Jer were both now in Midwest colleges; that my parents and sister were here; but, despite all that, this was an opportunity to remain with an agency I deeply respected only now I'd be 1700 miles away with a lot more freedom and opportunity to grow. Selling so hard, I forgot to lob in the end of winters.

"Everyone's divorced out there," she said.

I reminded her that amongst our Chicago friends there had to be at least fifteen divorces.

She told me to read Daniel a book. She wanted to take a long walk around the neighborhood.

⁂

Harper's eastside co-op was as grand as he was grave. Brad Roberts was much closer to him than I'd realized and Paul was taking hard the thought of what had to happen. With us seated around his comfortable living room, he glumly said he had spoken to Brad and, when questioned about his puzzling choice, Brad pointblank reaffirmed that Kelley meant more to the L.A. office than Honda. Blair, far crustier than Paul, sat there seething over the chaos his old friend was creating for the company.

For a bloodletting, the plan Paul laid out sounded as routine as ear wax removal. On Labor Day, five days hence, Gerry and I, packed for a long stay, would fly out from Chicago and meet up with Paul at the Westwood Marquis, two blocks from the L.A. office. The next morning, the three of us would march over, and after Paul met privately with Brad, he would call for a meeting of all the employees, around fifty at the time, to introduce their two new honchos, Rubin and Postaer.

"What about Kelley?" I asked.

"I thought you could handle that while I'm in with Brad." He clearly was not eager to commit double homicide.

"Paul, other than a hand shake in Nashville, he doesn't even know me. I can't walk into his office, flash a sheriff's badge, and can him just like that!"

"I suppose you're right. But I've never dismissed a creative man. What do I say to him?"

"He understands English, Paul. I'd begin with 'You're fired.'"

"All that will take a little more time." he said apprehensively, performing surgery not included in his job description. "Maybe you and Gerry should wait down in the lobby coffee shop. I'll send someone to get you when the troops are assembled."

Then came the part Needham top management always found unseemly. "Well, I imagine you boys want to know what we have in mind so far as remuneration and titles and so forth," Paul said with a faint smile. "Gerry, why don't you come with me to my study. Blair can talk to Larry out here." Swell, I thought. I get Blair, lovingly known around Needham as the resident tightwad.

Gerry and I laughed about it later. Here we had the top two guys at one of America's most esteemed advertising agencies and—for what was likely to be the turning point in our professional lives—each scribbled out our sketchy financial details on the back of a canceled envelope.

Welcome to L.A.

My finale in Chicago, Friday, September 4, 1981.

Keith was well aware of the meeting with Harper. He beamed his congratulations. Given my last three months of intransigence, he seemed relieved, a burden lifted off both him and Joel.

We talked about something Blair had brought up in New York between scratches on the envelope: he didn't know what they had out there in the way of creative staff; I might want to ask two or three people in my group to move out with us. I sought Keith's blessing on the three I had already identified on the flight back. He was gracious and agreeable, just as he was about the one favor I asked of him: when and if we heard good news from Anheuser-Busch, would he please invite me back for the Budweiser Light victory party?

Blair, as usual, had had the right idea. In Los Angeles, Gerry would encounter his own set of problems but at least he was familiar with a number of the players. In all likelihood, I would be walking into a hostile creative department, complete strangers, many imagining an ax in my hand. It made sense that I have a few people (*moles?*) known and trusted around me.

I spoke to Helmut Dorger—a Berliner, a bachelor, a buddy and one of my best TV producers—about moving to Los Angeles. In the five years at Needham, with our far more elaborate productions,

I'd learned to appreciate the logistic and financial importance of that position. He immediately agreed.

I spoke to my old shortstop, Bob Scarpelli, then working under Susan Downs as a copy supervisor. He was tempted but after discussing the move with his wife, very close to her Italian-American family in Chicago, he regretfully declined, a decision that in the long run worked out incredibly well for him.

And I spoke to Gary Yoshida. Separating him would be gut wrenching for his partner Dexter. But given Gary's singular talent and persona, intuitively, I was sure he'd be a perfect fit as lead art director on the Honda account. Other than the fact that he was married without children, I knew nothing of his predisposition to such a life change. After huddling with his wife, he called me at home the next morning, Saturday before Labor Day, to accept. Did he have any material questions? No, he said; he knew he'd be treated fairly. I was elated.

Evidently, Brad had always run the L.A. office like his own little island. Because of his substantial contribution to Needham's bottom line, he'd been able to keep management back East at a benign remove. But the whistle-blower had dropped one other bomb on Paul—Kelley's people, at this very moment, caught up in a not-invented-here frenzy, were determinedly working to fix something that wasn't broken: the clean, sophisticated look and tone of Honda's magazine advertising. Blair, like me, a big fan of the Honda campaign, implored me to stop that ill-conceived effort in its tracks. Somehow I knew Yoshida's affirmative answer would be profoundly significant, immediately, and down the road.

It was late Friday before the Labor Day weekend. The office had been let out early. My door closed, I was packing up the Royal and other effects in the cartons Mailroom Mary had just delivered personally. The move to Los Angeles would remain hush-hush until next Tuesday. I'd save the good-byes to my staff for my first trip back a few weeks hence.

Lil and I were invited up for dinner at the Rubins' sprawling old home in Evanston that Saturday night. My relationship with Gerry had been all business. Being thrown together now in a new and distant venture, we both thought our wives needed to meet. Though they were born on two different planets—Shanghai and Cincinnati—they got on fine. Bobbie's comments about the easy lifestyle, bountiful produce, nonexistent mosquitoes, et cetera, helped soften Lil to the idea of Los Angeles. She recommended a savvy real estate agent and suggested several likely house-hunting areas not far from the Westwood office.

Gerry had seen a glimpse of Yoshida's talent through his ingenious, albeit aborted, work on Campbell's new product assignments. He was as gratified as I to hear that Gary would shortly follow us out to Los Angeles.

SWS and now Needham/Chicago; in both cases I was gracefully exiting an untenable situation. SWS had been the tougher emotional pill. I had almost three times the tenure there and had made a measurably greater contribution. Needham was Keith's show. I understood that the first day we met. So this time there was no cause for melancholy. In front of me, courtesy of Needham, stood a large canvas mine to paint. I hoped I wouldn't make a mess of it.

⁂

THE BEWILDERED LOS ANGELES OFFICE staff had responded to the receptionist's p.a. request to immediately meet in the lobby, a jury-rigged assembly hall. Harper, Rubin and I entered from a side corridor. Some recognized Paul, many remembered Gerry, not a soul knew me.

It had to be the most uncomfortable ten minutes in Harper's life as he explained away both Brad Roberts, who had opened the L.A. office sixteen years earlier, and Richard Kelley, Brad's fair-haired protégé.

A few of the more courageous had taken the available chairs in the reception area; the remainder and the late arrivals stood behind them, the farther away from us, it seemed, the better. Their nervous coughs and shifting feet punctuated Paul's soliloquy. He did not recite a list of particulars, sticking instead to corporatese: "my dear friend Brad," "irreconcilable differences," "we'll carry on," "a bigger and better Los Angeles presence." I don't remember whether Gerry chimed in. I know I didn't. I just wanted this awkwardness to end.

When it did, Gerry and I briefly met with the "whistleblower," Bob Welch, a short, white-haired pugnacious guy I sized up as a handful. It turned out Paul's speech wasn't exactly what Welch wanted to hear. He had assumed he, not Rubin, who had actually reported to Welch on his first tour in L.A., would be anointed to Brad's job. For the moment, he kept his disappointment to himself, welcomed me cordially, suggested I look at the questionable ad layouts with him the next day and, oh yeah, Kelley has a company car that I ought to get my hands on—a limited edition Accord loaded with bells and whistles.

We three interlopers walked back to the hotel to sum up the morning over lunch before Paul headed out for New York. He told us he had offered Brad a face-saving position in corporate development that Brad refused, a response Paul no doubt had hoped for. As quoted in *AdAge*'s rather unwelcoming coverage of the "shakeup" at Needham/West, Roberts "perceived corporate development as so much eyewash." Very perceptive.

As for Kelley, Paul was impressed with that "fine young man," so much so he had munificently and unilaterally upped Kelley's intended severance package from six months to a full year. (I harked back to the financial portion of the meeting in Paul's apartment where I had drawn the short straw—Blair.) And he mentioned that Kelley had asked to keep his company car. Harper, who hadn't sat in the front seat of *any* car in years, readily agreed to what he considered a trivial request. "We can't do that, Paul," I interrupted.

"Welch told me it's just one of a few and needs to stay in the Honda family. Call a repo man or whatever and give him something else, but I get to drive that one." Welch, car guy to the core, hadn't thought to warn me—that contested Accord had a stick shift, a feature my left leg learned to hate (or loathe?) every time I clutched my way down to Honda on the jam-packed 405.

Another inheritance from Kelley was Harmony, his secretary. The next morning, the attractive young lady was waiting to escort me down to his former office. It was obvious yesterday's coup had shaken her. She showed me around the room, pitch black from carpet to ceiling (interior design by its twice removed occupant, the minimalist Bob Cox) but her heart wasn't in it. A few cool days passed between us before she informed me she had accepted a new job; nothing personal, she just felt too close to Kelley. I thought that was probably for the better since a number of Kelley's corps, no doubt more of her chums, would soon be relieved of duty and she'd be even more despondent.

A week later while I was in the midst of interviewing candidates to replace her—surprise!—Harmony called. Could she have her job back? What happened? I asked. Her new agency doesn't pay parking, she said matter-of-factly. Welcome to L.A. But how could I not reward such guilelessness? Harmony, come home. Parking's on us.

⁂

MY FIRST FULL DAY ON the job, I stopped by Welch's office. He pointed to a pile of Honda magazine layouts sitting on his conference table, what Kelley had been calling "the new look," he said. Along with some others still in the works, they were scheduled for presentation that coming Friday, the same day Gerry planned to introduce me to the key players down at Honda.

In a word, the new look was atrocious. The classically understated Caslon typeface had been broomed in favor of a blunt and clunky font I'd never seen before. It didn't matter what the headlines and copy said, the heavy-handed typography overwhelmed any meaning. Aesthetics aside, Welch said there was another problem. The typeface was owned by a British firm. For the agency to use it, every word would have to be set exclusively by them in London—in those pre-Internet days, an absurdly impractical and costly step. I rolled the layouts up and told Welch not to worry. The ads would be altered (Yoshida was arriving the following Monday) but we would have to put off the client presentation for a week or so. He thought I could easily get an extension when I met the clients on Friday.

The layouts under my arm, I headed down to the creative floor intending to personally introduce myself to the staff as I made my way to the black-on-black corner office. It was nearly ten but you could roll a bowling ball down the aisle so few people were present. Either they all were out on productions or the H.M.S. *Kelley* was a very loose ship. I did spot one emaciated soul leaning over his drawing board. Even from the hallway I could see the hideous-looking headline he was hand rendering onto still another "new look" layout.

He wasn't Kelley's British art director lieutenant, Paul Walter, who, according to Harmony, was out of town on a shoot. But he was one of them, apparent when we said hello.

I asked him what the thinking was regarding this new typeface. He flipped his hair back and said *they* all agreed Honda needed a facelift (the look Cox had created was all of three years old!). And that at a recent test drive of the latest Accord, there was this "chunk" when *they* shut the car's door, a solid sound *they* felt the new font aptly reflected.

He spoke with such conviction in that authoritative Brit manner, I could almost imagine a client buying into it. That could not happen! Graphic onomatopoeia? Perhaps. But in no way did it say Honda. I left him at his drawing board though I knew, among others, he, and that cockamamie typeface, were goners.

FROM FIRST IMPRESSION—THEIR LOW-SLUNG NONDESCRIPT headquarters mired in the industrial section of Gardena, itself a third-tier suburb—no one could envision that Honda, in less than a decade, would be acknowledged as one of America's most respected brands or that their flagship, the Accord, would become America's best-selling car.

Inside, the gray hallways were enlivened by post-War photos depicting the incredible rise of their founder, Soichiro Honda—a career path that made my own seem utterly insignificant. There he was working in his tiny shop attaching miniature motors onto used bicycles. Then, at his small motorcycle factory. And on to his first full-fledged auto plant. Interspersed were grainy shots of him participating at motorcycle and auto races, along with framed renditions of his inspiring quotes extolling quality control and customer satisfaction.

Gerry and I met privately with the president of American Honda, Yoshihide Munekuni and his head of marketing, Cliff Schmillen, two men who would determine my destiny in the coming years. Of course I was on guard greeting "Moon," the storied table thumper, but his wide smile immediately augured well. Cliff, a lean Oregonian in his late fifties, was as unassuming as any client I'd ever met. From his low-key demeanor you'd never suspect he controlled an advertising budget, sizable at the time, of nearly $50,000,000. While engaged in the discussion, Moon, a wiry hyperactive sort, spent much of our conversation behind his chair working on his takeaway with an imaginary golf club. Both he and Cliff were golf fanatics and as the topic turned to the game, and our handicaps (rank amateurs all), Gerry, a non-golfer, was left out of the conversation. That was fine by him—he already had their blessing. The objective of the meeting was for *me* to make the team.

Gerry did speak up concerning the reason we needed to delay the print presentation. He kept it positive. Larry and his new staff (a grand total of one—Yoshida—at the moment) wanted to put their own stamp on the advertising. I did let them know how much I admired the "We make it simple" campaign, not just the slogan but the simple honest look of the ads and that we had no intention of reinventing the wheel. They nodded approvingly.

Almost as an afterthought, Moon mentioned that Honda would be opening an assembly plant in America, in Marysville, Ohio, the next summer. They would be the first Japanese company to do so. And, for Honda, it was "just the beginning," he promised. The agency should start thinking about a corporate campaign announcing this "first." Volkswagen pioneered in Pennsylvania a few years earlier, he admitted, but their production quality remained consistently poor. Honda, he said almost mischievously, had learned from VW's mistakes—he did not reveal what those were—and he was positive the Accords coming off the line in Ohio would be the equal of those made in Japan. (VW's plant finally shut down in '88. I knew why. Back in Chicago I had purchased a Pennsylvania Rabbit and experienced nothing but aggravation. It was the last non-Honda car I've ever owned.)

We left Gardena to celebrate at a sushi place on the way back to Westwood. Not only had the people chemistry gone well but now we knew our client had made a monumental long-term commitment to America. And we, as their agency, had a mandate, a singular opportunity really, to help shape the history they intended to write.

⁂

THAT AFTERNOON, BACK IN THE office, I received a propitious phone call from St. Louis, not from my art student son—though there'd be many of those in the ensuing years—but from one of my inherited L.A. staff, a senior copywriter named Bob Coburn. He was out there on a shoot, halfway finished, a commercial called "Honda across America." From a nearby phone booth he said they were patiently waiting for "magic hour," actually a few precious minutes, when the sun's position would bring a bewitching glow to Saarinen's graceful arch, which, in the shot, was framed to halo over an Accord parked in the foreground.

Coburn had been accompanied on the cross-country shoot by Paul Walter, Kelley's right-hand man. The day prior I'd left a message for Walter at his hotel requesting that he leave the shoot and fly back to meet with me. The receptionist said he was already here waiting in his office. Undoubtedly he'd spoken to Kelley. There could be no mystery about the nature of our meeting.

But Coburn was a different story. Welch had given me a brief and positive rundown—he was a real talent, Cox's last hire, and not party to the British invasion.

In his mellifluous Virginia accent, Coburn filled in the rest. He hoped I hadn't made any hasty decisions concerning him. (I had not.) He said he only knew the Brits by osmosis and had no "i-de-ah" how Kelley had gotten his job.

(At that moment, the local trade press did not share Coburn's jaundiced opinion. In an article headlined "Resignations Rock Needham/West," *AdWeek* said "Kelley, 28, was the youngest creative director at a major agency in the local ad community. [Where'd I hear that before?] His creative contributions to Needham have been hailed by all of its clients." Not quite. But precisely the sort of reception Rubin had worried we'd encounter from the insular West Coast community.)

To make certain I did nothing rash, Coburn went on to let me know he had worked on VW at DDB in New York, had won all kinds of awards and was a "damn good copywriter." The latter, I soon discovered, was a colossal understatement.

Given the circumstances, my meeting with Walter was anticlimactic. Extremely loyal to Kelley, he did try to defend the improvements they were making to the "Honda look." But he understood my position. He willingly resigned and said he'd clear out by the end of September. Blair would've been proud of me. I offered Walter nothing close to Kelley's severance package.

Meanwhile, Yoshida was arriving Monday. Until all the Brits departed, we decided he should hole up at his hotel. From there, he could rework their ill-advised magazine layouts without the distraction of corridor sniping. He asked if he could lob in some new ideas. Absolutely, I said.

When I'd swing by his hotel room to keep him company and check on his progress, he was clearly doing everything I'd hoped for. Working with some of Kelley's headlines—mostly word plays on "simple"—he had brought back the uncluttered Zen-like look that had set Honda's advertising apart from the glitzy stuff out of Detroit.

But he had gone further. Among his pile of new concepts, one blew me away. He had taken opportunistic advantage of the unpopular 55 mph national speed limit initiated during the Nixon years. Filling the left-hand page of the spread was a photo of the ubiquitous speed limit sign. On the bottom of the right-hand page was a simple profile shot of a new Civic hatchback that happened to achieve a remarkable 55 miles per gallon. Above the car, in the classic Caslon typeface, Yoshida, an art director by trade, had nailed the premise with a perfect set of words:

"We just brought our gas mileage up to speed."

At that moment I was certain Gary would have a major impact on the agency's future.

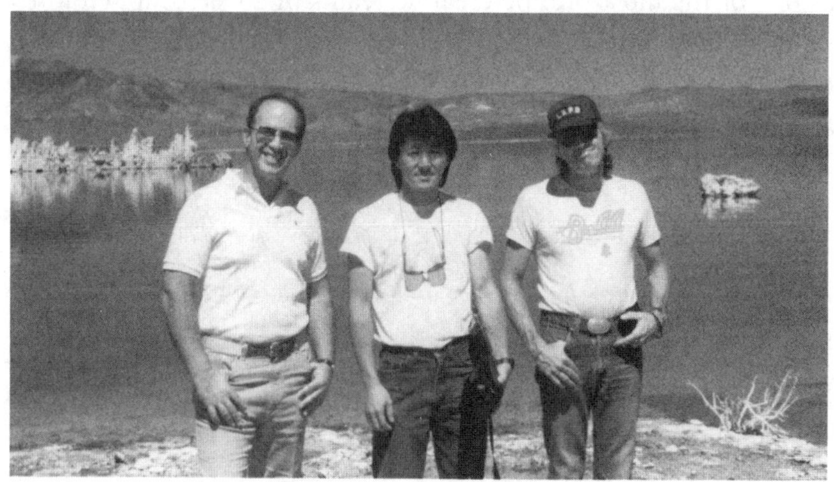

On a shoot near Mono Lake, California, with the brilliant creative team of Gary Yoshida and Bob Coburn, 1987

Ten days later, when Coburn returned from the lengthy shoot, I, like a marriage broker, introduced the two of them. There were uncanny similarities. Both were soft spoken. Both wore their hair to the shoulder, Gary's jet black, Bob's evolving to silver. Both were wearing lean black jeans and white tee shirts. Both were shod in identical K-Swiss classic white tennies. It was as if they'd called each other that morning to coordinate wardrobes.

There was no effusive backslapping between them. But in their own way, they appeared to hit it off. I rearranged office assignments so they could be cheek to jowl. While their offices were just steps from mine over the years I made it a practice to never intrude on their reverie unless asked. On those occasions they'd want me to sift through a stack of "i-de-ahs" for a current project and pick a few from the litter, for me a daunting yet exhilarating task. Almost never was there a runt in the pile. I'd tell them to save the rejects; with slight modifications, we'd likely find a home for them later.

Over the next fifteen years this symbiotic force—a sixth-generation Virginian and a Nisei from Chicago—continued to hit it off, winning award after award and gaining national recognition as one of the most prolific creative teams in advertising. From the first time they hunkered down over an assignment in either of their cave-like offices, shades drawn and lights dimmed, they became and remained, without question, our agency's greatest asset.

Another country heard from—Paul Walter's farewell memo, short and bittersweet:

"In 1776 the Americans won an important battle
and gained their independence.
In 1981 the Americans won another battle
and an Englishman gained his independence."

He kissed it off by inviting the entire creative department to a nearby pub for a drink after work that day. As clever as his parting shot was and as gracious as his offer seemed to be, I figured the darts, fueled by alcohol, might have my name on them. I took a pass on his offer of détente.

⁂

On a fine warm late January day, five months after leaving Chicago, the winters there a fading memory, Coburn and I were having lunch at an outdoor café a block from the office when the hostess, a budding starlet-to-be, came out to tell me Harmony was on the phone with urgent news.

Harmony: "Keith is on the line. I'll transfer him over."

Keith: "We got it, Larry! Budweiser Light. We got it."

Me: "Wow!"

Keith: "The celebration's tonight. We rented the ballroom at the Marriott. You're on the American 2:10 flight. And booked at the hotel. Just go as you are out to LAX. There'll be a town car waiting for you at O'Hare. We'll have a toothbrush and stuff in your room. You should be here by 9:00 and the party, I guarantee, will still be going strong."

He had kept his word.

And I did as I was told. Coburn gave me a congratulatory handshake before I rushed from the restaurant sticking him with the check.

It happened we'd had a client meeting that morning so I *was* wearing a light sport jacket over my usual L.A. get-up: an open-collared shirt and khakis. But in his exuberance and unflagging remembrance of a promise, Keith had failed to mention the predicted weather for Chicago that night: fifteen below; wind chill minus thirty.

When I pushed the exit door at O'Hare I thought my bare hand would freeze to the icy metal. Racing to the car, no more than a hundred yards away, my voice literally vanished, gone with the

Arctic wind. The driver's attempt at friendly Chicago conversation quickly became a mute point.

At the back of the packed ballroom, I rasped away the reason for my silent hugs and handshakes. Keith, at the podium, noticed my late arrival as he wrapped up his jubilant speech by recognizing all those who had contributed to this agency-altering* win. He asked me to come up and say a few words. I waved him off certain he thought—until we tried to converse later—my share of humility had spurted some in the sunshine of Los Angeles.

* Bud Light (née Budweiser Light) became the flagship account for Needham (now DDB), their Super Bowl commercials perennial favorites for the past twenty years. And whatever concerns Anheuser-Busch had about the potential cannibalization of "Big Red" by its skinny little brother have more than been realized. Today, Bud Light, not Budweiser, is America's best-selling brand of beer.

Short Takes

SHOCK NUMBER ONE: A NICE HOME IN LOS ANGELES—DECENT SIZE, good schools and, of course, convenient location—costs more than twice what we hoped to recoup from our comparable place in Chicago.

SHOCK NUMBER TWO: MORTGAGE RATES in the fall of 1981 are in the 14% range, two and a half times the interest we'd been doling out in Chicago.

SHOCK NUMBER THREE: L.A.'S CITY fathers, all no doubt ensconced at private clubs, found no place in their Westside plans for a public golf course. The closest, across from Fox Studios and six miles away, was Rancho Park, where more rounds are played each year than anywhere else in the world. The one Saturday I moseyed over there I was given a number and told I'd have plenty of time to warm up—a minimum of three hours.

None of these shockers had been taken into account on the back of Blair's envelope.

After several weekends alone with the real estate agent and one trip out for my wife, we quickly settled on a new Spanish-style house nestled in a cul-de-sac in artsy Santa Monica Canyon, across from reputedly the best public grade school in the city, a few minutes' walk from the beach and a fifteen-minute drive to the office. Peering down in full view was David Hockney's glistening white aerie perched atop the canyon wall. And, as we were told, one of my favorites, Richard Diebenkorn, lived and painted just up the road.

It was all picture perfect. Except for the math. Noodling the numbers I realized paradise came at a price. The house, the insane mortgage rate, real estate taxes, even something scary called earthquake insurance, all in, equaled a monthly nut for us five times higher than back in good old Chicago. And I still had no place to go whack a golf ball.

I sent a plaintive memo to both Paul and Blair. Attached to it was a photo of the house so they'd know we weren't talking mansion here. Gentlemen that they were, their response was prompt and fair on all fronts—a separate monthly check to cover the cost-of-living differential and approval of a country club membership.

Paradise found.

THE AFTERSHOCK OF THE OFFICE purge had passed. To my pleasant surprise the surviving creative cadre hired during past regimes was talented and highly professional. There'd be a few holes to fill but time enough to move rationally on those openings.

Moon and Cliff were more than pleased with the stack of ads Yoshida and I presented to them. Moon tried a little Japanese on Gary but found quickly that among his apparent skills, the mother tongue wasn't one of them. Still, we were off and running on the agency's premier account.

Just weeks into the flow, we were asked to pitch KABC radio, the top-rated talk station in Southern California. I gave the assignment to David Morgenstern, a contemplative, beard-scratching writer and his art director partner, a young lady with an improbably appropriate name: Holly Hood.

Their concept would feature the station's faceless on-air personalities, bringing them to life via tongue-in-cheek television commercials.

The station manager, George Green, a short, energetic man well known around town for his feisty three-minute editorials, took a particular shine to the spots for Dr. Toni Grant, their advice-giving pop psychologist. Her two-hour program ran midday, not in the lucrative drive-time slots, and boosting her ratings would be a boon for the station.

Since so many of the phone calls Dr. Grant fielded centered around questions of romance gone awry, the idea was to film her answering such calls, not in studio, but from a stagey boudoir set replete with silk and satin furnishings, a love seat in lavender, walls draped in lilac. Even her phone was campy, an old-fashioned candlestick model spray-painted pink.

Today, charitably, Grant would be called a "cougar." Then, in my eyes (I attended the shoot to hold George's hand), she was a middle-aged woman in denial, her thin upturned nose and implanted bosom likely sculpted at Cedars-Sinai. A classic prima donna, off camera she was demanding and petulant; in short, difficult.

She had dismissed our producer Carolyn Roughsedge's request for her dimensions so a wardrobe could be assembled. She said she would bring her own things, an assortment of satin tops and flouncy slacks we could alternate in the three commercials we planned to film that day.

After a prolonged session in make-up, she made her grand entrance onto the chilly set. The second she plopped down on the settee, I knew we were facing an issue with network clearance despite the fact the spots would run exclusively on their sister station, KABC-TV.

To put it bluntly, *sans* bra, her nipples bored into the satin like bullets. *How proud would Jerry Stern be of my latent prudery?*

I took David, Holly, George and Carolyn aside to point out the problem. George, Grant's boss, agreed but refused to confront his star on so touchy a subject. We nominated Carolyn, a no-nonsense woman of imposing stature, to relay our concern to Grant, who appeared annoyed by our secretive huddle.

Carolyn dutifully did as asked, then came back to report that Dr. Grant, now glaring my way, had given the standard pyscho-babble response: "It was my problem, not hers."

At that point, I walked over and, discreetly and diplomatically, told her she needed to go back to the dressing room and apply Band-Aids or whatever. If she couldn't bring herself to do that, we would have to cut bait and close down the shoot since there was no way her commercials would be accepted for airing on television. Meanwhile, George was staring at the ceiling full of interesting stage lights.

With that, she slid off the settee and pouted her way to the dressing room. In time, she came back out prim and proper and performed like a trooper.

When we wrapped, she hurried off to the waiting limo we had provided, thanking no one, but telling Carolyn to have all her wardrobe sent up to her Hollywood Hills address as soon as possible.

Wanting no foul-ups, Carolyn drove the clothes up the hill herself.

The next morning I heard what transpired. She rang the doorbell numerous times, waiting and waiting, in her hands the hangers full of slinky revealing garments owned by Dr. Grant, the on-air shrink famous for her barbed disapprobation of callers and their tales of woe over silly untenable relationships. Finally, wrapped in a large towel and dripping wet, Dr. Grant opened the door. She was in her Jacuzzi, she explained, the day having been such an emotional drain. And then a muscular man half her age, a towel around his hips, appeared behind her. Carolyn couldn't remember whether she introduced him as Rolf or Raul, only that Dr. Grant waved him away saying that all was fine at the door and she'd be joining him back in the boiling bubbles "in just a sec."

SIX WEEKS AFTER ARRIVING IN L.A., we received a stunning company-wide memo from Keith: after eleven successful years, McDonald's, without warning or provocation, had dismissed Needham.

Financially for Chicago, this loss was not in a league, say, with a Honda leaving us, but psychically for Keith, it had to be devastating.

Clearly, he was blindsided. As he said in the memo, "The record is there. The book has been written." Seemingly that wasn't enough. The entire U.S. account was going down the street to Leo Burnett.

When I called Keith to express my condolences, his incredible optimism (while it shouldn't have) took me by surprise. First, he joked that it was all my fault; if I had stayed in Chicago it would never have happened. Not a chance. Then he vowed he would spend the rest of his born days finding ways to entice McDonald's home. I wished him luck though, given the cantankerous nature of corporate ego, I knew as well as he did that the cat never came back.

(To my amazement, seven years later, Keith's willful tenacity paid off. Mickey D rejoined the Needham fold, not every nickel, but a majority of the business. The last I looked it's still there.)

Early on, besides the Brits, other legacies of Brad Roberts needed to be addressed. Flouting Paul and Blair's reservations, Brad, in an entrepreneurial frenzy, had established several "agencies-within-the-agency." And a peculiar menagerie it was: a yellow-pages agency, a job recruitment agency, and a retail agency; all run by free-spirited women, all rather ditsy from what little I saw; and all losing money. These are the sorts of things partners are for and Rubin stepped up to the plate.

What really set him off was a pile of parking tickets that landed on his desk. Evidently, the "yellow pages lady," flitting around town trying to line up clients for her dubious service, couldn't be bothered with parking meters or the ensuing violation notices under the windshield of her company-leased car. In short order, all three of Brad's "subsidiaries" were set free to park elsewhere and survive on their own. None did.

⁂

AND THERE WERE FENCES TO mend. In that unwelcoming *AdWeek* article, the reporter had extracted quotes of surprise and concern from clients at the agency's two other sizable accounts, the corporate side of ARCO and Crocker Bank.

Only now, with the advent of Honda's miraculous navigation system, has the mystery of downtown Los Angeles revealed itself. Back then, Rubin and I drove in circles for a half-hour trying to find ARCO's headquarters, for scaled down L.A., a building as prominent as the Empire State.

Finally, high up in the plush tower, we met with the guy who told *AdWeek*, "I had no warning that this was taking place. We've always had a strong working relationship with Brad and the creative department." For us, the first words out of his mouth were "You guys have eight strikes against you." Great.

Those were the days when solar energy was something you read about in the back of *Popular Science*. But ARCO (the Atlantic-Richfield Company) was already feeling heat from environmentalists and had embarked on building a grandiose grid out in the Mojave Desert, a perfect subject for corporate advertising. I asked Morgenstern to head up a team to work on it. Conscientiously, he kept ARCO's management busy for several years with ad upon commercial their lawyers invariably killed deeming all of them overpromising.

⁂

AT CROCKER, UP IN SAN Francisco, we found a more agreeable audience. While Richard Lyster, their VP of advertising had told *AdWeek* he had nothing but the highest regard for Roberts and Kelley, he did add that he understood "the Needham people coming in from Chicago are some of the agency's finest," and that he was "looking forward to working with them." Greater.

The bank traced its roots back to Charles Crocker, one of S.F.'s railroad barons. Their base was Northern California–centric and they were intent on expanding in the south, ergo a Los Angeles ad agency. In the early seventies, before Cox or Kelley, Needham had hit one home run for them, hiring Paul Williams to write not a jingle but a theme song for the bank's commercials. What he wrote, "We've Only Just Begun," was later lyrically embellished by the Carpenters, who sang it to the top of the charts.

Other than that bygone song, Lyster said, the bank had no real cachet especially in Southern California. Over lunch in their clubby, crowded executive dining room high above Market Street with views of both the Golden Gate and Bay bridges (I noticed faint cobweb traces on the bottle of wine our waiter poured), he asked us to work on a campaign to bolster their image and awareness.

The client was right. We learned from interviews back in L.A. that even among their own customers, at best, the bank was seen as safe but stodgy. The Crocker name meant nothing. For most, the bank appealed on location alone.

I leaned on Coburn and Yoshida with the hope they could come up with a mnemonic of some kind that would give the bank a tangible identity and us a solid hook on which to hang advertising. No easy task.

In short order, they came back with two simple ideas that worked as one. First, they thought the bank should change its name—just a little. Gary set out a sheet of drawing paper, the words "Crocker Bank" centered on it. With a tinge of the dramatic, he pulled out a Pentel and lettered "The" in front of the words and kissed them off with a period. Instantly, a new strength and importance came to the name. Not just any bank—now: **The Crocker Bank.**

Then they showed me a layout illustrated by Gary, his only visual a picturesque lighthouse beaming in the night. Bob had written a mantra of sorts, commanding copy, short and poignant. He referred to the bank as a beacon, a safe haven, a guiding light—

all attributes that would motivate their employees and customers alike. It *was* The Crocker Bank. And I knew we could sell it to them.

Gary had drawn an idealized lighthouse on a rocky cliff, pristinely white, capped by gleaming windows around the lantern room, at its cylindrical base a tender's clapboard house. Now to find a real live version we could feature in advertising. One would think along California's 840 miles of coastline there'd be dozens to choose from. But plowing through available source material—travel and marine magazines, even a cocktail table book on lighthouses—only one remotely filled the bill. Its location was ideal, ten miles south of Half Moon Bay, just sixty miles from Crocker's headquarters. From the old photo though, it appeared neglected and battered. We sent Helmut up to scout the location and bring back new pictures.

He reported that it was in far worse shape than the photo we'd seen, that the revolving lens was out of commission, and that these days the only functioning light was a blinking strobe attached to the dome. The house below was now a youth hostel serving hikers traveling the Pacific Coast Highway. Helmut said the man in charge would be thrilled to make it available to us for a reasonable price. And if Crocker wanted to refurbish the property, all the better.

Now back up to San Francisco for the light show. Lyster and then his legion of superiors, to a man, were enthralled with everything we proposed. Over the next four years—until the bank was bought by Wells Fargo (perhaps the new image helped seal the deal?)—we produced dozens of commercials and print ads up there, shooting The Crocker Bank's new symbol from every conceivable angle, in the fog, in the rain, in the black of night.

The merger did cost us a showcase account, not the last time that hard business reality would befall the agency. But the lighthouse still stands, a gleaming beacon on the rocky California coast.

FULLY DEVELOPING THE CROCKER CAMPAIGN was assigned to others in the creative department. Coburn and Yoshida had re-christened a lighthouse. Now another structure, Moon's new factory, was looming just months away. Who better than those two to make something of it?

It was dead of winter in Ohio. The factory still a construction site unsuitable for filming. And we all thought panning a camera across architectural renderings would appear distant and flat.

What Bob and Gary came up with was absolutely nothing. Nothing but brilliant. An empty screen—slightly shaded in gray to appease the networks' aversion to empty screens—was what one saw for the first twenty-seven seconds. At the very end, on a musical cue, the Honda logo dissolves up through the gray. To make perfect sense of all this nothingness, Burgess Meredith, in his whimsical way, teased out Coburn's words:

Introducing the 1983 Honda automobiles.
Well, they're not ready...yet.
However we're almost ready to start building
Honda Accords in America.
Right now, a new Honda automobile manufacturing
plant is going up in Marysville, Ohio
and it will be ready to build 1983 Honda Accord
4-door sedans this year.
Honda. (PAUSE)
You ain't seen nothin' yet.

In every way positive, for Honda and the agency, I hoped that last line was prophetic.

On Being Ernest

Months after the Budweiser Light news, Keith called again with more glad tidings. He said the Gallo wine business the Chicago office had recently won was proving to be a travel nightmare. Just getting to the client killed an entire day, a long flight to San Francisco followed by a two-hour drive to Modesto. If we were game, he thought he could swing the account to our office, only an hour non-stop trip on something called Aspen Airlines. No media, no account service, all they want is creative, he added reassuringly. Rubin was sitting beside me at the squawk box. When he heard the "no account service" part he gave me the high sign, all smiles.

Since arriving in L.A., I'd conducted enough interviews with job seekers—many with Gallo buried somewhere in their résumés—and heard enough horror stories to know Keith's kind offer was fraught with angst. According to an article in *AdAge* at the time, in their thirty years of advertising, Gallo had squeezed the juice out of fifteen well-regarded agencies.

Still, lodged in the brain of every adman there's an optimistic lobe, like the john who believes "surely this hooker won't charge me," a disregard of reality, a conceit that there is nothing so bad about a client a great commercial can't fix.

"I guess so, Keith," I said.

⁂

To know the E & J Gallo Winery, one first has to know where they're coming from. Were it in Texas, Modesto would be labeled a cow town. As is, it's a peach, apple and, most of all, grape town, which makes it more succinctly a company town called Gallo. Straddled to the north by Stockton and the south by Merced, it is, in other words, nowhere; secluded in the vast and verdant Central Valley surrounded by endless acres of fruit trees and grapevines, an unpublished amount of that acreage they owned outright.

At the time, the brothers Gallo appeared midway down the Fortune 500 list of the world's wealthiest people. If *Fortune* had any handle on their immensely valuable real estate, the Gallos would have leapfrogged dozens of names on that list. (Inadvertently I learned that just to produce a few of their non-grape brands like Boone's Farm and Thunderbird, they solely relied on their own 8,000 acres of apple trees, a land mass equivalent to seventy-five really spacious country clubs.)

The light shed on the town by *American Graffiti* a decade earlier had long faded. Modesto retained its insular stasis. You discovered at any bar in town, you were "from around here" or you were not, and after another bad meeting and still in your telltale shirt and tie, you dared not bad-mouth Gallo to a barkeep because every redneck in the joint was somehow connected by paycheck to the company and took whatever you said personally.

If one combines small-town suspicion of the outside world with Italian gravitas—tight-lipped business practices and loyalty to family—one begins to understand Ernest Gallo, president and reigning monarch over sales and marketing. (His brother Julio, whom I never met, ran production. He single-handedly established the price of California wine grapes. Independent growers were at his mercy. What he was willing to pay per ton in any given year became the prevailing price for the entire industry.)

Our meetings took place in a conference room down the hall from Ernest's corner office. The bank of windows in the modest-sized room looked out at the peacocks strolling the immaculate grounds of their headquarters. To stay in touch with the nature of their business, just beyond the lawns stood rows of giant holding tanks, like those at an oil refinery, except spotless and bright white, and glaring in the sun.

Despite the townsfolk's casual preference for tee shirts and blue jeans, Ernest was an immaculate dresser, pinstriped tailored suits, white shirts, conservative ties. His office staff wisely followed suit, albeit off the rack at Sears.

And he demanded promptness. Always, when we were led into the room, he and his entourage were already seated. (Where else did they have to go?) Ernest sat at the middle of the rectangular table, his back to the windows. To his right was son David, a nervous, crankily impulsive man in his forties fidgeting with his tie or his pencils. To his left, a few years younger than Ernest, who was in his mid-seventies at the time, sat Albion Fenderson, the titular head of marketing, in reality, Ernest's yes-man. Depending on the wine under discussion, five or six others, brand managers, research guys and whoever, had taken their places further along the table and around the two short sides. The agency guy—the outsider—was asked to sit alone directly across from Ernest, which put the blinding storage tanks smack in the agency guy's eyes.

Keith had warned me to go easy on the presentation intros; he, a commanding presenter, had been chastised by Ernest for lecturing too much. Besides being impatient and hard of hearing, Ernest had heard it all before anyhow. He knew it when he saw it, Keith said.

The meetings followed a highly predictable format:

- Ernest recognizes the agency guy's presence with a nod, then asks, "What have we got today?"
- A brand manager answers, "The agency has some ideas for (brand name goes here). The obsequious brand manager

never mentions that he has seen the ideas and approved them for presentation.

- Agency guy hauls out the storyboards and goes through the pretty pictures and reads the words without laying it on too thick.
- Ernest then starts around the room, putting each of his minions on the spot by asking their opinion of what they just saw and heard. Like weather vanes in a dead calm their responses, including the brand manager's, are noncommittal.
- Second to last, it is David Gallo's turn in the barrel. He sets down the object, often a paperclip, he'd been poking in his ear or, curiously, his eye and says, "I don't see anything here, Dad."
- Finally Ernest, pushing back his chair and rising to exit, says, "Well, I think the agency needs to listen better." Providing no insight or direction, then—or anytime previous—he leaves us all guessing.

⁂

We were paid a respectable fee of $75,000 per month to provide fodder for the Gallo gulag on brands like Andre Champagne and several new product concepts. Fortunately, one of our assignments was handled outside the purview of the formal meetings. All we had to do was write scripts, no storyboards necessary, for their long-running Carlo Rossi campaign. Each commercial featured none other than Carlo himself. I'd send Ernest a sheaf of scripts, he'd pick out a few, and I would then go up to Livingston, an industrialized grape-growing region south of Modesto owned in large part by Gallo, and direct the spots, which were always shot out in the vineyards.

Creatively, not my finest hour. But I liked Carlo, an unassuming carefree guy anyone would love as an uncle. One day on

On a break in the Gallo vineyards, with the star of commercial, the venerable Carlo Rossi, 1983

a mid-summer shoot when the vines behind us were just beginning to bear fruit, I asked Carlo what variety of grapes they were. "Hell," he said in his high raspy voice, "what do I know? I'm just a truck dispatcher." Which was true. Carlo worked for the company, related somehow through marriage to the Gallo family. Ernest thought Carlo's name held some magic and paid him a pittance to use it and his likeness on the label of a low-end jug wine, the "two-buck Chuck" of its day. Though he raked in the profits, I think Ernest—with delusions of grandeur for his corked and pricier brands—never got over the fact that Carlo Rossi, devoid of the Gallo imprimatur, was the second best-selling wine in America.

THERE WERE TWO SIDES TO Ernest Gallo. At work, he could become angry and vindictive. Albion's son was given a job as brand manager on Thunderbird, a cheap wine favored in ethnic neighborhoods. I happened to be up there the day Ernest learned through the grape vine that the young man, probably for good reason, was talking to a competitor. While he was out on the job interview that lunch hour, Ernest, without so much as a confrontational word, had the lock on the hapless guy's office door changed. With that, his right-hand man's son was *finito*.

Off campus, he could be a genial host. He invited me for dinner one night. His home was hard to find, he said. I was told to follow behind him and his anonymous twelve-year-old Cadillac.

He was right. I never would have found it, a long, oversized bungalow off a county road, well below grade and behind a thick stand of trees.

On every commercial we did manage to produce, Ernest always had the same complaint: while they looked okay when I showed them at the office, when he saw them at home on "regular TV" they were fuzzy and out of focus. I'd lay the blame on a weak station signal. Until I was ushered into their family room for cocktails and spied the tinfoil dangling from the rabbit ears atop his Zenith.

"Ernest," I said pointing at the problem, "now I know why your picture's so fuzzy. Tell you what. As a gift, let the agency have a real antenna installed on your roof."

"I could handle that myself if I wanted to," the multi-billionaire replied.

"Your commercials would look a lot better."

"Maybe so. But then people driving by could see the thing sticking up over the trees and know there's a house down here." Fair enough.

⁂

In the dining room, grapes and vines were everywhere: embroidered around the tablecloth, engraved on the silver, fired into the china and hung on the walls as subject matter for several large thickly textured paintings.

Ernest oversaw the choice of Gallo wines, a different one for every course, all from his own private stock, none that the company sold. He let the guests do most of the talking—a writer for a food magazine, one of his distributors and me—as he soaked in word from the outside world.

His chatty, scatterbrained wife, perhaps just months away from full-bore dementia, did chime in. Somehow Mrs. Gallo got onto the topic of mixed marriages. Much to Ernest's chagrin, she revealed how unhappy she was that her son David, "through the church" she said, was about to marry a lady (unsuspecting, no doubt) from Guatemala. To try to make her feel better about it, I volunteered that my wife was Chinese and we got along just fine.

"You don't have *children*, do you?" she blurted as though that would be a crime against nature.

"Yes, Mrs. Gallo, we have a son, almost five, Daniel."

"Oh, that's too bad."

Ernest was turning red. Anger? Embarrassment? Hard to tell.

"No, not really. Matter of fact, I have a picture of him out in my car." With that, I abruptly rose and headed for the front door. I desperately wanted a cigarette anyway and there were "No Smoking" signs all over the house.

The moment I reached the driveway, out of nowhere, two goons in dark suits, each wielding a Glock, had me surrounded. Obviously, Ernest hadn't had time to wave them off with a warning of some kind.

"Whoa, fellas, I'm a guest in there," I said, holding my arms up in surrender. One of them grunted an apology. The excitement over, they drifted back into the darkness.

I took two quick puffs, then grabbed my wallet out of the briefcase in my car and re-entered the house.

"Here, Mrs. Gallo. Here's how he looks." Daniel, incidentally, with his curly black hair, was an undeniably handsome little child.

She took the small photo over to the bright light of a pole lamp, the longest one I'd ever seen, necessarily so since the ceilings in the exploded house were at least eighteen feet high.

She stared and stared before pronouncing judgment. "Oh, he's not so bad," she had to admit. Ernest looked ready to muzzle her. Instead, I thought, he should provide her a seat at his conference room table.

⁂

We'd been slaving away on a new product called Polo Brindisi, a knock-off of several sweet, light-bodied Italian imports gaining inroads with the younger partying crowd.

Back and forth I'd go to Modesto, only to suffer one rejection after another. Desperate for resolution, I brought Bob and Gary into the fray though, until then, I had shielded them from the Gallo drudgery. As usual, they came up with a solid answer, an upbeat campaign involving lots of special effects and a memorable piece of music.

The conference room crowd of ten, having not the slightest understanding of the target market for the brand, decimated the concept, David leading the assault.

Next morning back in L.A. I was at the sink shaving my beaten face. Most of the decent ideas I ever had occurred halfway through that mindless routine. Looking in the mirror, I said to myself, "I don't want to do this anymore. And I don't want my people stuck with it either."

At the office I banged out a letter to Ernest resigning the account. I showed it to Gerry who, after hearing my latest lament, was completely supportive. I carboned Keith, Blair and Paul by regular mail knowing they would receive it days after Ernest. I did not want anyone talking me out of this.

Three days later, our receptionist called. "There's a Mr. Fenderson in the lobby. He wants to see you and Gerry." I lit up to let him stew down there for a bit.

We finally met in Gerry's office. The gist of his visit: Ernest refuses to accept your resignation; he wants to meet with you today. Albion showed us the three tickets he had for a flight up to Modesto that afternoon. He asked me to bring along the Polo Brindisi storyboards.

Gerry, the consummate account guy, shrugged his shoulders. The look on his face said it all—what've we got to lose?

⁂

Albion drove us to the headquarters but only Gerry and I were taken to Ernest's spacious inner sanctum, a first for me. Ernest was gracious, more outgoing than I'd ever seen him, shaking hands and gesturing for us to join him in his sitting area.

"What's the problem?" he innocently asked, the fifteen previous ad agency murders reduced, in his mind, to nothing more than involuntary manslaughter.

"Ernest, I have sons. You have a son." I felt like a petitioner in *The Godfather*. "It's difficult to talk about another man's son but I cannot work with David." Yes, it was cowardly leaving Ernest out of the equation but he seemed so undone by my letter.

"He'll change," Ernest said. He had to know that was physiologically impossible.

He turned to Gerry. "What are we paying you a month?"

"$75,000, Ernest."

"We'll double it." Not so much as a smile.

Gerry was instantly sold; he didn't have to work for these people.

"Do you have the Brindisi commercials in that bag?" he asked me.

"Yes. Albion said to bring them."

"Good. Then let's go to the conference room. They're all waiting."

Sure enough, the gang from the last bloodbath was assembled. Except this time David got up from his chair, came around the table beaming ear to ear and then, incredibly, hugged me like a long-lost brother.

Ernest interrupted the love fest. "Today we're going to break the pattern...those are the words you Needham people talk about, right?"

(Keith would've been proud. His unwanted lecture had obviously gotten through to Ernest. "Break the pattern" was one of Needham's six tenets for creating great advertising. Paul Harper actually wrote them years earlier.)

"Larry, I want you to take David's seat next to me." I could scarcely believe my own ears. Meanwhile I know Rubin is wondering what I've been bitching about...these guys are terrific.

Then Ernest asked me to present the Polo Brindisi boards again, the ones Coburn and Yoshida had labored mightily over. We hadn't changed a thing. In fact, they hadn't left my carrying case since the last disastrous meeting. I presented them as I had before, if anything not as deftly given the surrealism swirling around me.

"Okay, now I'll break another pattern." A mild titter of appreciation from his minions for Ernest's attempt at humor. "This time, I'll speak first," he said. "I think they're great. Wouldn't change a thing. What do you guys think?"

Each man in turn echoed Ernest's positivity, David close to gushing.

He asked if I had brought the production estimate. I found it, all two million dollars' worth, at the bottom of the big black valise. He barely glanced at it and asked me where he should sign.

Then, for all in the room to hear, he told me to just go ahead and shoot the three commercials. "We won't need to approve casting or wardrobe. Use your own judgment." The spots called for a cast of twenty young urbanites. "And you don't have to bring up anything in between...rough cuts, I guess you call them. Come back when they're finished and we'll have a look then."

What he just uttered was unprecedented. In the past they beat our casting and wardrobe selections to death. Leaving there with rough cuts unscathed never happened. And Ernest signing off on an estimate without nitpicking and quibbling over every measly line item was unthinkable.

Gerry and I kept our thoughts to ourselves until Albion dropped us off at the airport. Ever the optimist, and not bearing witness to the flipside, Gerry thought the day was a triumph. I told him I felt like we just robbed a bank.

⇝⇜

BOB, GARY AND HELMUT WERE speechless. They'd given this project up for dead. I told them not to improvise the production too much, the closer we stuck to the commercials as boarded and approved, the less chance for any second-guessing up in Modesto.

The completed spots were flawless, lively and fun to watch again and again. The casting was spot on, you had to love every last performer. And the finished music tracks drove home the oddball Polo Brindisi name in a hip and hypnotic way. I was proud of what they had wrought for so difficult a client, thought the campaign would be a nice change of pace on the agency reel and couldn't wait to take them back up to Modesto.

⇝⇜

A MARKED AND SOMBER CLIMATE change hung over the conference room when I arrived to show the commercials. David didn't hug me, in fact he didn't even look me in the eye. I thought perhaps they had just finished a nasty session with their other agency.

I ran the three spots making sure the volume was turned up so that even Ernest could get with the percussive music track. Uncharacteristically, he didn't ask to see them again; he always asked to see commercials three, four, five times.

I waited before the firing squad.

At last, Ernest spoke. "I don't see anything here. Does anybody see anything here?"

Silence.

He stared me down and said, "Well, I guess that's it," then stood and walked out of the room, the others trailing behind him. Nobody said good-bye.

I left the videocassette in the machine. He'd paid dearly for it—three months of a double fee and millions in production—just to teach me a lesson: There was no quitting Ernest Gallo until he fired you.

Politics

In 1984, the California legislature, seldom wont to swing at the high hard ones, left to the voters the controversial proposition of a state lottery. In their wisdom and after a vitriolic media battle of commercials pro and con, the people spoke in favor of fun and games.

I took no interest in the contentiousness at the time. Modest gambling was in my genes, strictly small-stakes poker and the ponies. I knew enough to know the odds of winning a lottery were astronomically slim and had no intention of personally participating, that is, until an RFP thumped onto Rubin's desk, a ninety-page Request for Proposal from the newly formed California Lottery Commission.

Given the pluralism that is California, they no doubt sent the RFP to every living, breathing advertising agency in the state. It seemed like a shot as long as a lottery win itself, but Gerry felt it was worth the effort.

Long shot story short, they awarded us the business.

The selection committee, comprised of bureaucrats and gaming professionals hired to run the lottery, chose us for several reasons:

- We had the stability and financial backing of a prominent national agency;

- The clincher for the electorate was the fact that one-third of all lottery proceeds would go to California's public schools, always hurting for money, and the committee immediately took a liking to a slogan I'd suggested, "Our Schools Win, Too." (Little did I know at the time what a stretch that was);
- Lastly, they loved the logo Holly Hood had designed—a bold golden **L** inside a money-green rectangle.

We were cranking away on their first "scratch and win" game, played on those dollar cards that leave rubbery gray residue under your fingernail, when word came down from Sacramento: the Commissioners—the political appointees—who had had nothing to do with the agency selection process, finally saw our logo and were uncomfortable with it. Gerry and I would have to go up there and convince them otherwise.

I put together a primer on what constituted a great logo design, borrowing quotes from legendary figures like Saul Bass; how, for instance, a great logo can be drawn from memory by a five-year-old, Holly's strikingly simplistic graphic a perfect example.

And political animals that the five starchy commissioners were, I told them the logo would appeal to the state's major ethnic constituents; that Latinos would immediately read "*Lotteria*"; that Asians would gravitate to the green and gold wherever they saw it posted.

"It's too simple. California's a multi-faceted state."

"How 'bout including a grizzly, like on the state flag."

"Can you add a picture of Governor Deukmejian?" (This was the most ludicrous suggestion. Despite the fact each of these men owed his honorary appointment to Deukmejian, the governor had been strongly and loudly opposed to the lottery.)

After hearing out the knee-jerk California boosters, there was one trick left in my bag I thought might win them over—a rough video version of an animated ten-second commercial we literally cobbled together the night before:

Open on a simple drawing of California map
in gold against green background.
Map begins to morph.
Map forms into Lottery logo.
Announcer: Now there's even more
to love living in the Golden State.
The California Lottery begins September 1st.

Then, when the ten seconds ended, the "Ah-Hah!" moment…

"Y'know, hadn't thought about it but that gold **L** does kind'a remind me of California," the head commissioner pronounced. His four cronies agreed. Their dollar-a-year job done for the day, off they went to lunch.

⁂

THE "SCRATCHERS" WERE AN INSTANT hit. Much like my experience with condominiums, the faster the 7/11's sold out of one game, the sooner we had to come up with a commercial pushing the next game. Success was killing my staff.

Meanwhile, a vocal minority of Californians who voted against the proposition continued to question the lottery's contribution to the state's education system via editorials, town hall meetings and letter-writing campaigns. We were asked to come up with a sugar-coated TV response to the naysayers.

The spot we developed featured a prototypical principal walking the corridor of her grade school. As she talked about the additional facilities lottery funds had provided, she gestured towards a classroom now filled with computers, a reinstated art class and so on down the hallway as cute little kids scurried to and fro around her. Since we needed to produce spots in English and Spanish, we found a bilingual actress who played the principal in both versions. Interestingly, without any directorial change, speaking Spanish, her delivery and body language were far more animated.

As was the reaction to the commercials from the California Teachers Association.

The lottery had taken in two billion dollars in its first full year—one pundit called it the most successful introduction in the history of marketing—which meant the schools' cut equaled six hundred and sixty-six million dollars. Our schools win, too, right?

"Wrong!" the teacher's union vociferously cried. Considering California's public education budget then was north of thirty billion, as far as they were concerned this "win" was a drop in the bucket. By the time school administrators finished raiding the cash register, the teachers proclaimed, the lottery proceeds had no tangible impact whatsoever.

In the midst of the brouhaha, the client caved. We were told to broom both the principal and my innocently written slogan.

⁂

Honda was turning out to be a dream account. Harking back to my old boss Jerry Stern, I began to wonder when the other shoe would drop. It never did.

They were on a roll. Their venture in Ohio was producing near-perfect vehicles, made by Americans. Each model introduction was met by critical acclaim and immediate sales success. And the annual dealer conventions—obligatory events in the auto industry—and often dreaded by the ad agencies called upon to present upcoming commercials—were, for us, near ego trips. Honda dealers, growing richer by the month, would actually pat me on the back. After serving penance amongst the Gallant Men of Olds, to now have these guys actually seek me out at cocktail parties to say, "Just keep doing what you're doing," was redemption incarnate.

For all the positive results in America, Mr. Munekuni received a well-deserved promotion back to Tokyo as head of Honda's worldwide sales operations. Fearing the unknown, Gerry and I had the typical ad guys' concerns over who would be named Moon's replacement, in our minds a tough act to follow.

Tetsuo Chino was not a car guy in the usual sense, neither a gear-head nor a flamboyant sales type. He was soft spoken, conservative and cultured; rather than cars, his first love seemed to be classical music. He and his wife—always seen in an Americanized kimono—became major supporters of the Los Angeles Youth Orchestra. With just a slight nudge from Chino-san, Rubin and I, not exactly regulars on the symphony circuit, became minor contributors ourselves.

He sat in, along with Cliff Schmillen and others, to our presentation of creative for the 1984 model year. He listened patiently and nodded approvingly as I went through a hefty assortment of commercial and print ideas. Only when I showed a magazine spread for the new Civic Wagon did he raise a question. The ad, conceived by an all-girl team of Carol Ogden and Pam Cunningham, was one of my favorites: a side profile across the spread of the extremely practical though somewhat clunky vehicle accompanied by a headline above the photo that said:

"But it has a great personality."

Mr. Chino asked me to explain the meaning of those words.

Experience is having heard it all before. And while this moment was not in league with Mr. Suzuki's "nookie" question, I still could hear a freight train coming. "Well, Mr. Chino, in the States we have a tradition," I began. "Someone knows a young man and woman and thinks they might enjoy each other's company. They are, we say, 'fixed up' on what we call a 'blind date.'" The others in the room are staring at me, grinning, wondering where I'm going with this. "Similar to 'arranged' marriages in your country." (That odious comparison I wished I hadn't uttered; for all I knew, his own marriage might well have been a fix-up.) "Anyway, Mr. Chino, sometimes, well, the young woman may not be, you know...beautiful. So the person arranging the blind date reassures the man by saying 'she has a great personality.'" *Whew.*

Convoluted as my explanation was, Mr. Chino understood.

"But our designers think it *is* beautiful," he calmly said pointing at the very clever ad as the headline began to smolder.

This being my first real encounter with him and surrounded by an audience watching me squirm, I did not feel it the time or place to debate the new president of American Honda. I moved on to the next creative execution.

Overall, it was a good meeting. They bought everything save for the ad in question. As the room emptied out, Cliff held me back and shut the door.

Cliff was an anachronism. There couldn't be a half-dozen other Americans whose résumés remotely resembled his. At the time, he was white-haired and golf-tanned; a beloved and loyal lifer at a company owned by the Japanese (a fact he often cautioned me to never forget). But back in WWII, Pacific theatre, he was a young naval aviator flying combat missions out of the Philippines over targets he would not discuss. For his heroics, he was awarded the Distinguished Flying Cross and five gold stars. He didn't reveal those either. I learned about them from his wife Mary, the only "Honda wife" who attended the conventions. She had a role. Dealers often button-holed good ol' Cliff to bask in his corporate glow or, more specifically, to seek out larger car allotments, a sign of good times but a request for favoritism that would compromise his position. Mary's job was to politely extricate her husband from those awkward dealer clutches.

When I was alone with Cliff in the conference room, he volunteered to fly one more sortie. "Larry, you did the right thing not arguing with him in front of everybody. But that's a damn good ad. Leave the layout with me. I'll go talk to Mr. Chino in private. Maybe I can change his mind."

In my life no client had ever made such a gracious or—given corporate politics—courageous gesture. I shook his hand and wished him well.

Carol and Pam were in my office at the end of that day. I had just explained what had happened to their ad, holding out hope that Cliff would come through. Still they vented, this talented and testy team. I knew I was right to have turned down their earlier request to attend the meeting with Chino. I was presenting the work of several groups; if I let them go, I'd be flooded with requests from the others. And the truth was I didn't trust, in particular, Carol's badgering lack of tact around Honda's new president. Just weeks before, I had complimented a piece of copy she had written and made the mistake of telling her "she wrote like a man," a desirable trait when the subject was automotive. Of course, she took it all wrong and huffed and puffed her way out of my office.

While she and Pam fretted in free fall, the phone rang.

"Go ahead, Larry. Run the ad," Cliff said with a mischievous smile in his voice.

I put my hand over the mouthpiece and turned towards them. "Mission accomplished, ladies." They didn't get the reference but nonetheless left victorious.

⁂

ONE OF MR. MUNEKUNI'S LEGACIES was the CRX, the first Honda designed in America by Americans. An aerodynamic two-passenger hatchback with plenty of zip and great gas mileage, it was inspired by rising gas prices and Moon's own experiences negotiating L.A.'s daunting freeways. To his mind it was the perfect commuter car.

I assigned the introductory campaign to Coburn and Yoshida. A lot of creatives would have taken the easy way out, accepting the client's "commuter car" terminology at face value and then just running with it. But Bob and Gary dug deeper. They felt the term was too limiting and would turn off young people—not yet suburban commuters—who might otherwise be turned on by the car's sexy styling. So they called it "The New Car," which elevated its stature and left its purpose to the imagination. They romanced it with idyllic night footage shot not on a log-jammed freeway but on an empty and tempting road high above a glittering city and added a haunting musical score. Sales took off. Love letters poured in.

We were privy to the letters, one of which caught my eye. Written by a young woman named Rhonda Fulker, an office worker at the University of Iowa in Ames, she raved about the CRX and the mileage she was getting, so much so that now she could afford to go home more often to visit her parents, who lived in a rural town named Fonda a hundred miles northwest of Ames.

Rhonda. Honda. Fonda. The commercial could've written itself. Instead, I asked Carol and Pam to apply some topspin.

What they came up with was as American as corn-on-the-cob and apple pie. In fact, that's exactly what it was:

Open on Rhonda driving her CRX down a road
bordered by cornfields.
Burgess Meredith (voice over): This is Rhonda,
the happy owner of a Honda CRX.
Rhonda loves her Honda. It's fun to drive.
Cut to close up of Rhonda's mother pulling apple pie out of oven.
Burgess: But the people who love Rhonda's Honda most
are her mom and dad...
Cut to road sign reading "Fonda. Pop. 846"
Burgess: who live in Fonda, 100 miles away
Cut to Rhonda pulling into dirt driveway
of parents' typical farmhouse.
Dog runs from porch to greet Rhonda.
Mom comes out holding pie. She sets it out to cool
then waves at Rhonda.
Burgess: and now see a lot more of Rhonda.
Singers: Honda

Notwithstanding complaints phoned in on location from Carol and Pam about the heat and humidity and, naturally, the bugs, the endearing spot for a neat little car was a huge hit both at dealerships and with the folks in Gardena. More significant though was its underlying message firmly planting the Honda flag in the heartland of America.

⁂

On that eventful day in Harper's Park Avenue apartment my partner came out of Paul's study with a special perk—a seat on Needham's board. Which was fine by me. The L.A. office was a distant outpost, a long way from Madison Avenue. It's one thing to be out of sight and mind (i.e., freedom, as evidenced by some of Brad Roberts's odd and unilateral decisions) but it's quite another thing to be out of the loop. Having Rubin on the board gave our office a presence in New York and me a proxy pair of eyes on the big picture back there.

Gerry returned from a board meeting in August '84 and told me that Foote Cone & Belding had made an offer to purchase Needham, an offer Harper presented to the group with some enthusiasm (it was a plausible exit strategy for him given his waning years). When Keith strongly opposed the loss of independence, even threatening to quit over it, according to Rubin, Harper immediately tabled the proposal.

Playing a little dumb concerning the crosscurrents in that boardroom, I sent Paul a note to lend my support to the decision he made. In part, I wrote:

> *"Knowing our marketability as an agency and the attendant financial implications for you and Blair, your steadfast position in this regard has to be the most noble stand in the history of advertising. I will never forget what you did <u>not</u> do."*

There's something to be said for toadying up to the big boss; by return mail, I received a formal letter from Paul Harper:

> *"I am delighted to tell you that you have been elected to the Board of Directors of Needham, Harper & Steers, Inc. This reflects a desire for stronger creative representation at the top management level. The company looks forward to benefitting by your counsel for many years to come."*

He closed by inviting me to the next board meeting in New York a few months hence. It turned out to be a momentous meeting for Paul and Keith and, inadvertently, for me.

⁂

There were twelve of us seated around the conference room table. I had a nodding acquaintance with all the others including the overseas contingent so while the occasion, for me, was auspicious, I did not feel like an outsider. I even knew the drill prescribed by Robert's Rules of Order. But none of that familiarity prepared me for what soon transpired.

Minutes were handed out and unanimously approved, Foote Cone's offer mentioned merely in passing. CFO Ed Haymes, a short New Jerseyan who spoke out of one side of his mouth (and would become, in time, Rubin and Postaer's home plate umpire) gave a favorable financial report. Old business was glossed over.

Then new business. Harper cleared his throat to make a motion. No posturing. No preamble. Head down and reading off a note card, he somberly pronounced his own demise. He moved that he should retire and take on a role as Chairman Emeritus and that Keith should move up to assume his position as Chief Executive Officer.

He looked up and quietly asked, "Is there a second to the motion?"

Who knew what maneuvering went on prior to this moment among Paul, Blair and Keith, but the rest of us were dumbstruck. I looked at Gerry and across to Hochberg, others were doing the same with their compatriots. Meanwhile, absolutely no one is taking Paul's bait.

From the way people began to turn toward me, I thought perhaps there was some unwritten rule that it was the new guy's place to step up to the plate.

"A second?" Paul repeated.

I raised my arm just inches above the tabletop. "I second the motion, Paul."

"Very well, thank you," he said. "It's been moved and seconded. All in favor say 'Aye.'" And so it went.

I'd had a minor role in helping Keith reach his goal as president of the Chicago office. And now, ironically, I had just seconded his way to the very pinnacle of Needham Harper Worldwide. In my old neighborhood (so far removed from where I sat at that moment) the phrase would've been "he owes me." But that wasn't it at all. I felt the baton had passed into the right hands at the right time. And we'd all be better for it.

Nevertheless, two years later, Keith would more than pay me back.

Regrets, I've Had a Few

Old Chicago friends have often asked me what's different about living in L.A.

To brighten their outlook, I provide the following odious comparisons: Los Angeles has a downtown missing-in-action; uninspired high-rise architecture; Persian-inspired McMansions; mile upon mile of flimsy stucco apartment complexes owned by anonymous limited partnerships comprised of movie stars who have neither laid eyes on the properties nor their dismal disrepair; arms-length neighbors and an undefined sense of neighborhood; nonexistent precinct captains; interminable drugstore check-out lines where the most picayune purchase is paid for with plastic; blazing brush fire coverage but never a mortgage-burning party; and constant reminders to prepare the household for the next "Big One."

On the plus side, naturally, there's the weather, the mountains, the ocean. And, thanks to Prop. 13, an inviolate annual real estate tax of 1% of your purchase price—a very good deal especially if you've lived in your house forever and are paying, say, $300 a year, while your neighbor who just bought that overpriced fixer-upper next door will pay $15,000—but not such a good deal so far as city services are concerned when, for instance, Los Angeles has just half the number of cops Chicago has "to protect and to serve" a land mass four times Chicago's size.

L.A. does boast one thing no other city can claim: the Laker Girls. Yes, they are surrounded by a very competitive basketball team. And, yes, they're younger and more wholesome than the Dallas Cowgirls. But what is most striking about the Laker Girls is that no matter how energized and intricate their choreography, they never stop smiling. Cartwheels, back flips, whatever their moves, they always land on their feet, advertising their orthodontia. How, every season, the Lakers manage to find a fresh chorus of twenty beautiful young dancers who can retain their bright white smiles through an entire two-minute time-out (which invariably, given television's commercial demands, lasts three minutes or more) is a casting miracle.

I know of what I speak. The last time I flashed a ready and sustainable smile, I was all of three years old. It just isn't in me. And with those who equate a smile with an approachable personality, my sour puss has often put me behind the relational eight ball, a curse I've tried to overcome by revealing my inner upbeat side in more tangible ways: a turn of phrase, a *bon mot*, a wisecrack. Often as not, they've backfired.

⁂

In Chicago, I was with a group from Needham out at Quasar, a relatively new client who made tabletop television sets. On this day, we were in their laboratory being shown a new and wondrous product they wanted to advertise. A serious engineer in a lab coat was demonstrating the amazing benefits of a microwave oven: quick cooking, thawing, et cetera. Someone brought up the question of the safety of this scary-sounding contraption. The engineer assured us there were no issues; but then, as a cautious afterthought, he added "Well, I suppose if a kid stuffed a kitten inside and pushed the Start button…" That struck me funny so I blurted out, "Then he could tell his mother 'I tout I tawd a puddy cat.'" Everyone but the Lab Coat laughed.

⁂

OUT HERE IN BURBANK, MY old buddy Anne Osberg, then in a big job as head of Licensing at Disney, brought us in to develop a TV campaign for the launch of "The Princess Collection," a mash of Snow White, Sleeping Beauty and Cinderella, their three big-hitter dolls along with, of course, all the little sweethearts' (un)necessary accessories.

Anne had approved our warm fuzzy storyboards. All that remained, she said, was to run them by her boss, a guy none of us had ever met. Throughout the presentation he was as animated as my accountant; she had warned me he wouldn't know a storyboard if it smacked him in the face. Finally, he weaseled out his judgment: "I don't know. It doesn't feel like Disney."

That set me off. We only became involved with them, a notoriously difficult know-it-all client, as a favor to Anne. The commercials, though right for the audience, were saccharine and trussed up in convoluted guidelines conceived by the hypocritical networks to protect America's youth. They would not appear on our agency show reel. I couldn't believe I was now forced to defend the work.

"You're kidding. It *reeks* of Disney!" I countered.

Poor Anne winced. And her boss left the meeting never to authorize the production expenditure. Ten years later, Anne, happily long gone from Disney and still a close friend, misses no opportunity to drop "reek-bombs" on me.

⁂

BECAUSE NEEDHAM NEW YORK LOST their flagship Xerox account in late '85 (a turn of events that had tremendous repercussions the next year), Keith requested a 7% reduction in payroll across all the U.S. offices. Despite the fact we were doing well, no immunity was given to Los Angeles. Which left me with the unpleasant task of singling out five creative staffers and then laying them off (a euphemism for "You're fired").

Over time I'd learned there's no good way to do it. I at least tried to be sensitive by meeting with the chosen victims in their *own* office, not mine. That way, they'd have a chance to gather themselves privately and be spared the knowing looks of others who might see them walking forlornly from my office. And selfishly, I'd be spared a drawn-out meeting; I could exit their office at will.

On this particularly onerous morning, scythe in hand, I had paid my call on three of the unsuspecting. Only a young team, two women, remained on my hit list. I caught up with them "concepting" together in one of their offices. In a vainglorious attempt to put a cheery spin on the inevitable, I stuck my head in the doorway and uttered a hackneyed phrase, emotions aside, absolutely perfect for the occasion: "Ah, two birds with one stone!" I exclaimed.

In today's litigious work environment, that utterance would lead to mediation, arbitration and the possibility of a jury trial. Then, it led to surprise, shock and tears in that order. (I still receive Christmas cards from one of them, the copywriter. She's doing quite well for herself in Boston. And she has told me, in retrospect, they both thought the line was deftly apropos.)

Another gaffe. My old friend from Suzuki days, Jerry Thompson, then in the printing business, came to our office accompanied by two fellow Native Americans involved in a start-up casino operation. Jerry thought we might be able to help his friends with the introductory advertising.

It seemed like a stretch, the casino somewhere in Northern Wisconsin. But it was nice of Jerry to think of us so as they say out here, I "took" the meeting.

Thompson had put on a ton of weight since I'd last seen him. That brought him in line with his buddies, both around 250 pounds. All three sat across from me, each in a black suit, bolo tie and turquoise-encrusted clasp, all sporting ponytails streaked in gray. I don't know what possessed me, maybe their strangely coordinated get-ups and my recollections of Tonto, but at the tail end of our discussion, to emphasize a point, I used the expression "Honest Injun!" The moment it tumbled from my big fat mouth, I knew it was a blunder. And their synchronized flinches made that very clear.

Jerry called later that day to ask a favor: though his guys would be taking their casino business elsewhere, and he knew I meant nothing insulting, would I write them an apology. Of course, I agreed. In the note I tried to explain that I hadn't used the expression since I was a kid and, back then, it was a noble oath of truthfulness with the same respectful connotation as "Honest to God." Which was the truth. But how men so physically large, in a business so cutthroat, could have their feathers so easily ruffled (oops, there I go again) is inexplicable.

✦

THEN ALONG CAME TACO BELL. Or as friend Anne—director of the account at TracyLocke before she joined Disney—called it: Taco Hell.

The get-acquainted meeting was being held in our impressive (thanks to CFO Ed Haymes's grudging acquiescence) new and larger quarters just west of the 405 on the east edge of O.J.'s Brentwood. Others on our side of the table were excited about the possibilities but I'd been to the fast food mountain, a five-year supply of Shamrock Shakes to prove it, and wanted *nada* to do with this pretender.

There were three of them, young, dark-suited MBA's, and not a Latino in sight. After an hour of patter—how great we were; how big they wanted to be—one of them turned my way to ask, "What methodology do you employ to determine the effectiveness of the advertising you'd be presenting to us?"

It wasn't a verbal parry. It wasn't even original. I stole it from Moshe Dayan—a simple visual response he gave a journalist when asked what secret weapon his country possessed that allowed them to survive while surrounded on three sides by avowed enemies. All he did was point an index finger at his forehead behind which presumably resided his brain.

I answered Taco Bell's ponderous question the same way.

And well before email or texting or Twitter, the account of my semi-forthright finger pointing had somehow made its way to Keith's office in New York by the next morning.

"Larry, they thought you were arrogant."

"It was a conflict."

"We lost McDonald's, remember?"

"Yeah, but I know you'll get it back."

I gladly share this last gaffe with my partner. He's the one who reminded me that Burgess Meredith was coming upon his tenth year as the voice of Honda's commercials.

We loved Burgess and his uncanny ability to weave whimsy into every piece of copy he read. He made our commercials better. He gave Honda an on-air persona, a warmth and friendliness, which was the envy of every other car company out there.

And he returned the love. Each summer he would invite the entire creative department up to his Malibu beach house. He dined us and wined us from his extraordinary cellar, for him not a showy repository but rather a heavily accessed storeroom.

To celebrate Burgess' tenth anniversary, Gerry and I decided to host a small party in a private dining room at the Regency Club high above Wilshire Boulevard in Westwood. Mr. Chino, Cliff and several other Honda execs accepted the invitation.

We knew there was a feeling among the highbrow at Honda that Robert Frost's poem "The Road Not Taken" reflected the company's maverick spirit. Burgess himself was fond of the poem and agreed to read it to the group at the party.

I waited for him down in the lobby. When he arrived in the new Honda he was provided every year and his "chauffeurette" (the old gnome employed a steady stream of young and attractive lady drivers) opened the door for him and he climbed out unsteadily, I foresaw problems.

As a famous award-winning actor he was treated deferentially by the Honda people, American and Japanese, despite his obvious and mounting inebriation. I hoped he had forgotten the part about the poem but, trooper that he was, he announced at a point well into the evening that, in Honda's honor, he would now recite Frost's immortal words.

He did perform it with gusto, at least those phrases he didn't slur, stumble over or flat forget. Rubin and I looked at each other in dismay; this night we had taken the wrong road for sure.

Afterwards, Gerry escorted Burgess down to his waiting car. Meanwhile, up in the elevator lobby, Mr. Chino had his own words for me.

"Mr. Meredith too old."

"It's true he's not a young man," I said fearing the worst. "But his voice in the commercials is still very strong."

"I think he's going to die."*

I had no answer.

"If that happens in the middle of the model year, then what do we do?" he asked.

"Well, Mr. Chino, God forbid, we'd replace his voice with some other actor's. Not a problem."

"No, no, Larry, big problem. In Japanese culture you cannot do that. Those are *Mr. Meredith's* commercials. We must stop running them. We must start over with new different commercials."

And so it went. With millions of dollars of television production staring at us just months away, and despite the talent I knew a sober Burgess still had, we began that fall television season on a less traveled path, the voice of Honda now a vigorous Daniel J. Travanti.

---

* In point of fact, Burgess did die—in 1997—more than ten years after Mr. Chino's dire prediction.

The Big Bang

Egalitarian that he was, Chairman Reinhard decided board meetings were no longer the sole province of New York; he added Chicago and Los Angeles to the rotation.

It was a Saturday morning in April of '86 and we were meeting in our new offices around our sleek new bird's eye maple, mahogany-edged conference room table. CFO Ed Haymes kept fondling the bull-nosed border before him in grudging admiration of its fit and finish.

After the prerequisites prescribed in Robert's Rules, a representative from each office including Germany, Australia and New Zealand, in turn, presented to the group a foam-core board full of numbers—their current financial status and optimistic year-end guesstimates. Rubin's board, by and large courtesy of Honda's steady growth, was the most impressive of the lot. Conversely, New York's grim post-Xerox figures could not be glossed over.

There were questions for Keith and Ed concerning Xerox's impact on the agency's future. (It wasn't idle curiosity. Though Needham was not a public company, board members—along with other key people like Coburn and Yoshida—had gone into hock when offered Needham stock.) The expected answers were given: Thanks to your cooperation concerning the recent "lay-offs," we'll live to see another day; and, New York is working hard to replace the business; and, so on. There were literally hundreds of years of agency experience sitting around the table. I wondered whether anyone actually thought hard work trumped timing and good luck when it came to generating new business leads.

Finally, the meeting officially adjourned. Haymes handed out the envelopes containing each board member's modest stipend. As the collegial group gossiped and gathered up their show-and-tell materials and checked itineraries for flights from LAX, Keith, completely out of context, lobbed an announcement into the camaraderie. "Gentlemen, there will be an extraordinary board meeting next Wednesday in New York beginning at 3 p.m. Please plan accordingly." No further explanation was given. Then Keith came over to Gerry and me and asked that we join him down the hall in Rubin's office.

WHAT FOLLOWED WAS THE MOST significant fifteen minutes in my and, no doubt, Rubin's professional life.

Keith was not a fast talker. Still, it was difficult to absorb the startling news he quietly now shared with us.

The gist was this: while Keith had fought the Foote Cone offer two years earlier, something new had come up that he found far more appealing—a three-way proposition whereby BBDO would buy not only Needham's stock (at a tempting multiple) but DDB's as well; the new holding company to be called Omnicom would then meld Needham and DDB into something called DDB/Needham (which Keith would run). There was another wrinkle—a third leg made up of various smaller agencies and consulting firms currently owned by the aforementioned trio.

Keith was making Gerry and me privy to all this, he said, because we were the most impacted by all these machinations and he wanted to give us time to cogitate before the surprise board meeting in four days.

Client conflicts are the bane of any agency marriage, even those infinitely smaller in scope than this megamerger. And (to our shock) Honda was the one major casualty the Omnicom masterminds could not prevent, though Keith avowed they tried.

I thought to say something in Honda's defense but Keith was wearing that "let me finish" look.

He assured us that all parties agreed jettisoning Honda was a huge loss and that there was no other client at BBDO, DDB or Needham with more upside potential, creatively and otherwise. But there were insurmountable roadblocks to retaining it.

For one, Lee Iacocca, the bombastic head of BBDO's massive, albeit beleaguered, Chrysler account, would not countenance his agency having a connection to any Japanese nameplate no matter how removed DDB/Needham might be. (That I could understand given the ass-kicking his company was taking at the feet of Honda and Toyota.) The other conflict was even more egocentric. DDB, which had fallen on hard times, owed its lingering creative reputation* to Volkswagen. And while VW itself was on the wane at the time, the thought of giving up their historic flagship in favor of upstart Honda was, for DDB, a non-negotiable deal point. (Nonsensical, I thought, until Keith reminded me that VW was also a mainstay account in a number of DDB's overseas offices.)

Now Keith laid out our options. He drew three circles on a notepad. Inside one, he wrote "DDB/Needham." In Los Angeles, they would be comingling the Honda-less Needham office with a then somewhat larger DDB office that already had its versions of Rubin and Postaer. But they'd find a way to shoehorn in the two of us and "some" of our people. In my mind, and I'm sure Rubin's, this was not an option.

---

* Ironically, three years later DDB/Needham was at the brink of losing VW. Keith and company "saved" the account at the last moment by creating the "*Farfegnugen*" campaign. The butt of many late night TV jokes and much maligned in the advertising industry, it was neither Keith's nor DDB/Needham's finest hour. And soon thereafter, they lost Volkswagen in the U.S.

In the second circle, he wrote the name "TracyLocke," an affiliate of BBDO, the agency Anne once worked for and still the tenuous home of Taco Bell. Keith said we could run their L.A. office. They would be a major component of Omnicom's third leg and, at the time, were bereft of a top management team. I knew I had already and unknowingly killed that option and was surprised Keith had forgotten my finger-pointing episode with the Taco Bell folks. Obviously he'd been busy with bigger enchiladas.

His third circle was a new world—and our oyster. Inside it, he wrote "R and P and Honda." It was what he would do if he were us, he confided. Just get Honda on board, assume the hefty lease on these offices, pay us a reasonable r.o.i. on your other accounts for a period of time, retain your own accounting and law firms, obtain financing, take over payroll and benefits, and change the name on the door. Dumbfounded, Gerry and I kept glancing at each other while nodding our heads like robins bobbing for worms.

Now, his emphatic words of warning. Since Omnicom will be a publicly traded company under the watchful eye of the S.E.C., other than your wives, he said, not a word of what we just heard to anyone else *including* Honda. He anticipated the vote by the board on Wednesday would be favorable given the multiple and the considerable force we would now be part of—Omnicom would leapfrog the Saatchis, the Interpublics, the Dentsus et al., to become the largest agency holding company in the world—what a cover story in awestruck *Time* would soon dub "The Big Bang." Following the Needham vote, the necessary public announcements would be made. Then, and only then, could we approach Honda.

When Keith left, we stayed back to discuss priorities, most crucial of course, that "approach." Gerry thought the best tactic would be to prevail on Cliff to arrange an unspecified but urgent meeting with the key players at Honda first thing Thursday morning, sufficient time to comply with S.E.C. insider rules but before the news sunk in on the West Coast. (The Omnicom people may have anguished unnecessarily. Highly independent Honda might well have had its own problems with this megamerger.) Gerry then would get on a red-eye from New York to arrive at Honda bright and early, hat in hand.

We weren't taking anything for granted. There were several relatively new additions on the Honda side: Koichi Amemiya, an executive vice president from Japan and Tom Elliott, being groomed to replace soon-to-retire Cliff as American head of marketing. We had cordial but scant history with them. They'd have a big say in all this, and the one thing we did not want to hear was: "Fine. We'll be sure to include you in our agency review." Without Honda on the roster we had no agency worth reviewing! For Gerry, the Northwestern drama major, it would have to be his finest performance.

And there was another important issue. We were company men. Neither of us ever thought we'd end up *owning* an advertising agency so neither of us had ever paid any real attention to the backroom aspects of our business. Ironically, Ed Haymes had only recently sent a young man out from New York to be our office comptroller, replacing a real dud left over from the Brad Roberts regime. Vince Mancuso was twenty-six at the time, previously in banking, and knew zip about advertising. But Gerry and I both liked his straightforward Bronx savvy. So to guide us through the mind-numbing tangle of financial red tape sure to follow, we'd be leaning heavily on a *kid*. Then again, considering the uncanny way events were unfolding, why not advertising's youngest Chief Financial Officer?

Keith painted the proposition in broad vivid strokes and gave it an emphatic endorsement. Then Ed laid out the financial implication for everyone at the table in New York and for the many other Needham stockholders. We would receive more than three times the book value of our Needham shares in exchange for publically traded BBDO stock that would then be re-christened Omnicom. While neither Keith nor Ed mentioned the Honda departure, seemingly the number crunchers had factored that into the Needham valuation. All said and done, the "ayes" had it including Gerry's and mine and the overseas guys who ended up attending the unscheduled meeting via several squawk boxes on the boardroom table. The markets were now long closed but we were all cautioned to keep this confidential until after tomorrow's press releases.

On the way down the elevator with Gerry I thought about Paul Harper—rebuffed in his attempt two years earlier to sell out to Foote Cone and who, upon his recent retirement, was required to cash out his considerable quantity of Needham stock at book value.

"Wonder how he's gonna react to this news. He just missed out on a 'triple' by a couple of months!" I observed shaking my head.

"I wouldn't want to be the messenger," Gerry replied.

THE MEETING AT HONDA WAS a resounding success. Corporate pride aside—according to Gerry they could not believe Volkswagen was chosen over Honda—they were extremely supportive of what we intended to do and only had two significant questions. Mr. Amemiya wanted to know "if our people would remain the same?" And Tom Elliott asked about our financial stability; did we have sufficient capital to be up and running immediately? To both, Rubin responded in the affirmative more out of confidence than certainty. No one asked what the agency's new name would be, which was good since we hadn't had time to even think about that.

Concerning Honda's two valid questions, we did have to act fast. To work with Vince on the financial issues, I suggested we bring in a golf buddy of mine, Dave Swartz, head of a medium-sized Los Angeles accounting firm. That Saturday morning, after absolutely whiffing my attempt at a drive on the first tee, Dave sensed something was awry. I took a mulligan, then filled him in riding down the fairway. He told me to calm down and enjoy this good fortune. He was sure his relationships with local banks would help us garner the letter of credit and operating capital we'd need. As events played out that summer before our official October separation from Needham, Dave was an invaluable counterweight in dealing with Ed Haymes on the myriad of details way over the heads of Rubin and Postaer.

Speaking of those two, we landed on a name without any deep think or bruised egos. For one thing Postaer Rubin & Associates sounded clunky, even to me. For another, in practice it would be shortened to P.R. making us sound like a public relations firm or that Commonwealth southeast of Miami.

As for the question about our people, we decided to throw an impromptu office party the following Monday evening on the sizable rear deck of Gerry's home in Pacific Palisades. Our people knew something was going on so the turnout, even last minute, was substantial. Gerry did most of the talking, mentioning that beyond Honda, our other clients, all informed by him on Friday, seemed to be okay with our reconstituted agency. Mindful of Mr. A, he went out of his way to assure everyone that their talents were appreciated, their jobs were secure and their existing benefit packages would be maintained.

Of the 139 employees of Needham/L.A. at the time, 138 remained with Rubin Postaer & Associates. The one naysayer? A junior account executive who decided his father-in-law's real estate company offered more security. (Until recently, it probably did.)

The Honda Way

Ten years earlier the SW/EL merger had propelled me out the door of an agency I'd thought would be my home for life. Now another merger has landed me in an office lobby where my surname, in crisply cast chrome letters, helps decorate the wall:

Rubin
Postaer
and Associates

Other than that—and the buttons popping proudly off my father's old cardigan back in Chicago—little had changed.

Except:

- Thinking about the 138 loyal associates, I'll be less inclined to blow my top in creative presentations gone sideways;
- Thinking about overhead, I'll start hiring new people in the creative department based on need rather than whether they remind me of myself at twenty-five;
- Thinking about Gloria Allred, I'll plan a new approach to office Christmas parties, arriving later and leaving earlier;
- And thinking about the press, I'll be more likely to return their phone calls.

Concerning the latter, the local media had had a change of heart. We were no longer L.A.'s resented carpetbagger regime. Suddenly we were fair-haired boys (evidently a "start-up" agency billing $100 million commands a modicum of respect). *AdWeek* headlined their coverage with "Rubin and Postaer: De-Merger Destiny." They followed that up a month later with "Balance of Power Suddenly Shifts in L.A." The *Los Angeles Business Journal* took a surprising stab at wit—if not political correctness—with their headline: "Former Needham Men Make Name for Themselves."

The *Journal's* reporter, displaying both an amazing grasp of the obvious and a limited vocabulary, wrote "On the surface, it might appear that Rubin and Postaer fell into something nice." *Mighty nice, actually.*

But good fortune does not radiate equally in all directions.

A few weeks after the official announcement of our "de-merger" I was in Chicago on business, focus groups as I recollect, and found my way to Riccardo's at the end of the day. I spotted the regulars ensconced in their usual big round corner booth. There were handshakes and congratulations and an introduction to an out-of-towner I hadn't recognized, the rather portly Sean Fitzpatrick, my counterpart on several G.M. brands at Campbell-Ewald in Detroit. He was feeling no pain. When he finally processed my name, the first words out of his mouth were "Well if it isn't the luckiest guy in advertising!"

I know an insult when I hear it. Fortunately, I didn't have to respond. Ralph Rydholm—the creative director at Tatham-Laird (then home of Pringles and Head and Shoulders), an Old Town neighbor of mine, and evidently Fitzpatrick's drinking buddy—leaned into the fray.

"Who's calling who 'the luckiest man in advertising'?" Rydholm screeched in his sandpapery voice. "You've done *one* half-decent campaign in your life (Chevy's "Heartbeat of America"). You fucked over a dozen music houses to come up with *one* okay jingle. And you're calling him lucky?"

The dressing-down by Ralph neutered Sean for the rest of the extended cocktail hour. But beyond the booze and perhaps a tinge of agency-envy, Sean was reflecting the prevailing sentiment in Detroit. We'd only recently learned about Lee Iacocca's petulance. And we saw more of Detroit's frustration when the AAMA (American Automobile Manufacturers Association), essentially the Big Three, unceremoniously threw Honda out of their organization though they were a bona fide American manufacturer.*

As an American working on Honda, yes, I have felt tinges of guilt about the faltering Big Three. But I've exonerated myself by comparing the manner in which Honda operates to the questionable business practices so prevalent out of Detroit.

The list is long. Rampant nepotism. Bloated bonuses. Union fraternization. Private jets. Chauffeured executives. Ignored inner city. Cloying patriotism. Deceptive advertising. Bait and switch. Blatant plagiarism (fast forwarding to just a few years ago, we ran an outdoor billboard for the Honda Civic which read "Life, liberty and the Pursuit." We entered it in a creative award show in Los Angeles. One of the out-of-town judges was the creative director on Cadillac. During the judging, he was overheard commenting favorably about that line. A year later it became Cadillac's slogan.) Misleading comparisons. Heavy retouching. Mouse-type disclaimers. Shifty product separation (the difference between a Buick and an Olds or a Ford and a Mercury was often nothing more than a front grille and the badges). Tainted sales results (without huge fleet sales to the rental car companies they own—and chauvinistic local, state and federal automobile procurement policies—in many cases Detroit's reported sales figures would be halved).

Speaking of Avis, Hertz, et al., the fact that those companies routinely flush out their inventory every three months adds a huge glut to the used car market and adversely affects the resale value of Big Three cars bought in good faith by real customers. And while

* In 1999, the AAMA changed its tune and its name. Now called the Alliance of Automotive Manufacturers, it accepts as members every company building them here. To date, Honda is the only major manufacturer that has spurned their olive branch.

rental car lots around airports are handy dumping grounds for unsalable Fords and Chevrolets, they also provide the public the opportunity to take a Taurus or an Impala on an extended test drive, a great idea as conceived in a Detroit boardroom, but a sampling program that often backfires, sending renters right into their nearest Toyota, Nissan or Honda showroom.

These are not arrogant observations. I've had dealings with Oldsmobile. And I've been to the mountain and seen firsthand how Honda works. They would never boast about it but in contrast to the Big Three, Honda is worlds apart.

For one thing, you can't rent a Honda. Even in a down market when it might be tempting, they do not engage in fleet sales. Durability differences aside, and they're substantial, rejecting the rent-a-car remedy keeps the resale value on a Honda higher, which makes for much happier customers and dealers.

"The Honda Way" is apparent at their headquarters. Substantively, it's a far cry from the old and modest Gardena location I first visited. Today, their associates enjoy a green and spacious campus setting in Torrance. But the rules, or lack thereof, remain the same. There is no executive parking area. It is first come, first parked. There are no executive suites. From the Japanese president on down, everyone works out of a half-walled cubicle. There is no executive dining room. Everyone who stays on site at lunchtime eats in the same clean, pleasant cafeteria, seating entirely open. There are no private jets. Everyone flies commercial (though that could conceivably change when the HondaJet they're developing in a plant near Kitty Hawk gets off the ground).

And no one that works there arrives in the back of a limo, a fact lost on a prominent national agency invited to solicit Honda's Acura division in the late nineties. An entourage, from both their New York and Los Angeles offices, pulled up to the main building in a pair of impressive limousines. Several Honda executives who happened to be in the lobby at the time duly noted the agency's grand entrance. It did not further their cause.

An inalterable insistence on customer satisfaction has always been the essence of "The Honda Way." My partner tells a story that makes the point. During his first tour of duty on Honda, in the midst of the OPEC-created oil crisis of '73–'74, he brought a finished commercial to the client for the 5-speed Civic CVCC. The car delivered, as the commercial proclaimed, better gas mileage than any other car sold in America, this at a time when lines of cars waiting for their turn at the pump stretched for blocks.

Mr. Munekuni watched the spot without comment. He then looked at a set of figures in his notebook and said, "I don't think so."

Gerry didn't quite know what to make of it until Moon explained. Based on their estimate of unit sales versus availability of inventory, there was no way Honda could meet the certain demand for this high-mileage Civic. In retrospect, Moon simply did not want to air a commercial that would contribute to customer disappointment.

In my time on the account, early on I saw another instance of Honda's customer-first philosophy. I presented a print ad for a new Accord Hatchback. Because its engine put out twenty-five percent more horsepower than the previous model, instinctively we made hay of the news. Again, Moon applied the brakes. He said he had driven the car and he hadn't felt like it had that much more power. Despite engineering factualness, he asked us to de-accelerate our copy claims. As good as the car was, he didn't want to overpromise in the advertising.

Compare this abiding ethos to the skullduggery out of Detroit; where, for just one example, a car equipped with all sorts of accessories is often advertised at a base sticker price. With the aid of a magnifying glass one can read the words of contrition at the bottom of the ad—the car shown includes extras *not* covered in the aforementioned (low-ball) price.

AS A COMPANY HONDA CARES about their cars, their claims and their customers. How are they then as a client? In a word, reasonable. At face value, that may not be the most reverberating adjective in the dictionary unless one has had to deal with the polar opposite: an *unreasonable* client (say, Gallo) whose iron whim, if allowed to prevail, will not just reverberate down the creative corridor but can shake an entire agency into disastrous submission.

At Honda, neither credit nor blame is bandied about. It's a workmanlike and resolute environment. Meetings begin and end promptly. Decisions are made. There is no phoning home for answers, a seemingly odd observation until one has worked, as I have, with other Japanese-owned companies (Kubota, Yokohama, Pioneer, SoyJoy) where no Stateside executive can make significant advertising decisions unilaterally.*

Most of all, Honda believes that given a good reason change is welcomed. *Reasonable enough.*

At their manufacturing plants the suggestion box is not mere decoration. They take those suggestions seriously and dig for more of them in regular morning meetings with the associates who work on the production lines.

At their headquarters, heels are not dug in either.

When we arrived in L.A., we inherited a slogan—"Honda. We Make It Simple"—conceived during Bob Cox's reign in 1978. Admiring it from afar, I never saw it as the brainchild of others and had no thought of abandoning it, an attitude no doubt applauded by the quartet who heard their voices singing (and the cash register ringing) at the end of every Honda commercial back then.

My creative department gamely coexisted with it; devising ways to amplify the "simple" idea in TV, print and outdoor; coining phrases like "Simple evolution," "Simple luxury," "Simple choice," simple this and simple that.

* Suzuki was another exception to the "phone home" rule. Remember what happened to their American decision makers?

But simply put, now in its fifth year, we were running out of phrases. And gas. Worse yet, there were good ideas I had to regularly reject because, preceding the slogan, they went bump in the night. "We Make It Simple" was making things hard.

Then, in late '82, Coburn, Yoshida and I went to Japan as part of what was called a "study group," the subject at hand an all-new Prelude, a low-volume niche vehicle favored in the past primarily by females. One look under the hood of this macho version, with its beefed-up power plant and advanced technology Honda engineers had neatly crammed into every available cubic centimeter of the Prelude's compact engine compartment and we knew—there was nothing simple about it.

Fueling our feeling that the slogan had outlived its value was what was happening at Toyota, the one manufacturer Honda saw as The Competition. They were spewing forth one new model after the other, threatening to drown out with oceans of advertising the awareness of Honda's smaller line-up in the marketplace.

Not anywhere near the financial powerhouse that was Toyota, Honda had only the Civic, Accord and Prelude—and Moon's CRX coming around the corner. We needed to stand up to the Toyota deluge by putting Honda's individual models on distinct pedestals. Ending our commercials with the "We Make It Simple" words and music prevented us from using that precious time and space for one last—and hopefully memorable—model mention (e.g., "The Accord LX…from Honda").

We now had our reasons. After hearing them, Rubin and the account people came on board though everyone in the room knew that asking a client to drop a slogan they'd invested millions promulgating was a dicey proposition especially when Honda dealers had "simple" plastered all over their showrooms. Anticipating that valid concern, we offered up an evolutionary segue. For the time being, we'd continue to end the commercials with the musical notes of "We Make It Simple" under Burgess Meredith massaging the model name. And as a final button, we'd have the singers belt out a one-word lyric: "Honda!" (Somewhere in West Hollywood wealthy studio vocalists were cheering us on.)

I smoked one last cigarette walking from the visitors' parking lot with Gerry and the head account guy Chuck Valentine, gathering my thoughts and my nerve. This was, as advertising moments go, a big deal. But I was armed with audio and visual examples of how we proposed to change the way their commercials and print materials ended. At least to me, it all seemed to make sense.

We met with an unsuspecting audience, Moon, Cliff, Tom Elliott and a few others. Gerry set the table by saying that we knew what we wanted to discuss was controversial but if we didn't think it was right we wouldn't be bringing it to them.

Then it was my turn in the barrel. I did *not* mention that my people had tapped out on every conceivable "simple" pun. I did tell them the greater truths though: that many good ideas that crossed my desk were stymied by the literal demands of the slogan; that their engineering was now far from simplistic; that their individual models needed more of the limelight to take on Toyota; and that their model line-up itself was expanding, and soon would no longer be, as when the slogan was conceived, the simple choice of Civic or Accord. Then I showed and played them the examples pulled from my black bag.

We were asked to leave the room so they could discuss it among themselves.

Ten anxious minutes later, we were called back into the conference room to be told they all agreed our proposal was more than reasonable.

Legends of Golf

My partner is not a golfer. Nor has any media director we've ever had been a golfer. Which meant that whenever *Time, Newsweek, USA Today, Reader's Digest, Golf Digest*—you name the gracious media host—extended an invitation to a high-ranking exec at Rubin Postaer and Associates for some glorious golf boondoggle, say to Pebble Beach, Hilton Head, La Quinta or even Augusta, guess who got to go?

Slimmer pickings in these days of skinnier magazines and tighter entertainment budgets, but back in the eighties and nineties those invites came so often that, in good conscience, I had to take a rain check on most of them.

As for Augusta National, there was no turning it down. Along with Cypress, it's the toughest ticket in all of golf. No amount of money will buy you onto that fabled course. One must be invited and accompanied by a playing member, in my case, that was Melvin Laird, Secretary of Defense in the Nixon years and one of the very few in that administration to leave office untainted.

Why him? He happened to be chairman of the charitable foundation established by the founders of *Reader's Digest*. Why me? Despite all my protests to the media department about running our big ideas on those pint-sized pages, they felt the *Digest*'s enormous readership triumphed over my inflated opinions. As a grateful guest, I did not express those concerns to Secretary Laird.

Instead, we had a wonderful weekend, a foursome of him and me, a sales rep from the magazine and a fellow Los Angeles adman, Denny Remsing, head account guy on Isuzu at Della Femina (remember the liar, Joe Isuzu?). We shared a four-bedroom cabin on the hallowed grounds close by the first tee.

From watching the Masters, I knew every hole by heart. That did little to help my game. Nor "Mel's." Even for Georgia it still was winter and we all were bundled up against the chill, our swings hampered by the bulky layers. Ol' Mel was nearly seventy at the time with perhaps a touch of arthritis and was having an especially difficult time getting his fairway shots up in the air. I noticed his irons. They were woefully dated. I mentioned that there was a lot of new technology these days and that he might want to look into it. "I know that," he said with a patient smile, "but they wouldn't have these on 'em." He held up his seven-iron to show me what was engraved on the back of the face—the impressive spread eagle seal of the Department of Defense.

A dusty shantytown right out of *Tobacco Road* surrounded the fences guarding Augusta National. Within, a verdant plantation beckoned the wealthy white golfers. The membership was a veritable who's who of the nation's business and political leaders though you'd be hard pressed to ever lay eyes on their mystery roster of who was who. Were you to encounter one of them anywhere on the property and had the temerity to proffer that member a business card, you would be chastised immediately and escorted off said property.

In the stately dining hall, all glowing wood and burnished brass—Mel in his green member's jacket, the rest of us in coat and tie—we were waited on like royalty by the liveried black staff. After dinner, the sommelier, who'd been there forever according to Mel, gave us a tour of the vast wine cellar. We'd already discovered during the meal, nothing off those meticulously labeled racks was less than *Grand* or *Premier cru*.

Then it was back to the cabin for a friendly game of gin rummy. A fireplace was already blazing in the central living room when we arrived, and remained that way all evening, fresh wood laid on and stoked by an attendant who appeared out of nowhere (a side door actually) at the right moment. Seated at the game table, my view faced the well-stocked bar and a large TV tuned to CNN, its sound on mute. As my gin partner, Mel was sitting across from me, his back to the picture, his attention focused on his hand.

It was Saturday night, January 16th, 1991. From the look on Wolf Blitzer's face and the cutaways to the somber foreign correspondents and the urgent streaming titles, it was clear the United States was preparing to blast Saddam out of Kuwait. The three of us with a view of the screen had set down our cards and were staring at history in the making.

"Hey Mel," I said, "looks like we're finally gonna kick some ass."

Still feeling the effects of the nippy day of golf, he turned stiffly toward the TV for just a moment, then back to the game.

"C'mon, play cards," he said slightly annoyed, "we're getting blitzed."

The next morning, before heading over for breakfast and another go at the golf course, a porter delivered an official-looking manila envelope, "TOP SECRET" and "For addressee's eyes only" rubber stamped all over its surface. Mel explained that he was still involved with the government—some sort of advisory council, he said—and received these "updates" all the time.

The man who conceived the lottery draft during Vietnam must've known this was one war we couldn't lose. He handed the unopened envelope to Denny and told him he ought to keep it as a souvenir.

IN 1989, WE LEARNED THAT Jack Lemmon was interested in becoming the voice of Honda, following in the footsteps of Burgess Meredith, an actor he greatly admired. In his illustrious career, Lemmon had never done a commercial. This was a talent and an opportunity we could not pass up. As part of the contract, he even agreed to appear at the upcoming annual dealer meeting in Vegas and at the next Honda Classic golf tournament in Florida.

No prima donna, his performance in the sound studio working on the new batch of commercials was flawless. That whimsical touch we'd missed since Burgess was back. And his surprise appearance at the meeting was a boffo hit. Dealers and their wives swamped him for photo ops and autographs.

But there's always one naysayer: in this case, a dealer who cornered me outside the convention hall.

"I'm not sure about your new guy."

"You don't like his voice? The man's won a couple of Oscars."

"That part's okay. It's his name. Lemon. Y'know, lemon *and* cars?"

"Ah, don't worry, Harry. He spells it with two ems."

At that point his wife, within earshot, whisked him away.

A few months later, I chaperoned Jack on the flight to the Classic. A known golf addict, he was looking forward to playing in the Pro-Am.

I saw how starstruck the dealers were. Now witnessing the reaction to him, on the plane and walking the concourse in Ft. Lauderdale, I got a close-up sense of what life is like for a movie icon. He chatted with all who stopped him and signed countless hat brims and boarding passes. It took us more than an hour to exit the airport.

The incursion on his personal space didn't seem to faze him; he couldn't have been more gracious; getting on in years perhaps he enjoyed all the fuss. Still, I suddenly understood the requirements of so many of L.A.'s less approachable: the bodyguards, the darkened limo windows, the forbidding twelve-foot hedges. The more I thought about it, the more I appreciated the anonymity of advertising.

Golf did have a new business side. Through a friend who invited me out to play Riviera Country Club, I met Bill Mow, the founder and chief honcho of Bugle Boy Industries. When he found out what I did, he was quick to say his products—mainly multi-pocketed "cargo" pants—sold themselves. One hundred fifty million dollars' worth, he added unasked. Whatever advertising he did, mostly outdoor billboards, was created in-house. He let me know he didn't care much for ad agencies or the fees they charged. I assumed he'd had a bad experience. Riviera's rules far more relaxed than Augusta's, I gave him one of my cards for the hell of it. By the end of the round, for whatever reason, he suggested I come out to his offices in Chatsworth.

For the meeting a week later, I brought along Gary Wenzel, our resident marketing guru, and a cassette of our recent commercials.

He was cordial. He showed us around the crammed cubicles and sizable warehouse, employees, mostly Asian, busily scurrying about, at least in his presence. And then we had our chat in his sumptuous corner office.

I told him he ought to consider television (knowing he couldn't accomplish that "in-house").

He said he never watched TV.

I asked him, just for ducks, if he had a video cassette player. He opened a cabinet full of electronics.

I played our reel.

As the spots appeared, he exclaimed again and again, "Oh you guys did that?"

"Bill, I thought you said you didn't watch TV."

"Well, I watch the news and golf."

Wenzel jumped in. "You've seen our spots because you're the market, age-wise anyhow, for cars and banks and we run them on things like the news and golf. But if we were doing commercials for Bugle Boy, we'd run them on shows you never watch, like MTV, Soul Train, maybe college sports."

Almost as an afterthought, he told us he was coming out with a line of blue jeans and asked what we thought it would cost to take on the "big boys" like Levi and Lee. I said that if the commercial was a home run, it might cost less than he imagined. And Gary suggested that we could find a few smaller test markets, run at different weight levels to replicate various national budget levels and, without spending a fortune, see how high was up.

Surprisingly, with no further discussion he agreed to proceed. I was sure he'd made up his mind before we arrived. The jean samples he showed us, conveniently nearby on his credenza, looked just like everyone else's. He surely knew that if he planned on convincing department store chains to hang Bugle Boy jeans on their already crowded racks, he would have to prove he was a serious player. Only television could make that point.

Driving back Gary felt exultant. He pegged Mow as sharp if not a wee bit crafty but thought we could work with him. We'd just witnessed his negotiating skill. When he asked what our credit terms were, Gary gave the boilerplate answer: net thirty days. Bill came right back with some story about how timing worked in his world and that he'd really need sixty days. Gary acquiesced (new business is new business). Only later did we learn that for Bugle Boy, sixty days actually meant ninety days or more.

Meanwhile since I had mentioned "home run" commercials, I gave the assignment to our clean-up hitters, Coburn and Yoshida. In their customary understated way, they knocked it out of the park:

Open on lonely road in the middle of nowhere.
A young man, early '20's, is standing at the side of the road.
He is wearing a tee shirt and Bugle Boy jeans.
Seemingly he's looking for a ride but he is not actively hitchhiking.
A black Maserati whizzes past him.
He stares straight ahead.
We hear screeching brakes.
Car re-enters frame, rapidly backing up to guy and stops.
Passenger side window slides down.
Guy leans toward car door as gorgeous 30-ish woman driver peers across to him saying:
"Excuse me. Are those Bugle Boy jeans that you're wearing?"
He looks at her and, with just a hint of flirtatiousness, says:

*"Why yes, they are **Bugle Boy jeans."***
*She says: **"Thank you."***
as window closes and car squeals off.
Nonplused, guy returns to upright position.
*Super: **Bugle Boy Jeans***

BILL MOW WAS SOLD, SAVE for two issues, one small, the other huge.

Instead of the Maserati, he wanted us to use his own Ferrari Testarossa (in my mind both an egotistical and money-saving request). No problem, except our producer, Gary Paticoff, warned that the rigors of production—take after take of the car roaring back in reverse—could play hell with Mow's transmission. Paticoff suggested we rent an identical vehicle and let insurance cover potential repairs. (If it mattered, and I think it did, Mow could still tell his friends it was his car used in the commercial). Mow relented.

His other issue was a major sticking point, the kind of predictable and unsettling client request that drives an adman to a fourth martini.

He wanted the guy to get the girl.

This request could not stand. It so clearly destroyed the idea—yet was so typical of the interference one encounters dealing with so-called creative geniuses in the fashion (and entertainment) industry—I chose not to argue about it, pacified him instead by saying we would cover the ending both ways, and counted on the obvious to prevail. If it didn't, we would end the relationship before it really began.

In the editing bay, the original idea leaped off the monitor. Everyone involved in the post-production process, mostly young guys in jeans, thought it was sensational. Though it was there in the outtakes, we never so much as looked at the guy getting the girl.

Fortunately, when we took the spot out to Mow, he had gathered a group of his own staff to watch with him. Almost always (Hunt's Skillet dinner the exception) a humorous commercial resonates even more in a roomful of people.

His sales guys loved it. His secretary loved it. His daughter Genevieve, fresh from college with a marketing degree, loved it (she, in fact, had discovered our male lead, a box boy at Ralphs, whom she was using as a model for some of their outdoor billboards). Even his wife who oversaw the bookkeeping department loved it. And Bill Mow, he loved it too, and never once asked for the whereabouts of his mind-numbing version.

The commercial wasn't just a resounding hit within Bugle Boy. It met the same reception when his sales guys showed it to department store buyers. Mow became so bullish he told us to forego Wenzel's test market plan; let's go for the jugular, he said, only tell your media department to sharpen their pencils.

We got lucky. A spot opened up on a nationally televised USC–Notre Dame football game—at a last-minute bargain basement price. We grabbed it. The introduction kicked off. And retailers immediately felt the effects.

Mow ponied up more media dollars—still not in Levi's league—but enough to keep the pressure building. Jane Pauley, on her show at the time called *Real Life*, did a segment interviewing teenagers about their favorite commercials. "Bugle Boy!" they responded; the girls, who seemed to relish the box boy's comeuppance, were the most vocal. In fact, while not at all directed at girls, Bugle Boy saw a big increase in sales of their "junior" line. A year after its first appearance on the game, Bugle Boy's total sales had quadrupled to six hundred million dollars. Nothing born in our agency, before or since, has ever achieved that level of instant success.

Armed with what was now a recognized national brand, Mow wanted to slice off a piece of Docker's business with a line of casual men's slacks. I gave the assignment to a hot young team in the agency, Jack Fund and Keith Weiman, who developed another interesting premise.

The TV starred Tony Griffin (Merv's son) and an adorable chimpanzee dressed in a classic business suit and tie. In the launch spot, which took place on an escalator in a shopping mall, Tony, wearing Bugle Boy casuals, is imploring the chimp to lighten up. He tells him that business wear was evolving and that he ought to get out of that...monkey suit. It was a timely message; businesses were moving to "casual Friday," and the campaign delivered even more than Mow expected.

Genevieve Mow attended the shoot. That was fine except she seemed to have picked up rather quickly a lot of her father's domineering ways, butting in during the day with unwarranted opinions. Additionally, I had made what turned out to be a fatal mistake. I suggested we do a "making of" video during the shoot that their sales force could show to buyers who'd get a kick out of seeing a chimp suiting up and cavorting around a shopping mall. I narrated the little video both on-camera and off. But began to get the distinct feeling that Genevieve thought, as a member of the Mow dynasty, she should have played my part. Animosity built between the two of us over the next few months that precipitated her continual nit-picking assault on the agency, this from a kid six months out of college.

Early on in our Bugle Boy relationship, Bill had introduced Gerry and me to his older brother. Harry Mow was the antithesis of Bill, a soft-spoken kindly man who was a commercial real estate developer and builder. It so happened that our lease of the Needham space was about to expire and we were looking to finally establish our own identity in new digs. Harry had the vacant land and approved plans (a major accomplishment in dictatorial Santa Monica) for a six-story building on Second Street, just a stone's throw from the beach. It was a great opportunity to headquarter in a highly desirable area and have a say in the interior design of the offices. (I prevailed on Harry to bore a hole in a corner of the concrete floor of my office-to-be so I'd have a putting practice target.) We signed on as the major tenant, enabling Harry to obtain favorable financing, which in turn meant a favorable lease for us. A win-win situation.

With that familial and contractual tie, not to mention the incredible success Bugle Boy was achieving, I thought I had license to discuss with Bill the deteriorating situation with his daughter.

Fatal mistake number two and one I should have anticipated given the Ernest and David Gallo denouement.

I phoned one evening from home after hearing about an especially aggravating exchange with Genevieve and left a message saying I needed to see him as soon as possible. Evidently he was still in his office. He called back within minutes and, detecting some urgency in my voice, suggested we have at it right then over the phone.

I can't give a verbatim, but the conversation went something like this:

"Bill, we're proud of our relationship. But Genevieve is creating problems and she's not yet qualified to be pushing my people around."

He became defensive.

"Bill, we don't deserve this treatment. We helped put Bugle Boy on the map."

Impugning his daughter was one thing. Taking credit, even partially, for his success was something else again. He became defiant.

"You're nothing but a fucking adman," he screamed.

"And you're Thomas Jefferson."

Click.

Click.

Now for my dumbest golf story.

John Marin, the senior member of *Time's* West Coast advertising sales office, one of the most avid if not adept golf fanatics in a community of golf-crazy magazine reps, and a good friend of our agency, happened to be on the board of a golf club manufacturer: Callaway Golf. John thought we might be interested in talking to them and arranged an appointment for me with the founder, Ely Callaway. John said they were then a small account but had major plans for the future.

I drove the eighty miles down to Carlsbad, home of practically every golf club manufacturer in the country. Ely (pronounced E-lee, he said) was one of the most charismatic client prospects I'd ever met.

A tall, lean, sun-creased good ol' boy from Georgia, in his early seventies at the time, his belt was notched with past successes. He had been president of Burlington Industries and let me know he'd gone head-to-head on advertising matters with the likes of both Bill Bernbach and David Ogilvy.

Upset he never made Chairman, he left Burlington in 1973 to oversee a vineyard he had started five years earlier in Temecula, California, in a climate no authority thought conducive to quality wine making. He proved everyone wrong by doing well enough with Callaway Wine to entice Hiram Walker to buy him out in 1981 for fourteen million.

Then, for a pittance, he purchased a tiny Carlsbad company making wedges and putters and used it as yeast to bake up what he now had, a well-regarded medium-size company. When he asked me to have a look at the magazine ads he "mostly wrote himself," it struck me that his tell-it-like-it-is declarative style could never be at one with our emotional approach to advertising.

Then he made a big production out of unlocking a drawer in his desk and bringing out a velvet sack he handled as though it held the crown jewels. Whatever was in there, it seemed he trusted me with the secret.

He untied the drawstring and pulled out an object. "Whaddya' think, Larry?"

It was a hollow casting of some heft, gray metal, no markings, its shape reminiscent of a driver head about to give birth. I didn't know what to think.

"I call it the 'Big Bertha,' same name as the big ass howitzers the Germans used in World War One. When our metallurgy guys get through refinin' it, I'm tellin' ya, it's gonna be the biggest damn thing the game of golf's ever seen!"

There were metal woods out there. I played with them. But they were half the size of this thing. It was so big it was silly. Golfers are desperate and gullible souls but I couldn't imagine Ely's ham hock sticking out of any sane man's bag.

"You'll have a field day writing copy for it, Ely."

"That's how I figure. But I'll need somebody to draw up the ads. I've got arrangements with all the golf publications. I don't need any media help."

So that was the deal. Another entrepreneur of a client with all the answers. A product with absolutely no prayer. And, worse yet, I'd have to beg an art director to grapple with Ely's exclamation points.

"That's not how we normally work," I said. "Let me talk it over with my partner and I'll get back to you."

After speaking with Gerry and thanking John Marin for the intro, I sent Ely a note. I wished him well but told him the assignment just wasn't right for us and that he ought to find a freelance art guy down there who could gussy up his copy.

Of course, Ely Callaway *was* on to something big. Despite the bombast of the advertising that ensued, his behemoth became the biggest thing that ever happened to golf, just as he predicted. Twenty years later, Ely's "big" idea—or one of its countless knock-offs—remains the weapon of choice of every professional golfer in the world. And the same is true of the unheralded millions of rank amateurs out there. Including me.

There are days even now when I think about the foot I had in Ely's door. But I console myself knowing he never once ran an ad for Big Bertha we would've hung on our agency's wall.

WHAT'S IN A NAME

THE AGENCY MOVED INTO HARRY MOW'S NEW BUILDING IN 1991. Optimistically, we took more space than we needed at the moment, all but the ground floor. There was ample room for growth. And the location was perfect. Around the corner, the burgeoning Third Street Promenade, lined with stores and restaurants, would give our people plenty of lunchtime and after-hour choices. And jutting into the Pacific, the famous Santa Monica Pier was just a short walk to the west. All things considered, we could remain there forever.

Checking out my ocean view a week after the move-in, I saw several workmen down on the sidewalk. As a gift to the agency, Harry had installed an eight-foot monument next to the entrance, three slabs of dark green granite forming a triangle. The workers were attaching stencils of our logo near the top of each slab. They were preparing to sandblast us into posterity.

I rang up my partner. "We ought to go down there and play sidewalk superintendents, Ger. The next time our names are etched in stone, we won't get to watch."

THE *FENG SHUI* OF OUR new digs, if you believe in such things, seemed all in our favor. Business was booming. Our space began to feel less ample.

Then, in 1994, my Augusta roommate Denny Remsing called. He'd been a car guy all his advertising life, though currently between jobs.

"Larry, there's big changes happening down at Honda. They've just brought in a new national sales manager, Dick Colliver. He's an old golf buddy of mine. You guys should talk to me."

We had a nodding acquaintance with Colliver's predecessor. Though he was not involved in decisions concerning national advertising, we worked closely with him on the annual dealer conventions.

At the time, Honda dealers were in control of local advertising. A city, say Chicago, with perhaps a dozen dealers, formed an advertising association (just as Oldsmobile dealers did in my past life) and hired a local ad agency. Across America there were eighty-six such associations, eighty-six ad agencies, eighty-six disparate local campaigns—mostly hardball in nature—muddying up Honda's national branding efforts. According to Denny, one of Colliver's first goals was to change all that. To bring dealer advertising more in sync with what we were doing on the national level he wanted to consolidate it in Torrance under his direction. And he had the blessing of Mr. Amemiya, who, in his travels, had had his fill of Honda dealer commercials (one he found particularly galling featured an exploding Toyota).

Nobody likes change. There was acrimony. But in the end, Colliver accomplished his goal. In turn, he awarded us the combined regional marketing account, a huge boost for us that helped mitigate the ire we incurred from eighty-six agencies around the country now bereft of their Honda business.

We hired Denny to head up our new dealer advertising division called RP alpha, opened seven regional service offices, and designated my old friend Jon Yarbrough—out of the film production business and working at the agency as an associate creative director—to run the creative side.

Jon would be ideal for the job. A workaholic, he'd have all he could handle and, given the budget constraints of regional commercial production, he'd have the opportunity to direct many of the spots himself. To help juggle the advertising requests that began coming in from all points, I prevailed on another old friend, Jack Hetherington, to move out from Chicago and play Jon's wingman.

RP alpha was a world unto its own. Just in L.A we had to recruit and hire a separate staff of account and creative people, media buyers, strategic planners and backroom support, in total more than forty new associates. Suddenly, 1333 Second Street was overflowing. We leased two available floors in the building next door.

Because "regional" bases its advertising budget specifically on ever-growing car sales, today it comprises a large portion of Honda's total advertising spend. Colliver's grand experiment has worked beyond expectations. Even those dealers disgruntled at the inception of his plan have come to acknowledge how a unified and cohesive advertising strategy has strengthened the overall brand image of Honda across America.

⁂

RETURNING FROM THE FIRST HOLIDAY break at our new offices, I found a Mac in my typewriter's stead. The Royal, a highly reliable manual, had been bodily removed and set aside on my credenza like a dead philodendron.

I'd carried it from Stern Walters to Needham/Chicago to Los Angeles. On it, I'd banged out a thousand memos and God-knows-how-many scripts, my only "apps" a bottle of white-out and a Xerox machine down the hall. And, just a month earlier, I had ordered a dozen spare ribbons when informed supplies of them were close to extinct. Even before computers, while everyone had switched to Selectrics, I had stuck with that manual. Early on in L.A.—a town akin to Guatemala when it came to public utilities—when electricity inexplicably shut down, a frequent event—I'd march down the hallway hollering (only half joking) at my incapacitated people: "If you had a manual, you'd still be functioning."

And now this. The dinosaur tamed. "You need to be connected," the office manager told me when I called to complain. "The whole place is wired. Except you. But we added something special to yours. Manual typewriter sound effects! You'll love them."

Yes, I'm writing this on a computer, a fifth-generation version of that first Apple shoved down my throat. And yes, I couldn't live without it or its cut-and-paste function. And yes, the entire agency, all eight offices, and the entire free world are now "connected." Furthermore, despite my obstinacy—my feeling that a computer screen was in no way a compelling canvas—our interactive group grew like Topsy in the mid-nineties. We needed to take even more space next door—this time the capacious ground floor encircled by a roomy balcony—where once a bank did business.

All that and yet I'll go to my grave knowing when the digital age pulled into the station, I was last to board.

THE ADVENT OF ACURA IN 1999 caused more growing pains. Our design group now was creating and producing annual brochures for every model of both nameplates, the equivalent in editorial pages to a year's worth of *Esquire* and *Atlantic* combined. Vince Mancuso, our CFO and resident real estate maven, found new space for the designers and their back-up across the alley on the Promenade in what was once the attic warehouse of a long-gone Woolworth's.

Our strategic planners had become a small army as well. Vince moved the think tank en masse to new quarters above the Anthropologie store down the Promenade a half-block away. For them, keeping an eye on consumer trends was now as easy as peeking out a window.

But net net the agency is spread over four locations. Notwithstanding considerable efficiency issues, the diaspora was bad for the collegial good. Gerry, Vince and I began looking at options.

We found the right location three miles inland, a park-like complex cater-corner from MTV's West Coast headquarters. No more ocean views. But we're reunited in a sizable three-story building surrounding a cozy central courtyard.

Since we'd need to revise all our stationery supplies anyhow, we decided to take a fresh look at our corporate identity program—in other words, the Rubin Postaer and Associates logo. Perhaps we'd update the typeface.

A committee is formed. They gather suggestions from every art director and designer in the agency, cull things down to a handful and ask to make a presentation to an unsuspecting Rubin and Postaer.

Dry coughs. Downcast eyes. Shuffling feet. And then the recommendation. "The committee feels we should make things simpler—y'know, shorten up the name a bit—to just RPA." They showed us several type and color treatments and pointed out their favorite, a stylized font in burnt orange. And gave us assurances. "'RPA.com is already our web address. And there'd be a transition period. The original name will still be there at the bottom of the letterhead. And we'll answer the phone the same old way. For a while."

Wait just a minute! I was thinking. A dozen years ago our name was etched in stone. And now we're initialized? Did some committee force Batten, Barton, Durstine and Osborn to sit through a similar slaughter? Did Doyle, Dane and the great Bill Bernbach suffer such diminution? But when I turned for Rubin's reaction and saw his graying temples just as he looked past my furrowed brow to my dear departed hairline, reality came home to roost.

"Are you guys sure about that burnt orange?" I asked plaintively.

"Yea, Boss, it's very edgy," one of the upstarts said.

In Memoriam

He consoled and counseled me on that long trip to New Zealand. He willingly donned the silly black hat for our Hubba Bubba tap dance. He delivered on his promise to make sure Paul and Blair considered me for the transfer to Los Angeles, when and if. And during our first five years in L.A. he was generous with his notes and calls of congratulations for one thing or another we were doing out here.

Just months after Jim Fasules retired at sixty-two to realize his fly fishing dream, he was asked to join a group of DDB/Needham execs, along with several clients and prospects, on a whitewater rafting excursion to British Columbia. He and his wife Lenore were at their fishing retreat in Montana when the call came from Chicago. *We've got one spot open and, hell, you're a lot closer to Canada right now than the rest of us.* There was no way Jim would turn down a chance to relive old times around the advertising campfire.

Then it was my turn to get a call from Chicago, from my friend Jack Hetherington with horrendous news. He had just learned that the raft—arguably overburdened by twelve grown men—capsized in the roiling rocky rapids of the Chilton River. Jim, another Needham friend Gene Yovetich, and three others perished the previous day, August 1, 1987.

Gerry and I flew back to attend two of the funerals.

First, Gene's. He was an account exec I worked closely with on General Mills. Just forty-one, big and athletic, it was hard to believe he was not one of the seven survivors. (No one from Needham including Jack would discuss details of the tragedy. Seemingly there were concerns over potential legal issues.) Solemn is the only word to describe Gene's Serbian Orthodox service; hundreds stood for two hours in the baroque and stifling church on the Northwest Side as several priests in heavily brocaded vestments intoned a mass in a language only members of Gene's immediate family understood. Gene's wife Karen did host a gathering of friends that evening at their townhouse in Lincoln Park. The atmosphere while subdued was certainly not somber. All of us felt Gene would have much preferred that second venue.

Lenore had asked that Jim's service be a celebration of his life. Held at the First Congregational Church in Glen Ellyn, the setting was light and airy and almost cheerful. Family members and friends shared anecdotes that captured the spirit of Jim's quirky and ebullient nature. There were tears but there was gentle laughter too.

Jim was a fishing buddy of Norman Maclean, who wrote *A River Runs Through It*. If you were a client or friend of Jim's, then he had given you a copy of that book signed by the author. I still have mine.

An excerpt was included in the simple memorial program:

"The river was cut by the world's great flood and runs over rocks from the basement of time...I am haunted by waters."

White Mile, a made-for-TV movie loosely based on the incident, ran on HBO in 1994. Alan Alda starred as the trip's organizer. The producers acknowledged Jim's Greek heritage by naming his surrogate Nick Karras, played by the character actor Robert Loggia.

Three years later, I was the guest in a threesome at Bel Air Country Club when the starter, by happenstance, asked if we would mind adding a fourth to the group. It was Loggia.

It turned out he was a fellow Missouri J-School grad. We had a lot to talk about. Including Jim Fasules. I admitted to Loggia that I wasn't familiar with every role in his long career but I assured him he never stood in for a finer human being than Jim.

MAKING NEWS

Theme music, title and super: ***Nov. 22, 1988***

Anncr: ***From ABC, this is World News Tonight with Peter Jennings***

Close up of Jennings

Jennings: ***Good evening. We begin tonight with what has been in some respects the worst kept secret of airplane design in many a year.***

Cut to close up of Air Force general,

pull back to reveal B-2 Bomber in front of

Edwards Air Force Base hangar.

Jennings: ***Today the Air Force has finally given the world a glimpse of its so-called Stealth Bomber, the B-2.***

General: ***I'm proud to present the first B-2 Bomber.***

Jennings: ***If the sight of the Stealth Bomber seems vaguely familiar to you...yes...***

Cut to scene from Honda commercial showing facsimile B-2

Jennings: ***this is the Honda commercial that has been running for quite some time. Maybe someone at the ad agency had a cousin who worked for Northrop. At any rate, if you've been wondering how close Honda came...***

Cut to horizontal split screen,

Air Force B-2 version on top,

Honda's version below.

Jennings: Very close.

⁂

I SWEAR WE HAD NO spy planted at Northrop. What we did have was an assignment to develop a new commercial for the CRX-Si, not the biggest seller in Honda's conservative arsenal but certainly the sexiest, zippiest and most youthful. Like Chevy's Corvette or Nissan's Z, it cast an aura across the entire model line-up. Over time, Honda had come to expect one big commercial idea after another for the CRX from us. To help vent the pressure, that "can-you-top-this?" expectation, there was one thing we could count on from the client: when it came to creative latitude on CRX, the sky was the limit.

Latitude aside, you don't just pluck good ideas out of thin air like butterflies. So where do you find inspiration, especially with a deadline looming?

Jack, my first boss at SWS, who no doubt had run one race too many, relied on a file cabinet full of ads he'd torn from old magazines. When he needed an idea, he'd sort through the meticulously organized file folders until he found a headline he could creatively adapt (or steal intact*).

Movies inspire some creative people; the film industry calls them sequels; we call them parodies.

---

* I once fired a creative team for plagiarism. They didn't just swipe ideas from competitors, they began submitting scripts highly reminiscent of commercials our own agency had done in the past. When they sued for wrongful termination, I showed the mediator exhibit after exhibit, proof positive of their wrongdoing. "Forget about it and settle," he advised. "You don't stand a chance at trial. Juries think advertising is nothing but plagiarism."

A trip to an art gallery can trigger an idea; just observe how many lame layouts have Mondrian to blame.

One of my sons, a bachelor, seeks the answer doodling on cocktail napkins; if nothing else comes of it there is always the possibility a curious woman on the next barstool will strike up a promising conversation.

The act of shaving has worked for me—and others I've discussed this with—though how original thought comes while staring at an object as familiar as one's own face remains an enigma.

If all else fails, more than once I've thumbed through a dictionary in hopes a word of inspiration would magically rise out of the gray; that's how "Solo Suzuki" came to be.

Rarely, though, does a big idea shine through your windshield as you drive up the 405 in the company of your two creative stars.

Coburn saw it first. "Check out that license plate," he drawled.

In front of us was a CRX, black, maybe two years old. The clever owner's vanity plate read "STLTH." It might've read "BINGO," so quickly did Bob and Gary begin to free associate.

There'd been much speculation in science and aviation magazines about the "Stealth." It would be made of composite materials invisible to radar. It would fly at great speed and height. It would end the Cold War. But what it would look like no one knew for sure.

Bob suggested I turn off the freeway and head over to Culver City where he knew of a large hobby shop. Scouring the model kit shelves, they found it—Revell's newly released version of the stealth bomber, a scramble of black plastic pieces inside a cardboard carton.

Back at the office, Bob assembled the delta-winged model while Gary drew up the storyboard. Knowing the first question the client would ask, we brought in Gary Paticoff, our head producer, to figure out how the words and picture could be brought to life for less than a gazillion dollars:

Dramatic music under.
Overhead shot of tarmac as Stealth moves into frame
Cut to low shot as mysterious plane comes to stop

Anncr: Shrouded in secrecy for years,
the Stealth Bomber will soon
be introduced to the public.
Cut to overhead as black CRX enters frame
and moves toward Stealth.
Anncr: For the record, we introduced ours first.
Cut to reverse shot as, CRX drives under wing of plane
and comes to rest in foreground.
Super: CRX-Si and Honda logo

Paticoff talked to various Hollywood model makers. The consensus was a cinematic version of the miniature Stealth model we showed them could be fabricated using a frame of aluminum tubing covered in tightly stretched and painted canvas. Approximately two-thirds the size of what we guessed the real Stealth's dimensions might be, ours would have a wingspan of a hundred feet (anything larger, even partially disassembled, would be difficult to transport and, worse yet, would dwarf the compact CRX on the TV screen). The cost to build and ship it to the film location, an emergency airstrip close by the Miami airport, seemed reasonable, all things considered: around a half million dollars.

What remained was to sell it to the client.

⁂

Bingo again! The ban on aircraft production during the U.S. occupation had only whetted Japan's obsession with flight. And showing Honda the Revell model and carton alleviated any concerns they might have had about compromising America's military secrets. We were given an enthusiastic go.

Lugging our Stealth from L.A. to South Florida, its delta wing divided and strapped alongside the fuselage on a flatbed truck, created major lookie-loo traffic jams. Once reassembled at the location, more significant reaction developed. Military aircraft overhead spotted our prop sitting peaceably on the airstrip. They reported the sighting to higher-ups whereupon our shoot was visited by a carful of FBI agents. We assured them we were friendly forces and they left, but there's no doubt a report reached the Secretary of the Air Force. Knowing the gist of the Honda commercial soon to air, they rushed the long-overdue unveiling of the real McCoy, as Peter Jennings observed, though as he rightly added, Honda still beat them to the punch by several months. (The plane shown on the newscast was actually incomplete. When the Air Force rolled it out that day, news people were not allowed to walk behind the Stealth because its tail section was not ready for prime time.)

The spot, however, was a smash hit, for Honda, for their dealers and for the agency. Along with its magazine counterpart, the campaign garnered a number of creative honors including the coveted Sweepstakes Bowl at L.A.'s Belding Awards Show. And it may have contributed to a slight reduction in the U.S. defense budget as well.

Soon after the ABC news report, I received a call from the chief designer at Northrop. I thought I was about to get a tongue-lashing. Instead, he asked how we built our version of the Stealth and what it had cost. My answers seemed to set him off. "For years I've been telling management that we didn't have to spend *millions* building mock-ups just for show 'n' tell to the Brass. That we could've made them the same way you guys did. But no one would listen." He asked if I would reveal the name of our Hollywood model maker. And thanked me.

TODAY, WHEN THE AGENCY NEEDS to see and drive an upcoming model, we motor ninety miles out to the secluded test facility Honda has built in the Mojave Desert. But back in the spring of 1989, to get our first look at the next-generation Accord necessitated a flight to Tokyo and a bullet train north to Utsunomiya, an industrial town where the client had both a manufacturing plant and test track.

None of us—Gerry, Bob, Gary, two account execs, myself—minded the long journey. The U.S. accounted for sixty percent of Accord sales worldwide. It was Honda's bread and butter and therefore ours. We'd heard great things about it. We'd be working with it for the next four years. And we couldn't wait to set sight on it.

For six jet-lagged hours we were sequestered with the Accord project team in a barebones conference room. We saw no photos of the car. Rather schematics, cross-sections, statistical data and bullet points flashed by on the screen, the text all in Japanese as was the narration by designers and engineers responsible for various aspects of the vehicle. Each of their sentences was repeated one by one in English by an ardent young lady translator.

Halfway through the seminar, they gave us a break. Led over to the factory lunchroom we, and a long line of white-clad factory "associates," waited our turn to be ladled a bowl of udon soup topped with tangy fishcakes. Rubin, Yoshida and I dug in; Coburn, the Virginian, was not so eager.

Finally, in late afternoon, we were escorted to an outside viewing area next to the test track. For comparison's sake, they had on display a mix of current Accords (which everyone of us had in our garage back home) alongside the day's subject matter: a small fleet of the much-anticipated 1990 model.

I scratched my head and whispered in Gerry's ear, "Which one's which?" He had no idea. Nor did Bob or Gary. We had just spent six laborious hours learning about the advanced inner workings of the all-new Accord. Yet now, staring at its exterior, not one of us could spot a discernible design change from its predecessor, a serious obstacle when the agency's mission was to bring factual hoopla—and visual impact—to the introductory advertising of this crucial vehicle.

During the obligatory "walk-around"—marveling at the jam-packed engine compartment and spacious trunk, testing out the leg-room from the rear seats, admiring the ergonomics from behind the steering wheel—the hosts in white coats closely gauged our positive reactions. Apprehension over the vanilla exterior we kept to ourselves.

Out on the test track, the car leaped to life. Honda was truly the little engine company that could. It was incredible how much torque and horsepower they could coax out of four cylinders. Since we all owned the old model, the improvement in acceleration, handling, sound reduction, even braking was palpable. Spinning around the track at 110 mph, an introspective Yoshida in the passenger seat, I tried to lighten his mood. "Somethin', huh Gar? This'll be a slam dunk." From the corner of my eye I saw him manage a meager smile. "No problem," he said none too convincingly.

⁂

So this is what we had on our hands: a stunning model clad in dated clothes. You really did have to test-drive this car to appreciate it—an automotive industry bromide if there ever was one and one we'd never had to contend with in the past. Once again, Coburn and Yoshida to the rescue. They took that shop-worn proposition and turned it into a riveting work of art:

Light-hearted classical music under
as we open on wall of art gallery.
Bird's eye view of 1990 Accord suspended on wall,
bracketed by a modern sculpture
and an abstract painting. Viewing bench in foreground.
Young man walks into frame.
He gazes at the Accord.
He sits on bench to gaze some more.
He gets up, walks to car, opens driver's door
and, amazingly, climbs in, shuts door
and drives Accord along wall, out of frame
leaving only telltale tread marks on wall.
An old woman carrying shopping bag
enters frame and stares quizzically at tread marks.
Anncr: You have to drive it to believe it.
The new Accord from Honda.

No other spot we ever produced created so much buzz. We fielded phone calls from a gaggle of journalists all asking the same question boyish John Tesh asked—seated next to gorgeous Mary Hart—on the TV show *Entertainment Tonight*: "How did they do that?" They had sent a video crew to our offices for the answer. Using a mechanical drawing of the set, I explained that we had learned how Hollywood filmed Fred Astaire's famous tap-dance-on-the-ceiling routine and that we employed the same trick.

The art gallery wall and floor were installed within a forty-foot-high revolving steel drum. The Accord and the other *objets d'art* were securely fastened to the "wall" while it was in the "floor" position; then the drum turned ninety degrees bringing the car to vertical. The camera was locked into place directly across from the car. As the actor approached the car door, the drum slowly turned downward so that both the actions of him climbing in and the Accord driving off appeared to defy gravity. The set was revolved back to its original position allowing the little old lady to stroll in and do her thing.

Today, computer-generated effects could accomplish what our Rube Goldberg contraption did—for a twentieth of the cost. Then again, with Avatarian magic *de rigueur*, no viewer these days would give "Art Gallery" a second glance. And I wouldn't have had my eight minutes of fame* (in full make-up) on the *CBS Morning News* interviewed by Charlie Rose. Nor would I have received in the mail a TV screen shot of the back of my then slightly balding head taken by Marv Stern, a supposed friend, who was watching CBS that morning, his Polaroid camera at the ready.

Most importantly, launched with a less newsworthy commercial, the Honda Accord might not have become that year, for the first time ever, the best-selling car in America.

---

* I wanted Coburn and Yoshida to make the trip to New York for the TV appearance. They deserved the limelight but turned it down. Camera shy, I guess.

Then the awards—so prevalent in our industry—began rolling in. We had entered "Art Gallery" in the Cannes Commercial Film Festival, and encouraged by the tons of hardware it had already won in various U.S. contests, including an unprecedented three separate Clios (best car commercial, best special effects, best musical score), we decided to invest in a trip to the south of France to bask in further glory.

Cannes is a world unto its own. Bare flesh beachside. Extravagant parties thrown by the major agency conglomerates. And the morning ritual checking the politically motivated international judges' latest verdicts, known as the all-powerful "short list," posted at newsstands and in the lobbies of all the swank hotels.

The morning of the final posting, Bob, Gary and I chose to stretch out the arrival of certain victory. We took a stroll along the strand of sand trying not to stare at the early morning sunbathers. Now to the postings, where something was amiss. Like three worshipers at the Wailing Wall, our heads bobbed up and down the lengthy columns. "Art Gallery" was nowhere to be found. *Ce n'est pas possible!*

I cornered a festival official and asked if there had been a typographic omission. No, I was told, a Brazilian judge had pronounced that a similar idea had appeared in his country several years earlier and that we had obviously plagiarized it. The American judges—no doubt all with their own big agency agendas—did not come to our defense.

The three of us had been to Cannes once before, in 1986. At that time we had a sure Gold winner, a commercial for Bayless, a chain of supermarkets in Phoenix.

Their marketing director, a fan of McDonald's advertising, somehow had ferreted me out. "We've revamped our antiquated stores. We're up against all kinds of big name players. We need to make a splash. I've got $200,000 to spend on a commercial, y'know, a 'food, folks and fun' kind of spot you used to do for McDonald's."

Coburn and Yoshida had a better idea. Let's do a bunch of low-cost commercials singling out the fifteen best-selling items in the stores. They'll be witty and worth watching (a first in supermarket advertising history), but we'll always provide time for a special offer of some sort. The client bought in and couldn't wait to see the storyboards.

The spot we were counting on at Cannes was the best of the Bayless batch. It opened on an unwrapped roll of toilet paper. An announcer, quirkily British, intones "Right now at Bayless, bathroom tissue is on sale." At that point a super came up showing a bargain price. Then a hand reaches in and tugs out the roll's inner cylinder as the announcer adds with somber sincerity "And, with every roll of bathroom tissue, you'll get a cardboard tube absolutely free!"

Bayless experienced amazing results with that commercial and the others; comparable sales rose over six percent, in that world a phenomenal increase.

At Cannes the t.p. spot did garner a Silver Lion. There was an outcry, loudest from the French contingent (who have a toilet paper obsession). How did it not win a Gold? How, in fact, did it not win Best of Show? *Je ne sais pas.* Even *AdAge*'s report of the event questioned the judges' decision. My guess is the spot, which cost less than $10,000 to produce—not to mention the agency—were seen as too small potatoes for a big-time award.

This time, five years later, no Silver, no nothing. We were flat robbed. In silent protest, we pushed our return flight ahead two days, out of Nice at nine the next morning. And though Bob wanted to drown his sorrows that last night he did not care to mix it up with what he perceived as the perpetrators. He asked me to join him far from the maddening crowd. We found a disco kilometers from the epicenter where not a soul spoke English nor had a thing to do with advertising. Finally, at 2 a.m., I reminded him we had an early flight and strongly suggested we head back to our hotel.

There were no taxis. Using each other like supportive lampposts, we made our way down the narrow winding streets.

Along the way we encountered small fleets of rowdy foreign sailors—Polish, German, God-knows-from-where—making their way back to their ships and, to a man, emboldened and intoxicated. There were looks; there were sneers; there was, given Bob's angry mood, the fear of imminent physical contact. At that moment I was willing to trade the loss of a Gold Lion at Cannes for the cushy safety of my sagging hotel bed. As luck would have it, the latter won out.

Bitter Endings

Virtually every organization—fraternal, service, social, trade—throws an annual fundraiser under the guise of honoring someone with enough celebrity or clout to fill a venue. Tuxedo rental shops love these galas. Invitees attend begrudgingly. Valet parking for hundreds of cars arriving and leaving all at once a nightmare. Waiting in line for a drink torture. The roast beef or sole inedible. The speeches interminable.

Perhaps the only time such an event is tolerable is when you're the honoree, or in this case, Gerry and I, named Co-Leaders of the Year by the Western States Advertising Agency Association in 1990.

With Gerry arm-twisting the media community, a record crowd showed up that night at the grand ballroom of the Beverly Wilshire, around 900 people, despite a rare and pouring rain.

We were there in large part thanks to the string of award-winning hits Coburn and Yoshida had produced for the agency. In my acceptance speech, I acknowledged their enormous contribution, even insisting they stand to take a bow (which they hated).

It was a far cry from the icy reception the ad community had given us nine years earlier. But the truth was we were doing better than most of the agencies in town. If we had an Achilles heel it was this: no matter how much new business we attracted, Honda's ever-increasing budget would always make them our dominant account.

With my agency partner Gerry Rubin basking in glory as Co-Leaders-of-the-Year at the Beverly Wilshire Hotel, 1990

We were, and remain today, "Honda's agency," though, as my partner is wont to remind me, that's far better than the alternative.

Still, from my perspective, new business was a must. The variety of clients is what separates advertising from most other occupations. We do not spend our working lives solely fixated on widget sales or root canals. One day, yes, it's a car to promote; the next day, a pair of pants; the third, a bank's new certificate of deposit. Especially within the creative discipline, variety keeps minds fresh and makes coming to work more, dare I say, fun. Winning new business is not so much a case of making money as it is a chance to spread our attention deficit around.

LANDS' END AHOY!

It began in the early sixties as a marine supply store located on the edge of the murky north branch of the Chicago River. The founder, Gary Comer, an avid sailor, began to add sailcloth outerwear and other apparel to his offerings. Mail order sales soon outstripped business at the original store. Came the dawn and Comer built offices and an enormous mail order distribution center in Dodgeville, Wisconsin, fifty miles northeast of Madison.

In the early nineties, Comer semi-retired to Tahiti. He lived on what was described as a massive teakwood schooner equipped with every known electronic gadget. Comer enticed his friend Dick Anderson, whom Gerry and I worked with at Needham/Chicago where he was Media Director, to come up to Dodgeville and take over the day-to-day operations of the company. Anderson, in turn, asked us to join the party. He did warn us Dodgeville was not an easy commute from L.A.

Dick wanted to increase the role of magazine advertising at Lands' End. He admired our print work for Honda. In his mind, Lands' End and Honda shared like values and a similar target market. Our job was to bring a fresh new look to his ads (marching orders don't come better than that!). We would report in to Karl Vollmer, an old-school copywriter who worked part-time at Lands' End supervising their internal catalog development. Karl had Needham connections too. I befriended him there when he freelanced as a speechwriter for several Needham bigwigs including Dick Anderson. I liked Karl, the only grandfather figure I ever knew with a command of the King's English.

Dick was right about Dodgeville's inaccessibility. We flew the one non-stop a day from LAX to Madison on Midwest Express, a strange little airline started in Wisconsin by Kimberly-Clark, the Kleenex people. One class. Two-across leather seats. Pleasantries provided by plump rosy-cheeked flight attendants who looked and acted like every woman manning the phone order headsets at Lands' End.

The flying was fine. Driving the rest of the way in the dead of winter was the scary part. Wisconsin was practiced at plowing snow; their problem was where to put it. That meant the narrow county road to Dodgeville was often bordered on both sides by white cliffs twelve feet high. It was both hands on the wheel for a harrowing two-hour drive that otherwise took forty minutes.

Rubin wisely chose to join me on one summery excursion out there. Always the consummate account guy, he thought it was time he made an appearance at Lands' End. Never one to miss an opportunity, he suggested we leave a day early so we could have dinner in Madison with one of his cronies, an influential and extremely successful Honda dealer. As it happened Gerry's friend was under the weather; his son and heir apparent stood in for him that evening. He was a free-spirited bachelor in his late twenties—a man about Madison. After dinner he took us on a tour of the college haunts. Among the many choices along Regent Street, we ended up in a bar called Bucks (an obvious couplet just three beers ahead).

My oldest son Steffan had graduated from Wisconsin ten years earlier. Given the move to L.A., I'd never had the chance to visit him there. I'm not one for parapsychology, but a paranormal relationship, a synchronicity, has always existed between Stef and me. When he was young, we'd test it out using playing cards guessing who held what. Our degree of accuracy consistently beat the odds. And now, through the beery aroma in Bucks, I strongly felt his presence. Back in L.A., I called to ask if he'd ever spent any time there. "Dad, I helped pay the rent in that joint."

Meanwhile our Honda host had had enough. He said he was tied up at the dock near our hotel. We walked down with him to have a look at his boat. He pointed out the flickering lights where his condo was located on the far shore of Lake Mendota. He didn't board any of the boats docked there though. He hopped on a Jet Ski bobbing next to the pier, said his good-byes, then roared off into the night and the pitch black waters.

Unfortunately, that daredevil spirit did not wend its way to Dodgeville.

We had developed a solid strategy agreed upon by all hands at Lands' End. Rather than creating omnibus ads reminiscent of their catalog pages, we would single out an item, say a polo shirt or a cable knit sweater, come up with a clever headline, then wax poetic about the quality minutiae of its construction; far more copy than anyone might care to read, but an impression left that Lands' End took their products seriously. Which they did. And all ads led to a phone number and the rosy-cheeked ladies waiting either to take an order or send out a catalog. Karl, who loved long copy, was very supportive of our work.

But Dick Anderson was a different story. As Needham's media guru, he had been astute and adventurous (with clients' cash). He embraced new publications and took pride in supporting them; there was always an insertion for one of our clients in every promising magazine's premier issue. And he never backed away from a new TV show he thought had merit, controversial or not.

Now, running Lands' End, his own money as it were, he went conservative on us. "Make the logo bigger. Show more products. Cut the copy." Knowing Dick as well as I did, I had no difficulty debating him. But I had the distinct feeling there was another opponent, an absentee critic, floating around the South Seas somewhere, steering the rudder of Lands' End via shortwave radio.

Despite two years of very smart advertising created by a crew of my best people, and countless revisions and meetings and more revisions, the relationship foundered (the founder still at the tiller?) and finally sunk.

In the mid-nineties ARCO reappeared in our lives. The corporate work we inherited when we arrived in L.A. was long gone, their lawyers had had their way. But now we were invited to compete for their retail gasoline business along with what turned out to be the real plum, their am/pm mini-markets.

Pitted against the incumbent and several other agencies, we won the account. ARCO gas was the low-price leader in California, about a dime less than the majors. The only time they felt the need to advertise was in late spring, weeks before the peak summer driving season, when they and everyone else jacked up their price per gallon.

am/pm was more problematic for them. Attached to their gas stations, but operated by independent business people (mostly foreign born), the stores were seen in the research we conducted as little more than a poor-man's 7/11, a place to grab a pack of smokes or a can of beer. Well more than half their goods were opened and/or consumed before the customer climbed back in his car.

The task for advertising was to give am/pm a tangible identity—a destination status—using as bait the wide assortment of name brand products they had on hand. The proposition we shelled out to the young male target market was pure straight talk: don't just go there because it's next to a gas station, go there because it has:

"Too much good stuff."

While it was true the agency owed much to Coburn and Yoshida, gratefully we had other creative teams who could tackle high-visibility assignments. For am/pm, David Smith and Joe Baratelli were my go-to guys. David was a Joplin native, a J-School alum and a facile copywriter. Joe, a Detroiter, began at the agency as a junior in our design group working on Honda brochures. In time, they teamed up and started to give Bob and Gary a modicum of healthy competition.

Their launch spot for the "Too much good stuff" campaign became a cult hit in California, a simple premise beautifully executed:

Open on young couple parked in am/pm lot.
Girl: John.
Guy: Yeah?
Girl: Say it.
Guy: I'm only gonna buy two Cokes.
Girl: No Fritos.
Guy: No Fritos.
Girl: No beer.
Guy: Okay.
Girl: No Hershey bar.

Guy: No Hershey's.
Guy gets out of car. She calls out to him:
Girl: Be strong. I love you.
Guy enters store. He's overwhelmed by the shelves
full of colorfully packaged junk food as music swells.
Time passes.
Cut to him entering car carrying two Cokes.
She kisses him.
Girl: Good job.
Guy: Thanks.
Girl: Let me smell your breath.
Super logo and "Too much good stuff."

NEVER BEFORE HAD A CONVENIENCE store been feted by humorous storyline commercials. am/pm stores experienced an immediate surge in customer count. We kept the pressure on with a number of other spots designed to elevate am/pm as a bona fide destination. One of my favorites in the series went to great lengths to make the point:

Four young guys enter am/pm store.
Clerk looks them over a tad suspiciously.
Clerk: How you doin'?
Guy: We're on a road trip.
Clerk: Where from?
Guy: Fowler (a podunk town south of Fresno).
Clerk: Fowler, eh? Where you headin'?
Guy: (Gesturing around store) ***Here!***
Guys leave with bagful of junk food.
Outside store, one guy apes store clerk.
Guy: Where you headin'? Duh.
All four laugh.
Super logo and "Too much good stuff."

AM/PM HAD BECOME ANOTHER SHOWCASE account for us. Sales were up over eight percent, an unheard-of gain in their category. The campaign won a Gold Effie, an award clients actually care about since it is based not just on creativity, but on effectiveness as well. And, thanks to an unusual incentive agreement, the agency picked up a sizable bonus check every December.

Things were going well for us. And maybe too well for the client. Out of nowhere, British Petroleum made a purchase offer that ARCO couldn't refuse (beware that other shoe!).

To this day, ten years later, BP has not put their name on either ARCO gas stations or the am/pm markets (prescient of them given recent events in the Gulf of Mexico). They did, however, change agencies.

Gerry and I were asked to breakfast by BP's recently installed marketing director, an eager and amiable Scottish woman. We thought her purpose was to personally present our well-earned annual bonus. Instead, between controlled sobs, she told us that Sir John Browne, the head of BP, insisted she replace us in favor of Ogilvy, their worldwide agency. (Ogilvy's L.A. office was woefully weak at that juncture. She admitted the change made no sense but said it was "either us or her job.")

There was a certain irony in all this. Just months prior, Sir Martin Sorrell, founder of the advertising holding company WPP (Ogilvy being one of his holdings) had come a'courtin'. Gerry and I had no interest in selling out but, in deference to his knighthood, we agreed to meet with him clandestinely one late afternoon in a back booth of the Bel Air Hotel restaurant.

Sir Martin, a short, squat Brit, reminded me of Leo Burnett. He appeared invigorated as though fresh from a massage and a facial. We did not. And he had done his homework. He knew far more about us than we knew about him. If he was privy to a potential BP purchase of ARCO, he didn't let on. Though he did try to put the fear of God into us by idly wondering if we'd heard the "rumour" that Ford (a major client at J. Walter Thompson, another of his holdings) was about to buy Honda. We knew that was absurd; if anything, it would've been the other way around.

As one of the last remaining independent ad agencies of any size, we'd been asked to this dance before, meeting with senior representatives of conglomerates from all quarters: France, Japan, the U.S.—and now Great Britain.

Their scripts were eerily similar:

The man pulls an org chart from his Hermes attaché. He points out our rectangle. He talks about the "global family" we'd be part of and tells us whom we would e-mail for answers. The man feigns ennui discussing our clients. He does not ask what they might think of all this or suggest any tangible benefit for them. He knows what they represent—chips on a green board of chance. He does pay homage to our product and assures us there would be space provided on their corporate website to display one or two of our executions.

He never talks money. Seemingly, sordid deal points would be left to others in his purview. Rubin and I are relieved; having heard that every man has his price, we didn't want to know ours.

Sir Martin was by far the slickest of those we'd encountered. He had parlayed controlling interest in a shopping cart manufacturer (Wire and Plastic Products) into WPP, an advertising giant holding a mind-boggling stack of blue chips. Dealmaker that he was, he could not fathom our kneejerk negative reaction to his proposition. Finally, he gulped the last of his tea, glanced at his Patek Philippe and asked how long it would take his driver to get him to LAX at that hour. Clearly there were places to go and more reasonable people to see.

What he and the others didn't understand was how influenced we were by Honda's fiercely independent heritage; how, early on, they had dared to spurn their cautious government's request that they stick to motorcycles and not rock the boat of U.S. trade relations by becoming still another Japanese auto manufacturer. We knew Honda expected that same independent spirit from their ad agency just as we knew our partnership with them could never be peddled on the street.

SOON AFTER OUR ARCO DEMISE I got a condolence call from an editor at *AdAge*. I unloaded my anger over the blatantly undeserved dismissal but did not mention my fatalistic feeling that somehow the British had evened the score with us. He suggested I have my say publicly, a letter to the editor, which he assured me they would publish.

What I wrote per se is lost in the ether. I know I managed to make a sovereign connection between Sir John Browne and Sir Martin Sorrell and to observe how two knights would always beat two rooks (like Rubin and Postaer).

Sorrell must've had people sleuthing publications in search of his mention because the day after my letter appeared in *AdAge* he sent me an email. Like an old friend, he commiserated over the ARCO loss though an implicit "I told you so" surely lurked between the lines. He did point out one slight factual error in my letter: BP's bullheaded leader had received a promotion; no longer Sir, he was now Lord John Browne.

That promotion only took the Lord so far. Several years later, amidst a hue and cry only the British press can muster, he was "outed," literally and figuratively, by BP's board when they discovered he had been funneling unaccounted-for corporate funds to his assistant—a male half his age.

Vengeance was mine.

Though not entirely.

Sir Martin still owns Ogilvy.

Ogilvy still has ARCO and am/pm.

And, a decade later, am/pm still uses our slogan.

Perhaps even Lord Browne took "Too much good stuff" to heart.

⟡

MONDAY, SEPTEMBER 10, 2001. FIVE of us from the office are on a flight to Chicago for a most unlikely new business pitch.

The prospective client was a consortium of strange bedfellows—the four big breakfast cereal makers: Kellogg's, General Mills, Post and Quaker—who, for the first time ever, had anted up a sizable joint advertising budget the goal of which was to increase sales of their ubiquitous and colorful boxes stagnated by soaring retail prices and morning hour inroads from the likes of McDonald's. They wanted their version of the successful dairy industry campaign, a "Got Cereal?" approach, if you will.

RPA was one of four agencies asked to the dance. It promised to be a big and newsworthy account. Despite the traumas we knew were likely to ensue from not just one packaged goods client but a *phalanx* of them, we had gone all out to win this business and had in the overhead compartments black bags stuffed with compelling and humorous TV commercial ideas. We liked our chances. And would be second in the barrel the next day—9:15 sharp they said—in a meeting room at a "Willy Loman" hotel near O'Hare. To be on our game, we had just one nightcap in the lackluster bar off the lobby, then headed for our rooms.

This was a cereal account that would not rely on critters snapping, crackling and popping. Every one of the clients already had a stable full of cartoon characters. Here was the potential for a really smart, even hip, campaign.

The next morning, I showered, shaved and dressed quickly, without so much as turning on the *Today Show*. I wanted to be downstairs, at the ready, in case the first agency finished early.

In the lobby, of course, it was bedlam. Dozens of hotel guests and employees were staring up at a TV set hanging over the bar, many of them sobbing. Just as I pushed into the crowd, a plane pierced the second tower. I flashed on my son Daniel then working in New York a mile from the scene on the screen. I immediately stepped aside to call him. Unbelievably, he answered and told me he was on the roof of his office building with his camera.

I spotted the consortium's acting chairman, the marketing director of one of the four cereal companies. And I recognized several people from the first agency to present, now glued to the tube like everyone else.

The potential client and I commiserated over what we were witnessing for a minute or so. He then looked at his watch and asked if we were ready to present (by now my compatriots were behind me, black bags in tow).

As the first tower began to implode floor by floor, I asked, over the shrieks in the lobby, if this was really the appropriate time for an advertising presentation.

He said that bringing his group together again at a later date was problematic, that they had come from all over the Midwest to attend this meeting, that they all had busy schedules and that we had to carry on.

I then confided that everything we planned to show him and the others was built around humor. You know, funny stuff.

He said they were capable of dealing with the circumstances. I didn't believe him but kept it to myself.

I beckoned to my guys. We entered the conference room and proceeded to have the most downbeat meeting I've ever attended. No one in the room—they or us—had heart for any of it.

Not surprisingly, we did not make the final cut. Then again, neither did any of the other agencies. There are no monuments to committees and this makeshift group was no exception. In the end they decided they couldn't decide on anything and the idea of a united campaign on behalf of a bowl of cereal imploded too.

The Client

One reality should be woefully apparent by now: the agency business, even more than modern marriage, is mercurial. And while a lot of marriage vows these days have expunged "'til death do us part," that oath, or anything close, has never appeared in an agency agreement with a new client. With frighteningly few exceptions, the honeymoon inevitably unravels for a myriad of reasons: client contacts move on; companies cash out; egos collide. Never in my experience though was our agency fired for the most valid reason of all: because our advertising was objectively bad. Nor has any client who dismissed us gone on to run advertising created by another agency that I wished we had done.

That said, there is such a thing as a happy and enduring relationship. For us, of course, the partner has been Honda.

We share their independent spirit. We share in their highlights and hiccups. And most of all, we share with their people a fervent commitment to the company's success in America.

On Honda's side, no one epitomized that commitment more than Tom Elliott.

Like many at Honda, Tom was a lifer. With an engineering degree, he began at Honda in product planning, moved out into the field to gain experience working with dealers, then came back to headquarters in the marketing department as understudy to

Cliff Schmillen, our main client contact. When Cliff retired just three years after we arrived in L.A., Tom took over. And then some.

He was deeply involved in the development of their "second channel," the Acura division in 1986. When we first heard about it, I remember scribbling down a headline I thought would be perfect for its launch: "What Honda did with $25,000." But we were soon told that they sought true separation from the Honda brand and that we would not be considered as the Acura agency. In fact, Tom asked us for names of competitors who could likely fill that role. Fifteen years and several agencies later, Tom, in his wisdom and perhaps out of frustration, point blank handed us the Acura assignment.

❧

TRACKING BACK TO MR. HONDA'S love of the sport, the company had always been involved in racing—from gritty dirt track motorcycle events to prestigious worldwide Formula 1 venues. But they had never ventured into the All-American world of open-wheel racing, namely the Indy 500.

Tom, a motorsport fanatic himself, was put at the helm of Honda's effort in 1994. My old client Andy Granatelli, long out of racing but ever the warhorse, got wind of Honda's intentions. He called to tell me there was no way Honda could successfully compete on the Indy circuit without his expertise. He asked for an introduction to Elliott. Out of courtesy, Tom spoke to Andy. It was thanks but no thanks.

About subsequent events, an entire book could be written. From a modest start providing hand-made racing engines to several prominent teams; to building a fully dedicated engine manufacturing facility in Valencia, California; to piling up victory after victory; to putting a damper on the enthusiasm of other engine suppliers like Ford and Mercedes; to today, where the Indy 500 has become the most level playing field in all of sport considering the fact that every one of the thirty-three starters on Memorial

Day is powered by a Honda engine (the equivalent of every team in the N.B.A. starting a Michael Jordan clone at shooting guard). Tom's acuity and Honda's engine prowess have absolutely stolen the show.

For a decade, we had the task of keeping up with their success by creating "win ads" every time a Honda-powered car took the checkered flag, a near-weekly occurrence. It became a cottage industry at the agency. They'd win on Sunday, we'd crank out headline ideas on Monday, get Tom's approval Tuesday, then whip out finished spreads to *USA Today* and the racing weeklies to appear that Friday. At times it felt like I had finally made it as a sports editor.

Ironically, now that every Indy car is Honda powered, bragging rights seem a moot point. Much to the dismay of the publications accustomed to the incremental media dollars—though not so disappointing to our harried creative department—we no longer run those weekly "win ads."

BUSY AS HE WAS, TOM always kept close tabs on his ad agency.

Even on his numerous trips to Japan, instead of movies he'd pull out his red pen and plow through our copy, be it a paragraph for a spread in *Time* or the reams we wrote for Honda's many brochures. His crimson ink was infamous at the agency; copywriters cringed when they saw it snaking through their hard-wrought words. Mostly he had a good point, or two, or three.

And he never missed a meeting when he could "look at some ads" (everything was an "ad" to him including radio, TV and outdoor). Though not fluent in our lingo, he was an eager and quick learner. Early on he asked to attend one of our music sessions, something clients generally avoided for fear of being unduly swayed by the show biz moment and buying into something they really didn't like.

But Tom wanted to fill his learning gap. No problem, I said. Except the music house we relied on at the time—as good as there was in Los Angeles—was run by a wild man named Don Piestrup. A renowned jazz composer, he had written a string of haunting scores for our Honda spots. His singular talent and usual coterie of hirsute musicians were fueled by very good French wine stored in a fully stocked and unlocked wine closet. Don owned the building. Racking up costly studio hours meant nothing to him. Music sessions went on and on as Don, wineglass in hand, and his arranger alongside, wrote and rewrote until well into the night when they finally got it right. We'd sometimes rent an RV and park it outside the studio so we could wait out Don with a catnap.

The chaos of Don's studio and the hushed environment around Tom Elliott's office were as different as Black Sabbath and Beethoven. For Tom's visit, I implored Don to clean up his act.

Which he did. The studio was spotless, the wine closet locked and Don's hair plastered down like a choirboy's. The final sheet music was actually resting on the stands *before* the band took their places. After Tom was introduced and given a front row seat in the booth behind the engineer and his exotic mixing board, Don strode into the studio, picked up a baton I'd never seen him use before, tapped it on his stand, and led the group through a perfect thirty-second score. Don had the band do several more takes (to give the visitor his money's worth), and then popped his head into the booth to ask Tom what he thought. Tom thought it was great.

Outside, heading to our cars, Tom said he was surprised at how buttoned up Piestrup was. He imagined the process of songwriting would be far more chaotic. I think he was disappointed.

⁂

TOM WAS THE MOST DECISIVE client I've ever known. In the storyboard presentations for the "Stealth" and the "Art Gallery" commercials, both major productions, he okayed each idea instantly.

No inquisition of the staff seated to either side of him (unlike Ernest Gallo). No standing ovations, either. He just liked what he saw and that was that. His only question, out of curiosity given his engineering background, was how were we going to pull them off. He never asked how much. The pencil sharpening he left to Eric Conn, his tough but reasonable staff sergeant.

Over the years, strategic planning became the ploy *du jour* in the agency business. Any agency worth its salt had always employed some sort of research department. Just as secretaries were rechristened "assistants" over the years so, too, did researchers become strategic planners. As such, their crutch was no longer statistics alone. Planners delved into the psyche of shoppers much like anthropologists digging for pottery shards. The preamble to creative presentations, once the role of account executives, was now the planner's sacrosanct responsibility. Account execs by nature kept their target profile low and their setups short and sweet. Conversely, armed with PowerPoint, planners tended to justify and amplify their deep think to death.

I'd observe Tom as he stroked his whitening mustache listening politely to the drawn-out strategic prologues. Occasionally he'd jot down a note or two (though he might have been doodling). The meeting would then take an intermission while I arranged the storyboards in question along the presentation rail in salesman-like order. On his way out to the coffee station, invariably Tom would pat my shoulder in passing as if to say I'm counting on your ads to liven up Act II.

⁂

TOM BORE A STRONG RESEMBLANCE to Bob Keeshan (Captain Kangaroo) though he did not share the Captain's gushy persona.

As close as he ever came to high praise was in a testimonial he agreed to do on behalf of the advertising industry itself. He was pictured in a magazine ad sponsored by the 4A's (American

Association of Advertising Agencies), arms crossed, leaning against the side of an Accord. As background, an array of some of our best Honda print work was affixed to the wall behind him. There are several backhanded bouquets to the agency buried in his comments. See if you can find them:

"The difference between advertising and an accelerator
is our engineers could probably design a viable
alternative to the accelerator.
I've heard it said more than once from an adjoining
airplane seat: 'Gee, Honda has such a great reputation.
Why do you guys have to advertise?'
Other than how awkward it would be explaining the change
to our ad agency, I go on to say that Honda's reputation is
primarily based on personal experiences
customers have with our cars
and dealers. And what those customers tell others.
Call it favorable word of mouth.
Frankly, the only problem is,
not everyone gets the word.
So we advertise.
Hopefully, we do it in a way that distinguishes us
from our competition, which is considerable.
One media pundit recently observed that Honda had
'arguably the most consistent advertising campaign in the industry.'
I won't argue with that.
We stay the course because it works.
It works because it reflects our reputation.
Twenty-five years ago you couldn't buy a Honda with four wheels.
Today the Accord is the best-selling American-made car.
We can't pin that success on advertising alone.
Anymore than we'd pin our hopes on a future without it."
—Tom Elliott, Exec. V.P., American Honda

The Super Bowl has become as much an advertising contest as it is a football game. The business press can't wait to report the TV commercial casualty count. Monday morning network news can't wait to flash the flops. And next to the water cooler—especially clients' water coolers—far more talk involves the commercials than the usually forgettable game. For all those reasons—none of which having anything to do with advertising effectiveness—creative directors fortunate to work on a client big enough to buy into the Bowl pull out all the stops. Including me.

I'd never subscribed to the gang-bang school of creative assignation. My m.o. was always one assignment, one team. But this was different. This was late 1997 and the upcoming game would be Honda's—and our—first ever foray into TV time so costly. Every last person on my staff wanted a shot at the Super Bowl spot. More to the point, the vehicle itself, a compact SUV called the CR-V, was an extremely important launch for Honda.

So I threw it open to all comers.

And saw a ton of good ideas.

One, however, stood out. Conceived by our youngest team, Todd Carey and Vince Aamodt, the idea not only worked on its own as a TV commercial but it had "legs," which would carry it over synergistically to the Internet, then a newfangled marketing tactic.

Simply put, the spot showed off the CR-V as it bored through the pages of *USA Today*, past the snow on the weather page, the mountains of the travel section, and so on. There was no announcer copy. (To me, that made sense since so many fans watch the game in a noisy party or sports bar setting and can't hear the words even if they wanted to). For the Internet, we would replicate the CR-V's television action on the home page of the newspaper's website—employing somewhat primitive animation albeit advanced technology for its time. Of course, none of this would've been possible if *USA Today's* editors had not got past the journalistic credo of separation of church and state.

With the blessing of Rubin and the account guys, I filled two black carrying cases in an unusual way for the trip to Honda. In one, I stuffed five of the other storyboard ideas, any one of which we could have lived with. In the other, I slid in only the *USA Today* concept.

Waiting for us in the client conference room was an overflow crowd (Honda's people were not immune from Super Bowl fever). Stoic Tom, in his customary seat at the center of the long table, seemed amused by his staff's chatter of anticipation.

There was no big setup from our side, just some mediaspeak about the negotiated cost of the commercial time (still the price of a large house on a small lake) and which quarter of the game our commercial would appear.

Then I stood holding a case in each hand. Looking directly at Tom, I said, "We've got two bags today. In this one," hefting the over-stuffed bag, "there are five really good concepts. In this one," gesturing toward the far thinner bag in my left, "there's an idea we really love. Which one you want me to open first?"

Without hesitation, Tom chose the thin bag. I showed the spot, eighteen well-drawn frames on three boards. And paused.

"Do you want to see what's inside Bag Number Two?"

"Nope," Tom said. "I like that one. *USA Today's* on board?"

"Yes," I replied.

"Then let's go," he said.

Meeting adjourned.

⁂

TOM WAS FAR MORE CIRCUMSPECT when it came to Acura. He was there for its birth. It was his baby. And though, as a Japanese luxury car, it had come to market first, Toyota's Lexus and Nissan's Infiniti soon rolled out.

By pure chance, Acura's debut could not have been better timed—right on the heels of a reverberating and devastating *Sixty*

Minutes report on Audi's unintended acceleration problems. Real or not, Audi's sales plummeted. And early sales for Acura (priced in Audi's ballpark) more than took up that slack.

On the other hand, Lexus and Infiniti have presented big and ongoing challenges for Tom and his ad agencies. Both brands have two-upped Acura by offering eight-cylinder engines. To this day and for good reason, Honda engineers have steadfastly believed that their powerful and efficient six was all anyone needed. True enough, but not in the minds of some luxury buyers who equate an eight with heightened virility. Therein lies Acura's Achilles heel, then and now.

When the reins were passed to us in 1999, we put together a separate Acura group headed by a senior creative team, Mark Erwin and Wendy Knox, who had a great track record at the agency delivering a number of memorable Honda campaigns in the mid-nineties. They had coaxed the Coen brothers off their rising Hollywood star long enough to direct a funny and cinematic series of Accord spots. They had persuaded the highly protective Keith Haring estate to allow the use of the late artist's iconic images to light up the successful introduction of the Odyssey minivan. And they had enticed photographer William Wegman to put his charming Weimaraners to work in a follow-up Odyssey campaign—the first time the dogs ever appeared in TV commercials. Tom was well aware of Mark and Wendy's talent and contributions.

Now, on Acura, they set about to top the current campaign, which was dark in tonality, fact-laden, devoid of humanity.

Their group worked diligently to brighten things up, to inject life, to take Acura out of somber urban settings and onto the road headed for aspirational destinations: Key Largo, Taos, Palm Springs.

In that and subsequent campaigns, there was a line Tom wouldn't allow the agency to cross: humor. In his mind, and maybe so, anything that smacked of wit was the province of Honda. As an agency, our inclination, our strength really, was saying it with a smile. Rubin maintained that a smile added ten percent to the ticket. But Tom, who appreciated as much as anyone a good sight gag or punch line in a Honda commercial, wasn't buying it when it came to Acura. In his mind, and senior Japanese management's as well, Acura was serious business. Where humanity ended and humor began was always a bone of contention. Where there's contention—I've learned the hard way—the client (to remain a client) needs to win.

And while Acura sales have steadily climbed, it remains a work in progress: a continuing priority for Honda to develop product to compete with the deeper pockets feeding Lexus and Infiniti, not forgetting Mercedes and BMW; an ongoing endeavor for the agency to develop advertising that meets the client's expectations—and our own.

⁂

TOM ELLIOTT RETIRED IN 2005. He and his wife Anne bought an RV decked out as slick as a rock star's. They spend much of their time touring the sights of North America and finding their way, of course, to wherever an auto race of any stature is taking place.

His departure marked a turning point for me as well. After more than two decades working closely with the key contact at the most important client in my life, the thought of starting over with a new regime seemed daunting and, for RPA's best interests, unwise.

I began to plan the passing of the baton.

⁂

WHILE WRITING THIS CHAPTER, AN email arrived from Tom. It was as if he'd been standing over my shoulder. In all the years we worked together never once had he communicated with me via computer.

Seeing his name on my screen was a shocker; reading the message even more so.

It was an invitation to become his Facebook friend.

My Three Sons

I hope this doesn't jinx them, but it's 2011, still not the best of times, and all three of my kids are gainfully employed. What's more remarkable—since not one of them majored in it or ever so much as asked me about it—all three work in advertising. At agencies. Mind you, not mine. I may be the only person in the business rooting for three competitors.

Genetics can't explain it. No admen hang over my head on the family tree. Proximity? Osmosis? Maybe. Or did they merely seek out—as I did—an attainable avenue of self-expression?

Steffan, the oldest, a liberal arts major at Wisconsin, was a rock concert critic for several Madison free papers. Right out of school he landed a job as a copywriter at Leo Burnett (a far more condensed timetable to the big leagues than his father achieved). He moved up the ranks there over a twenty-year span bracketing a one-year stint at Needham. I never quite fathomed the reasoning but Needham recruited him hard when I moved to Los Angeles. He resembles me. Perhaps that's why he bolted back to Burnett after so brief a stay—too many "Little Larry" references. These days he's Chief Creative Officer at the Chicago office of Euro RSCG, a multinational agency.

I was sixty when the first of his three lovely daughters was born. My dad asked at the time how it felt now that I was a grandfather. I said I felt too young. "*You* feel too young?" he blurted.

"You made *me* one when I was forty-eight!" At the time, that had never occurred to me. My bad.

Jeremy, Stef's younger brother by fifteen months, is Creative Director on various projects at JWT New York, one of Sir Martin's many holdings. He spent more than a decade as an art director at Goodby Silverstein in San Francisco, an Omnicom agency and arguably the most creative in their portfolio. Jeremy has a BFA from Washington U. in St. Louis (where he gave the commencement address, the first art student ever to do so) and an MFA from UCSB. I thought he would become a famous painter and emblazon the family name on the walls of MOMA. Or maybe become a talk show host. But advertising beckoned. Jer has one son Jasper, who, at present, is charged with carrying forward our singular surname.

In retrospect it should come as no surprise to me that both Stef and Jer are slugging it out on the creative side of advertising. As kids, they wiled away the Chicago winters collaborating on their very own comic books; Jer, a mini Michelangelo, drew the superheroes while Stef's intrepid words ignited the space inside the bubbles.

Daniel, their half-brother and a generation younger, is a sports fanatic. Considering he's half Chinese, it's strange that he's considerably taller than Stef and Jer, a fact not lost on them. He played high school basketball, a very accurate outside shooter, and now, in his early thirties, still plays pickup ball with his old teammates.

That he too ended up in the business is a true head-scratcher. He has a double degree from USC in political science and international relations. After two interesting but dead-end jobs out of college, he took a summer off to study the mother tongue in China.

We had a family tradition—Chinese on Sunday at a restaurant near Marina del Rey. When our regular waiter heard Daniel was going to China, he handed him the business card of an American he somehow knew named Dan Mintz who had founded DMG, an ad agency in Shanghai. Between language classes, Daniel met with Mintz, who gave him a freelance assignment—ferret out the athletic mindset of Chinese youths (Nike was a DMG account) and write a report.

One thing led to another and as Daniel became conversant in Mandarin he also became Director of Sports Marketing for the agency escorting the likes of Kobe and LeBron around Shanghai. More recently, he was given the additional job of "rainmaker," sniffing out new business prospects in the States—including the movie studios—that have a desire to enter the tempting but tricky China market. So he's bi-continental now, shuttling back and forth between L.A. and the Middle Kingdom. His mother is happy he's home at least half the time these days and he's racking up a ton of airline miles.

⟡

WHEN WE FORMED RUBIN POSTAER and Associates, I called my father to give him the news. The first words out of his mouth? "Good. Now you can hire the boys." (He was referring to Steffan and Jeremy. Daniel was just eight at the time.)

I tried to explain the problem to him—as I have subsequently to a number of acquaintances who, like my father, don't really understand the advertising agency business but who have shared with me the same nepotistic thought.

An advertising agency is not a grocery store. Or a brokerage house. Or a trucking firm. It is a business that defies certitude. There is no right or wrong. There is personal opinion. And taste. It is possible to impose opinion and taste on a team of egocentric creatives who see your name on their paycheck twice a month but to induce acquiescence from opinionated flesh and blood would be folly. And that's not even taking into account office politics and the suspicions of favoritism that would surely swirl through the corridors of the agency.

Much as togetherness might have appealed to me from time to time, I knew it would never work. My sons knew it too. Not one of them has ever asked me for a job.

⟡

Of all the creative honors we bestow on one another, the Kelly Awards, sponsored by the Magazine Publishers of America (MPA), always seemed to me to be the most significant—the winner received not just a shiny trophy but a serious cash prize—and the most legitimate. I know first-hand how simon-pure the judging process worked. No schmoozing with other judges. No politicking. You quietly walked around the tables that displayed the twenty-five finalists—theoretically the twenty-five best magazine campaigns of the previous year. You graded them based on creativity and effectiveness, handed in your score sheet and departed. If your agency happened to have something on the table, that entry had been blacked out on your ballot. In my experience as a judge of other award shows, none of those stringent Kelly rules applied.

I was not asked to judge the 1997 Kelly's. I learned of the finalists just as everyone else did—by reading the list released by the MPA. And was blown away by what I saw. As *AdWeek* put it, "The Postaer family has tripled its chances of winning the coveted $100,000 at this year's Kelly Awards." Steffan's Altoids campaign was a finalist. As was Jeremy's Porsche campaign. As was our

My three sons at the 1997 Kelly Awards: Daniel, Steffan (the winner), "Pops" and Jeremy

agency's Honda Civic campaign. It was a unique happenstance for the Kelly's and a once-in-a-lifetime moment for me.

The MPA rotated the venue for the award presentation dinner each year: New York, Chicago, Atlanta, etc. This one would be held (conveniently) at the Santa Monica Museum of Flying. Of course, Stef and Jer came in for it; and I brought young Daniel along as a cheerleader.

It was gratifying to see Jeremy as jubilant as Daniel when the grand prize was finally announced and Steffan went up to accept it.

I'm not one to adorn walls with stilted shots of celebrities surrounded by fawning ad folk (me among them). Just three meaningful photos hang in my home office.

In one, I'm standing alongside Andy Granatelli in his raincoat at the Indianapolis Motor Speedway—the famous "Gasoline Alley" sign behind us—going over the next scene of a commercial we were shooting there. It was late May in 1969 and a few days later Mario Andretti handily won the Indy 500 driving Andy's STP Oil Treatment Special.

Soichiro Honda playing sommelier; an unforgettable moment

In another, the year 1990, I'm seated at a business dinner. The guest of honor, the lively and fun-loving Soichiro Honda—wearing a white server jacket he appropriated from a willing waiter—deftly pours wine into my glass from a bottle cradled in his arm. It was the last time anyone in the room saw Mr. Honda. He passed away the next year.

The third, shot right after the Kelly's, shows the four of us in our obligatory black finery standing side-by-side and beaming ear to ear. As any father who's had three sons voluntarily follow in his footsteps might readily understand, when and if the "Big One" hits Los Angeles, I grab this photo first.

EPILOGUE

RIDING A BIKE ALONG CHICAGO'S LAKESHORE, OFTEN WITH ONE OF my sons bringing up the rear in a kiddie seat, I'd see the emphatic warning posted on the stonework walls leading into Diversey Harbor. Though hardly words to live by, the phrase stuck. A mystery novel? A Frostian poem? A clergyman's Sunday sermon? But as evocative and memorable as those words were for me, in all the years of writing headlines and copy—or caustic memos—I never found a place or purpose for them.

Until now.

Unless you're the Invisible Man, it is physically impossible—boating, flying, driving, bicycling, jogging, walking—to cause no wake. Churned-up molecules of your past presence always trail behind. Yet, as the fates have it, and with no cause attributable to me whatsoever, almost every milestone of my life has disappeared without a trace.

Recently, I drove a rental, doors securely locked, to see what had become of my father's grocery store. 3142 S. Indiana Avenue is now one address on a block-long stretch of neat dark-brown brick townhouses capped in white stone. The entire neighborhood, a near slum then, is gentrified. Nearby, they've even leveled Comiskey Park, my old haunt, replacing it with something called U.S. Cellular Field in a similar shade of brick. *Say it ain't so, Joe.*

Navy Pier—the first two years of higher educational hell for me—is today a major tourist attraction. Near its rehabilitated entrance that massive Ferris wheel lights up Chicago's evening skyline. At its far end, a mile into the lake, just past the spot where I did detention in French, is a large meeting facility. Honda hosted its dealers there a few years ago. Our new commercials received far better grades at that convention than did my conjugations long ago.

Polk Bros., where I earned my way through college, is no more, eaten alive by the Best Buys of the world.

Goldblatt's Department Store, which deserved to die, did.

The Army Security Agency, its intercepting prowess no doubt stumped by the advent of devious digital tricks, was merged in 1976 into a larger military intelligence-gathering agency called INSCOM of which I know nothing.

In 1993, a zillion trees were spared when the presses stopped churning out Sears catalogs. The reason for the demise was not Internet shopping (though in another decade it would have been). At the time, the culprits were the likes of Wal-Mart and, following Sam Walton's lead, the mall developers who began mining gold on Sears' claim—small town and rural America.

Stern, Walters (you recall the SW/EL part) went asunder in the mid-nineties. When he retired, Jerry Stern, my second father now deceased, sold his stake to several employees who, suffering delusional grandeur, rented overpriced space in a slick new high-rise, got in over their swelled heads and, from what I heard, just walked away from it all.

My beloved Needham has gone through several name changes; today it is simply called DDB. Were I to walk the halls there now, I've been warned, I wouldn't recognize a face—or the place. Keith Reinhard is Chairman Emeritus and, deservedly so, lives comfortably with his wife surveying the New York scene from a condo seventy stories on high.

Finally, there's my alma mater. Once they discovered me buried in their archives, I have been invited to Columbia several times to speak to students, in assembly and in one-on-ones.*

On my initial trip back to the school I encountered two more missing milestones.

Driving down Broadway, I saw that Puckett's, my first real client, was now a chic women's store called Breeze.

Then, just as I did more than fifty years before, I was walking the halls of J-School seeking out the Advertising Department.

I found no sign of it. Perhaps they'd been relocated as part of their recent expansion program. I'd already determined the newspaper presses were moved elsewhere. That unmistakable smell of printer's ink no longer permeated the corridor.

I asked a passing co-ed if she could direct me to the Ad Department. As though coddling her grandfather she politely gestured at something over my shoulder. "Sir, I believe you're standing in front of it," she giggled. "It's different now."

What could be so "different"? I turned to read the words on the plaque. In a well-spaced sans serif font (no doubt Futura) it read:

Department of Strategic Communications

Quite a mouthful, I thought; wonder how they shorten it?

---

* In early summer of 2010, the School of Journalism pronounced me one of the winners of a Missouri Honor Medal for Distinguished Service and asked that I attend the award ceremony in frigid late October. I hesitated about taking the flight—particularly when told by the travel agent I would have to drive the last leg, that all too familiar and lonesome road to and from Columbia, because the feeder airline out of St. Louis, like so many other things, no longer operates. My reluctance dissipated when I learned that an early recipient of the medal was Winston Churchill. *Okay, you talked me into it.*